# LEARNING DISABILITY/MINIMAL BRAIN DYSFUNCTION SYNDROME

# LEARNING DISABILITY/ MINIMAL BRAIN DYSFUNCTION SYNDROME

## Research Perspectives and Applications

*Edited by*

**ROBERT P. ANDERSON, Ph.D.**

*Professor of Psychology*
*Texas Tech University*
*Lubbock, Texas*

*and*

**CHARLES G. HALCOMB, Ph.D.**

*Professor of Psychology*
*Director, Experimental Psychology Program*
*Texas Tech University*
*Lubbock, Texas*

CHARLES C THOMAS • PUBLISHER
Springfield • Illinois • U.S.A.

*Published and Distributed Throughout the World by*
CHARLES C THOMAS • PUBLISHER
Bannerstone House
301-327 East Lawrence Avenue, Springfield, Illinois, U.S.A.

This book is protected by copyright. No part of it
may be reproduced in any manner without written
permission from the publisher.

© 1976, by CHARLES C THOMAS • PUBLISHER
ISBN 0-398-03395-1
Library of Congress Catalog Card Number: 74-34302

*With* THOMAS BOOKS *careful attention is given to all details of manufacturing and design. It is the Publisher's desire to present books that are satisfactory as to their physical qualities and artistic possibilities and appropriate for their particular use.* THOMAS BOOKS *will be true to those laws of quality that assure a good name and good will.*

**Library of Congress Cataloging in Publication Data**

Main entry under title:

Learning disability.

    An outgrowth of the Conference on the Learning Disabilities/Minimal Brain Dysfunction Syndrome, held at Texas Tech University in 1973.

    1. Learning disibilities—Congresses. 2. Minimal brain dysfunction in children—Congresses. I. Anderson, Robert P., 1924-  ed. II. Halcomb, Charles G., ed. III. Conference on the Learning Disabilities/Minimal Brain Dysfunction Syndrome, Texas Tech University, 1973. [DNLM: 1. Learning disorders—Congresses. 2. Minimal brain dysfunction—Congresses. LC4661 C749L 1973] LC4704.L42      371.9'2      74-34302

ISBN 0-398-03395-1

*Printed in the United States of America*
HH-11

# CONTRIBUTORS

**PEGGY T. ACKERMAN, M.A.**
*Research Associate
Behavioral Laboratory
Department of Psychiatry
University of Arkansas Medical Center
Little Rock, Arkansas*

**ROBERT P. ANDERSON, Ph.D.**
*Professor of Psychology
Texas Tech University
Lubbock, Texas*

**BONNIE W. CAMP, M.D., Ph.D.**
*Assistant Professor
Pediatrics and Psychiatry
University of Colorado School of Medicine
Denver, Colorado*

**VIRGINIA I. DOUGLAS, Ph.D.**
*Professor of Psychology
McGill University
Senior Psychologist
Montreal Children's Hospital
Montreal, Quebec, Canada*

**ROSCOE A. DYKMAN, Ph.D.**
*Professor of Psychiatry
Director of the Behavioral Laboratory
University of Arkansas Medical Center
Little Rock, Arkansas*

**ROBERT B. DOYLE, Ph.D.**
*Psychology Service
V.A. Hospital
North Little Rock, Arkansas*

**STEVEN M. HIRSCH, Ph.D**
*Administrator, Technical Programs, II
Alcohol and Drug Abuse Section
Texas Department of Mental Health and Mental Retardation
Austin, Texas*

**T. STUART HARRIS, M.D.**
*Assistant Professor
Child and Adolescent Division
Department of Psychiatry
University of Arkansas Medical Center
Little Rock, Arkansas*

**CHARLES G. HALCOMB, Ph.D.**
*Professor of Psychology
Texas Tech University
Lubbock, Texas*

**MAX KAPLAN, M.D.**
*Associate Clinical Professor of Ophthalmology
Assistant Clinical Professor of Pediatrics
University of Colorado School of Medicine
Denver, Colorado*

**PAUL C. LAYBOURNE, M.D.**
*Professor of Psychiatry
Associate Professor of Pediatrics
Director, Division of Child Psychiatry
University of Kansas Medical School
Kansas City, Kansas*

**PHILIP H. MARSHALL, Ph.D.**
*Assistant Professor of Psychology
Texas Tech University
Lubbock, Texas*

**JEANETTE McGREW, B.A.**
*Research Associate
Behavioral Laboratory
Department of Psychiatry
Little Rock, Arkansas*

**MARY R. PARUCKA, Ph.D.**
*Director
Day Treatment Center for Children
Family Service and Child Guidance Center
Topeka, Kansas*

**JOHN E. PETERS, M.D.**
*Professor of Psychiatry
Director, Child Study Center
University of Arkansas Medical Center
Little Rock, Arkansas*

# Contributors

**GERALD M. SENF, Ph.D.**
*Associate Professor
Special Education and Evaluation
Research Director
Leadership Training Institute in Learning Disabilities
University of Arizona
Tucson, Arizona*

**ROBERT L. SPRAGUE, Ph.D.**
*Professor of Psychology
Director
Children's Research Center
University of Illinois
Champaign, Illinois*

**PHILIP A. TATE, B.A.**
*Research Assistant
Department of Psychology
Texas Tech University
Lubbock, Texas*

# PREFACE

The purpose of this volume has been to face the problems of research related to children who have been defined as Learning Disabled or Minimal Brain Dysfunctioned. We have elected to use both of these broad diagnostic terms; the former is representative of the psychoeducational approach, the latter of the medical viewpoint. Both terms, however, suggest a child who has behavorial deficits which markedly reduce his or her effectiveness in achieving developmental, educational and social goals.

The book is an outgrowth of a Conference on the Learning Disabilities/Minimal Brain Dysfunction Syndrome sponsored by the Graduate School and the College of Arts and Sciences, Texas Tech University and the Departments of Pediatrics, Psychiatry and Ophthalmology, Texas Tech University School of Medicine. We are most grateful for the support and assistance of Dr. Robert Moore, Acting Chairman, Department of Pediatrics and Dr. George Tyner, Dean of the Texas Tech School of Medicine who helped create an interdisciplinary focus to this work.

It is hoped that this volume can stimulate the thinking of students and researchers in the field along innovative and interdisciplinary lines of inquiry.

R.P.A.
C.G.H.

# CONTENTS

*Page*

*Contributors* .................................................... v

*Preface* ........................................................ viii

*Chapter*

    I.  Introduction
        *Robert P. Anderson* ............................... 3

   II.  Model Centers Program for Learning Disabled
      Children: Historical Perspective
        *Gerald M. Senf* ................................... 10

  III.  The MBD Problem: Attention, Intention
      and Information Processing
        *Roscoe A. Dykman and Peggy T. Ackerman* .......... 27

  IV.  Counting Jars of Raspberry Jam
        *Robert L. Sprague* ................................ 94

   V.  Psychiatric Response To the Minimal
      Brain Dysfunction Child
        *Paul C. Laybourne, Jr.* ........................... 126

  VI.  Effects of Medication on Learning Efficiency
      Research Findings Review and Synthesis
        *Virginia I. Douglas* .............................. 139

 VII.  Visual Efficiency and Learning Disabilities
        *Max Kaplan* ..................................... 149

VIII.  The Effects of Perceptual Motor Training
      on Reading Achievement
        *Steven M. Hirsch and Robert P. Anderson* ........... 162

IX. A Review of the Research on Concept Formation
and the Child With Learning Disabilities
*Mary R. Parucka* .................................. 182

X. The Vigilance Task and the Measurement
of Attentional Deficits
*Robert B. Doyle* .................................. 188

XI. Research With the Smart Reading Program
*Bonnie W. Camp* .................................. 204

XII. Two Blinded Studies of the Effects of Stimulant Drugs
on Children: Pemoline, Methylphenidate and Placebo
*Roscoe A. Dykman, Jeannette McGrew, T. Stuart
Harris, John E. Peters and Peggy T. Ackerman* ........ 217

XIII. Memory Analysis: Short- and Long-Term Memory
in Learning Disabled Children
*Philip H. Marshall, Robert P. Anderson
and Philip A. Tate* ................................ 236

XIV. Future Research Needs in Learning Disabilities
*Gerald M. Senf* .................................. 249

XV. Methodological Problems in Working With
Special Populations
*Charles G. Halcomb* .............................. 268

# LEARNING DISABILITY/MINIMAL BRAIN DYSFUNCTION SYNDROME

## Chapter I

# INTRODUCTION

ROBERT P. ANDERSON

THE PRESENT VOLUME represents a summary of the major papers presented at a conference on the Learning Disability-Minimal Brain Dysfunction (LD/MBD) syndrome sponsored by Texas Tech University and the Texas Tech University of Medicine. The Conference took place in October, 1973. The objectives were threefold. First, an effort was made to provide a vehicle for the sharing of ideas about ongoing programatic research among investigators representing different disciplines. Second, the application of research to clinical and/or educational practice was considered in the light of various theoretical models and research programs. Third, an effort was made to provide some fresh perspectives for future research explorations.

The need for the conference grew out of the conviction that research investigations concerned with the study of children categorized as Learning Disabled (LD) or Minimal Brain Dysfunctioned (MBD) have proliferated in a somewhat erratic fashion during the 1960's and early 1970's. Moreover, there appears to have been a noticeable gap between the conclusions drawn from research and the application of these findings to clinical and educational practice. Part of the difficulty has stemmed from the confusion in terminology, and part from a lack of coordination and communication between disciplines. The need for remedial procedures which could be applied immediately to the pressing problems of children has also served to create a gap between research and clinical application.

A great deal has been written in a descriptive sense about LD/MBD children by writers representing the disciplines and subdisciplines of psychiatry, neurology, ophthalmology, speech pathology, occupational therapy, special education, physical education, and clinical, educational, school, developmental and counseling psychology. The research in the field has also been carried out by a broad spectrum of investigators representing these various disciplines. Unfortunately, the synthesis and integration of research findings has not always been carried out with the enthusiasm and productivity which has characterized the work of writers concerned with speculation about etiology, diagnosis, and how-to-do-it remediation.

The research minded investigator should seek information from a wide variety of sources. A perusal of research literature representative of only one discipline can lead to the development of a very narrow perspective concerning research on a LD problem. The divergency and scattering of research findings has presented some realistic problems noted in the disciplinary narrowness of inquiry, the failure to take into account the results of previous studies in the design of new projects, and the duplication of lines of inquiry. There has been relatively little interdisciplinary fertilization of research ideas compared with the extent to which non-research oriented speculations have been shared by persons from different disciplines.

Myklebust (1968, 1971) in his two volumes *Progress in Learning Disabilities,* Walzer and Wolff (1973) in their compilation on *Minimal Brain Dysfunction in Children,* and the proceedings of the conference on Minimal Brain Dysfunction published in the *Annals of the New York Academy of Sciences* (1973) are notable exceptions to the general lack of interdisciplinary research sharing. The serious investigator cannot ignore these works as sources of reviews for research concerned with a wide variety of topics related to the learning disabled child.

The Texas Tech Conference was designed to hit controversy head on. No attempt was made to gloss over problems. In this regard, divergent and controversial points of views were explored.

## Introduction

As the reader will note in several of the chapters, the informal objective of provoking controversy was achieved. Thus, a number of ideas which have dominated the thinking of both lay and professional workers concerned with LD/MBD children were challenged. An outgrowth of this free ranging sharing may be viewed from three perspectives. First, a healthy skepticism developed about much of the research which has been carried out. Second, systematic reviews of the literature serve to explicate the overlapping character of the research from the various disciplines. Third, ideas were generated based on the descriptions of ongoing research programs which focused on the need for more programatic research and studies based on theoretical models of the syndrome.

The research side of the conference, and subsequently this volume, were organized to present various points of view and theoretical models of the LD/MBD syndrome. Reviews of the literature related to the topics of medication, concept formation, memory, and perceptual motor training are presented. In addition, several current research programs are described in detail. Finally an effort was made to look at approaches needed in future research programs. A brief overview of the chapters follows.

Senf has presented a historical perspective of the Learning Disabilities movement related to program and research development. He argues generally for increased vigor in the definition of population parameters. Over the past decade of practice and research, the characteristics of specific groups studied have changed. Thus, a population of learning disabled children in the early 1960's may not be representative of a population of learning disabled children studied in the 1970's.

Dykman and Ackerman developed a theoretical model of information processing which was designed to explain the cognitive intellectual functioning of the MBD child. The model developed by Dykman, *et al.* derived from their earlier work concerned with attention deficits. Not only does the model present a basis for systematic research exploration and testing of the assumptions underlying the model, but a vast amount of seemingly divergent research findings in the area have been synthesized in the review.

Sprague has taken to task the "bureaucracy" which has evolved related to the needs of children with learning problems. Besides providing a fascinating overview of the research conducted by his colleagues and himself, Sprague has focused on the problem of relevancy. That is, he is concerned that research interest in diagnosis and the prediction of future behavior has diverted attention from what he considers the important aspects of training and remediation.

A series of implicit assumptions concerning learning disabled children have evolved both in the lay public and among many professionals. For example, one implicit assumption is that aggressive, restless children are neurologically hyperkenetic. If this assumption is accepted, then an adequate response should be derived from traditional, medical and educational forms of treatment. A second implicit assumption which has marked much of the practice with children is that academic achievement which is lower than expected from parental expectations is the result of a neurologically based learning disability. Dr. Paul Laybourne has challenged these narrow viewpoints of children who are functioning behaviorally and academically at less than peak efficiency. He has presented a strong case for looking at the total child in light of the social and psychological factors which may be contributing to the alleged learning disability. Laybourne recognized a tendency to make automatic assumptions about the nature of a child's learning deficit without first raising questions which bring to bear a wide range of possible psychologically or neurologically based causes.

Virginia Douglas, representing her co-workers at McGill University, has presented a review of the psychological research in the controversial area of medication for the child defined as hyperkinetic. She has argued that hyperactivity is too broad a concept. Rather, the child should be defined as having an attention-impulsivity syndrome. Douglas is a skeptic. She, like Sprague, has focused her research efforts on how children can be taught to compensate for their disability, particularly in the realm of their attention-impulsivity problems. The reader will note a disenchantment with use of medication as a primary means of permanently modifying disturbing behavior patterns.

Kaplan has examined the role of the visual apparatus in reading problems. While recognizing that faulty vision may contribute to a child's frustration and slow down the rate of readiness, he pre-

## Introduction

sents a convincing case, backed by research evidence that perception is more important in the development of reading skills than any measurable defect in the basic receptors system.

Hirsch and Anderson have examined literature related to perceptual motor training. A systematic attempt was made to examine a series of studies concerned with the efficacy of perceptual motor training as a means of positively affecting academic achievement. Their position is represented by a definite bias; that is, perceptual motor training in all of its various forms does not significantly alter the cognitive structures underlying the development of reading and language skills. It was concluded that perceptual motor training has not been validated as an effective technique for altering cognitive development. This conclusion has implications for a wide range of perceptual motor training activities carried out in school; in other words, the training exercises may not be accomplishing the objectives they were intended to achieve.

The limited range of studies in the area of concept formation of learning disabled children has been examined by Parucka. She raised the question of whether or not children who are learning disabled solve problems in the same way as nondisabled children. Parucka has supported the proposition that LD children appear to learn concepts under contingencies of reinforcement which are different from the contingencies needed by normal children. Doyle traced the use of the vigilance task as a means of exploring attention deficits in LD children. The studies were carried out at Texas Tech University and represent a programatic research effort.

Perhaps one of the most challenging research efforts presented at the conference concerned the work of Dr. Bonnie Camp. She based her research on several assumptions. Stated very simply, the child cannot read at expected levels but he can learn to read more efficiently. The etiology and nature of this condition is basically not relative to the learning problem. Finally, under appropriate contingencies of reinforcement the child will learn. This study provided a fascinating exploration of a remedial approach based on the learning theory framework. Camp has not become bogged down in questions concerning etiology, but has simply attempted to provide a means of helping with a particular behavioral deficit. In many ways, her work challenges the elaborate plan for remediation developed in many educational settings. She supports the position taken by Douglas and Sprague that the main emphasis in research should be on evaluating the effectiveness of modifying the behavorial deficits which provide the stigma of disability to many of the LD children.

Dykman and his co-workers at the University of Arkansas Medical School showed in two carefully controlled studies how the effects of medication can be evaluated. Their results point up the need for extreme caution in the application of various medications. There appears to be no doubt that while drugs can affect the cognitive functioning of the child, they do not represent a panacea.

Marshall, Anderson and Tate presented the results of their study in short term memory. It was demonstrated how the well developed techniques of experimental psychologists can be adapted to a learning disability problem. This type of study points to the need for more inter- and intradisciplinary types of research whereas questions raised by the clinician can in essence be explored through the methodologies and theoretical assumptions provided by colleagues in related disciplines.

Senf has considered future research needs. He points up the need for more collaborative research between the pure researcher and the practicing clinician. Senf has raised the question of whether or not investigators are wasting their time by not asking relevant questions and if the proliferation of programs has far outstripped the evolution of evaluative types of research programs. Basically he is raising the question of accountability. Finally, Halcomb has explored the needs for interdisciplinary research with an emphasis on the need to use modern technological advances in related disciplines as a means of developing more sophisticated research.

Partial answers to the question of what has been done, what is being done, and what should be done in the future has been provided by these chapters. It is evident that there is much to be done, particularly in the realm of evaluating the efficacy of various types of treatment techniques, and in experimental basic research. A greater understanding of "how" the LD/MBD child learns and the effects of various types of environmental contingencies on the learning process should provide the broad focus for future research.

## REFERENCES

De La Cruz, Felix, Fox, Bernard H., and Roberts, Richard H.: Minimal brain dysfunction. *Ann Acad Sci, 205,* 1973.
Myklebust, H. R. (Ed): *Progress in Learning Disabilities.* New York, Grune & Strattion, 1968, Vol I.
Myklebust, H. R. (Ed.): *Progress in Learning Disabilities,* New York, Grune & Stratton, 1971, Vol II.
Walzer, Stanley, and Wolff, Peter, H.: *Minimal Brain Dysfunction in Children.* New York, Grune & Stratton, 1973.

## Chapter II

# MODEL CENTERS PROGRAM FOR LEARNING DISABLED CHILDREN: HISTORICAL PERSPECTIVE

Gerald M. Senf

It is important to know about the historical background of the presently functioning federal programs for learning disabled children because it tells quite a bit about how the category "learning disability" has changed over the last decade owing to the development of the subspeciality within education called Learning Disabilities. It is very important from a research perspective to recognize that the educator's conception and applied orientation has changed year by year. If researchers accept into their studies those children designated by the educators as "learning disabled," they are going to be continually in a state of flux. The researcher must achieve a measurable definition of the disability to be studied if knowledge is to be advanced.

At the present time there is an enormous problem of interpretation created by noncomparable samples subsumed under the same disability label. The sample compositions vary with the passage of time, as the brief history of Learning Disabilities will illustrate. Sample composition also varies geographically. For example, the widespread inner-city educational difficulties have often been categorized similarly to those possessed by a small percentage of affluent suburbanite children despite obvious differences in their functional nature. In my experience, research done at pediatric and neurology clinics has utilized quite different learning disabled children from children drawn from special education schools. In turn, these youngsters have differed from those designated within the public school setting. Children called learning disabled vary from state to state and from one locality to another. The use of the label is frequently more dependent upon administrative and quasi-legal concerns than with a conviction about learning disabilities per se. This line of reasoning is developed more fully in a later paper. Chapter discussion in this review is limited to a description of the present federal effort on behalf of learning disabled children beginning with its recent history.

## BRIEF HISTORY OF LEARNING DISABILITIES

### Early Beginnings

The history of the field of learning disabilities may be traced as a subspeciality within education to 1963 when a steering committee was appointed to organize a symposium on "The Child with Minimal Brain Dysfunction" by the National Society of Crippled Children and Adults and the Neurological and Sensory Disease Control Program of the United States Public Health Service. At this point in time, the emerging field of "Learning Disabilities" was derived from two major schools of thought, one medical-neuropsychological and the other psychoeducational.

The medical-neurological thread is the older of the two, stemming from the neurological theorizing of Samuel Orton (1937) and earlier investigators such as Morgan (1896) who sought physically based explanations for inadequate school performance, specifically in reading. This orientation gained it widest acceptance in the hands of Strauss (Strauss and Lehtinen, 1947; Strauss and Kephart, 1955) through whom the concept of minimal brain damage was introduced into the educational arena. Since this early work, research on brain-behavior relationships and other physical bases of learning problems have continued, primarily outside the field of education, e.g. in neuropsychology, pediatrics, and pharmacology. The general influence of Strauss and his colleague Heinz Werener are presently still felt through their influential students, who include Newell Kephart (1960,

1963) and William Cruickshank (Hallahan and Cruickshank, 1973).

The second thread represents, in part, a reaction against this etiology oriented "medical" approach stressing instead an educationally relevant psychological description of the disabled child's functioning. Focusing more heavily on treatment, i.e. educational remediation, the psychoeducational model seeks to measure the child's educationally relevant skills and prescribe appropriate remedial activities individually tailored to the child's specific strengths and weaknesses. This orientation is based in psychology, though the immediate historical precedent derives as well from other subspecialities within education, such as mental retardation and remedial reading (Snef, 1973).

The steering committee for the symposium on the child with Minimal Brain Dysfunction proposed three task forces. The first concerned itself with terminology and identification. Though authored by a psychologist (Clements, 1966), the first task force was dominated by medical-neurological thinking, the resulting choice of the term "Minimal Brain Dysfunction" reflecting this orientation. The second task force reviewed available services and authored a report (Haring and Miller, 1969). The third task force reviewed relevant research, its title, *Central Processing Dysfunction in Children,* reflecting its authors' educational orientation (Chalfant and Scheffelin, 1969).

In the same year, 1963, Public Law 88-164 allocated training funds for special education. Learning Disabilities were not so named but training funds were made available under the rubric crippled or other health impaired who by reason thereof require special education and related services. At the same time, Samuel Kirk was the chief of the Bureau of Education for the Handicapped (BEH) through which the federal monies were dispersed. Dr. Kirk, one of the authors of the Illinois Test of Psycholinguistic Abilities, appeared to be favorably disposed toward a psychoeducationally-based concept of learning disabilities and as Bureau Director allocated money for teacher training programs in learning disabilities at Colleges of Education.

In 1964 a parent-professional group, the Association for Children with Learning Disabilities (ACLD), was formed. In searching for a name, ACLD was reportedly influenced by Kirk who championed the term "Learning Disabilities" over the term "Minimal Brain Dysfunction" due to its focus on "education and training rather than on etiology" (Kirk, 1970). In adopting the educationally oriented designation for their organization, ACLD moved themselves closer to education than to medicine.

In 1973, ACLD was ten years old with a membership of over 20,000. It sponsors a very well-attended annual conference each year and has local- and state-wide chapters which exert considerable influence on both state and federal legislation related to learning disabilities and/or special education. In fact, ACLD was purportedly instrumental in obtaining passage of the Learning Disabilities Act of 1969, the legislation presently supporting the Model Centers and the Leadership Training Institute in Learning Disabilities which shall be described later in this chapter.

It is important to note the growth of an educationally-based concept of disability (apart from the medical-neurological orientation) supported by federal legislation, federal money, and the institution of teacher training programs, and an active parent-professional organization. The term "learning disabilities" became fashionable. Being more acceptable to educators and parents than "Minimal Brain Dysfunction," the classification quickly became overly, if not indiscriminately, applied.

A couple of years later, in 1966, a unit on Learning Disorders and Interrelated Areas was added to the Division of Training Programs within the Bureau of Education for the Handicapped, U.S. Office of Education. For the first time the term "learning disabilities" acted as a categorical funding base for teacher training programs at universities. A conference of the administrators of each of the eleven funded training programs followed immediately. Dr. Corine Kass, Professor of Speech Education at the University of Arizona and conference organizer, stated that "a strong feeling of growing professional identification . . . ," permeated the conference even though . . . , "problems surrounding a label and definition were not yet resolved" (Kass, 1970).

So, in the mid 60's, special educators were carving out a domain called Learning Disabilities. It is important for psychologists and physicians, both practitioners and researchers, to recognize that many of the tasks and responsibilities of other professionals were being undertaken by learning disability specialists. New role relationships were being instituted.

The following year an advanced study institute at Northwestern University forged an educational definition of learning disabilities to supercede the medical one of Task Force I (Clements, 1966). Kass and Myklebust (1970) published the definition in the *Journal of Learning Disabilities.*

The educational definition forged at the Northwestern Conference can be contrasted with that of the medically-oriented Task Force I. Task Force I searched the literature to reveal thirty-eight terms which described the minimal brain dysfunction syndrome (MBD). These included organic aspects such as organic brain disease, cerebral dysfunction, and minimal chronic brain syndrome. Other terms referred to a segment or consequence of the total syndrome such as the hyperkinetic behavior syndrome, character impulse disorder, dyslexia, perceptually handicapped, aphasoid syndrome, and attention disorders. The MBD syndrome included, "Children of near average, average or above average general intelligence with certain learning or behavioral disabilities ranging from mild to severe, which are associated with deviations of function of the central nervous system. The deviations . . . manifest themselves by various combinations of impairment in perception, conceptualization, language, memory, and control of attention, impulse or motor functions" (Clements, 1966). Note that the definition included an etiological statement about who was to be included in this group: those who manifest "deviations of function of the central nervous system." A further search of the literature yielded ninty-nine symptoms often associated with MBD, the ten most frequently noted in descending order of occurrence were: (1) hyperactivity, (2) perceptual-motor impairments, (3) emotional lability, (4) general coordination deficits, (5) disorders of attention (short attention span, distractibility, perseveration), (6) impulsivity, (7) disorders of memory and thinking, (8) specific learning disabilities, as in reading, arithmetic, writing, spelling, (9) disorders of speech and hearing, and (10) equivocal neurological signs and electroencephalographic irregularities. Despite the apparent protean nature of the disability, Task Force I suggested that clusters within the ninty-nine symptoms likely do exist, pointing to the hyperkinetic syndrome, primary reading retardation, and the aphasias as examples.

Those familiar with traditional taxonomic diagnosis will recognize the methods of Task Force I. It is admittedly different from educationally oriented diagnosis. Task Force I stated that "The objective of medical diagnosis is to demonstrate the existence of any causative factors or disease or injury capable of amelioration or prevention. The educational diagnosis involved the assessment of performance and capabilities . . . to make possible the establishment of appropriate remedial programs of management and education" (Clements, 1966).

They might have added that taxonomic diagnosis (categorization) represented by medical diagnosis also serves to form units for research within which lawful patterns can empirically be determined, by the variables related to "causative factors or disease or injury" or to other nonorganic variables of interest such as remedial programming. The taxonomic approach, I would argue, is well-suited for psychoeducational research as well as for etiological research. At any rate, the etiological emphasis did not appeal to special educators; the empirical search for symptom patterns has only recently begun, typically under the impetus of noneducational personnel.

The growing isolation of special education's subfield of Learning Disabilities was epitomized by their search for an educational definition and the ensuing professional developments. The definition they forged emphasized the educational nature of the problem, its psychoeducational underpinnings, and the necessity of special education remedial techniques. They wrote:

> Learning disability refers to one or more significant deficits in essential learning processes requiring special education techniques for remediation.
> 
> Children with learning disability generally demonstrate a discrepancy between expected and actual achievement in one or more areas, such as spoken, reading, or written language, mathematics and spatial orientation.
> 
> The learning disability referred to is not primarily the result of sensory, motor, intellectual, or emotional handicap, or lack of opportunity to learn.

Significant deficits are defined in terms of accepted diagnostic procedures in education and psychology.

Essential learning processes are those currently referred to in behavorial science as involving perception, integration, and expression, either verbal or nonverbal.

Special education techniques for remediation refers to educational planning based on diagnostic procedures and results (Kass and Myklebust, 1969).

The only reference to etiology is exclusive rather than inclusive. The broad language, not at all dissimilar to that later utilized by the Federal Advisory Committee for legislative purposes, has allowed room for considerable interpretation on the part of diagnosticians. Incidence estimates, for example, range from less than 1 percent to greater than 30 percent. Diagnostic unreliability and considerable confusion at the applied level have resulted. For instance, one federally funded program for learning disabled youngsters was providing resource room assistance for seven to fifteen children with not a single Iowa Test of Basic Skills score below the 30th percentile. The point being made is that variability in a learning disability sample's characteristics will be the rule rather than the exception. Similar to research on various psychopathological conditions such as schizophrenia, neurosis, and psychopathy, learning disability research will have to evolve its own definition (measurement techniques) if it is ever to discover generalizeable principles. These issues have been discussed at greater length in a recent publication (Senf, 1973).

The educational definition may most accurately be viewed as a symbol of professional identity rather than as a set of classificatory principles for the practitioner. In a similar vein, 1969 saw the creation of the Division of Children with Learning Disabilities (DCLD) within the Council for Exceptional Children. Journals evolved to further intra-group communication, creating a communication apparatus for educators separate from the medical and psychological professions.

Leaders in the learning disabilities field quite understandably wanted to take the lead where they felt they had the most to offer the children in question. McCarthy (1972) argued this position most succinctly in pointing out that a learning disability is typically first noted in the educational arena and that the educator must deal with the problem thirty hours per week. With education seen as the "base of the triangle" of service to learning disabled children, McCarthy argued that educators should be primarily responsible for remediation with psychologists, physicians, and others being viewed as support personnel.

The loss of the interdisciplinary focus has had severe costs, especially in research areas. For example, I was asked this past year (1973) to give a talk at the annual CEC Conference on research directions in learning disabilities. It turned out that there were only four talks of a total over 100 that could be considered as research related. The Research Committee of DCLD for the second year in a row did not make a report at the annual business meeting. One asks, how does an organization which has presumably taken the lead in educating children with learning problems support its opinions if it does not do research? Does it draw upon the allied professions, or does its isolation result in its serving learning disabled children with ideas drawn from the 50's? This is somewhat of a rhetorical question. I certainly think learning disabilities is basically adrift even though there are some indications that DCLD may set about reducing the isolation which has occurred.

## Recent History

The most recent history, that enabled by the Learning Disability Act of 1969, can now be described. Through the efforts of the Association for Children with Learning Disabilities and many interested professionals, Congress passed the so called LD Act of 1969, incorporating it into the Elementary and Secondary Education Act of 1970 as Title VI-G.

That act was to provide somewhere in the neighborhood of 85 million dollars over four years for the training of professionals, for research into learning disabilities, and for service to learning disabled children. The first year of funding, 1970 to 1971, no money was allocated. Out of a second year authorization in the neighborhood of twenty million, one million dollars were actually provided. The Bureau (BEH, OE) decided, purportedly without much input due to the time constraints, to disperse these funds directly to state departments of education for establishment of model centers called Child Service Demonstration Programs. Eight CSDP's, each in a different state, were funded, the notion being that the money should be distributed across the country, each state getting one model center. The Bureau also spent money for a Leadership Training Institute in Learning Disabilities (LTILD). The reasoning here presumably was assistance from a central organization which in turn could learn from the CSDP's ideas useful to programs in other states.

I joined the (LTILD) group in its second year, 1972 to 1973. That year the funding had risen slightly and there were twenty-three CSDP's in twenty-three different states. Each program was granted between $125,000 and $150,000 for two years, a small sum for most state departments of education. BEH was apparently cognizant of this fact but viewed the grants as seed money to catalyze the states' thinking about programs for learning disability children and to enable them to try out trial programs. Successful programs were to be replicated during the second year of funding and eventually supported by state and local monies.

## Child Service Demonstration Projects

At present, there are forty-three Child Service Demonstration Programs in forty-one different states plus Puerto Rico and a North Carolina based project operated by the Bureau of Indian Affairs. Because of the nature of the VI-G funds, learning disabled children must be served by the program. Each state must interpret the meaning of the term learning disabilities, both in constructing an appropriate program and selecting children for service. Some programs acknowledge service to other handicapped children or to children who could be termed learning disabled but have some additional handicapping condition. For example, at least one project is serving culturally and economically deprived youngsters, two are serving socially and emotionally maladjusted children, and at least two of the projects have educationally mentally retarded children being serviced in the same setting as the learning disabled. Some programs operating in states that distinguish between learning disabled and brain damaged children are serving both under this legislation. Other programs, because of their theoretical and practical nature, provide help to non-handicapped children as well. Such programs are typically those employing consultant assistance to regular classroom teachers, the beneficial effect of the consultant's suggestions purportedly aiding in the curriculum planning for all of the classroom's children rather than just the one or two minimally handicapped youngsters.

Though the funding is allocated to state departments of education, they typically designate a local education agency to operate the model center. The degree of both involvement and control by state level personnel varies widely, some maintaining control of day to day decisions at the state level while others subcontract the bulk of the funds to the local education agency.

The keynote of each program, being funded through the Service Branch of the Bureau of Education for the Handicapped, is its specific strategy for delivering services to the learning disabled child. Typically, the programs have a child service focus, though some incorporate teacher training and parent involvement as major aspects of the total program. The majority of the programs deal with elementary school children. About one quarter of the projects with a direct child service component stress some form of mainstreaming, that is, reincorporating or maintaining learning disabled children within the regular classroom context. Not a single project advocates the sole use of initiation of a self-contained classroom program. Parenthetically, the research minded reader should note what such programs must mean in terms of the types of children being served. The readers with a medical orientation most likely cannot believe that the severe MBD child whom they see in their offices can possibly be returned to the regular classroom. In fact, they are not. Rather, less severe cases, perhaps heavily represented by corrective reading cases, minor emotional problems, slow learners, and so forth are now being labelled learning disabled. The implications for the selection of research samples has already been noted.

While nearly all projects incorporate mainstreaming, there may or may not exist other options for placement, such as special personnel consulting to the classroom teacher, resource room placement for part of the day, a previously available self-contained class placement for extremely difficult problems if they arise, and auxiliary personnel for specific handicaps such as in hearing and vision.

Selection of children for the programs generally has followed one of two procedures, either teacher referral or some form of mass testing. The Evaluation Research Component at the Leadership Training Institute has initiated an examination of the selection methods used by CLDP's in order to understand more clearly what procedures are being used in the field to choose children for these special programs. Because the data are not yet collected I can only speak from my experience in dealing with a large number of the programs. Typically, regular classroom teachers are asked to identify learning disabled children with the federal definition being used as a guideline. A follow up assessment is then used to eliminate mentally retarded children from the program and to determine whether there are grounds for calling the child learning disabled. Typically, all that is required in practice is that the child's IQ on some measure be within one and sometimes even two standard deviations of the mean and that he be achieving below his age expectancy. Seldom does a project even adjust the child's expected achievement score in terms of IQ (Vandevoort, Senf, and Benton, 1972). Typically, the screening procedures utilize both testing and teacher referral as well as the vagaries of parent pressure and administrator assignment of children. While the selection procedures are not necessarily haphazard, they are extremely variable so that the researcher who selects unquestioningly the diagnosis of learning disability is courting serious problems.

The remedial programs likewise vary considerably from one program to the next. While none of the programs are devoted exclusively to the contingency management brand of behavior modification so prominent in programs for mentally retarded youngsters these days, one program is totally committed to precision teaching. Based on the work of Ogden Lindsley of Kansas, this program, operating in the state of Washington, has been directed by one of Lindsley's former students until this year. Because of the brevity of this presentation, I shall not take time to define the procedures involved in each of the remedial programs I shall mention. Those not familiar with the terms I shall use can get a brief overview in another recent paper (Senf, 1973).

The majority of programs utilize what is known in special education as the diagnostic-prescriptive approach. Here, the learning disabled specialists utilize a wide variety of diagnostic tests to assess perceptual motor functioning, language functioning, auditory discrimination abilities and other psychological dimensions thought to be important for school achievement. Working with the child's strengths in order to remediate his weaknesses, the specialist will then construct a remedial program tailored to the individual child. Depending on the training or theoretical background of the specialist, sometimes the remedial program emphasizes strengthening the aberrant underlying processes such as weak visual-motor ability while others direct themselves toward the deficient school skills themselves, modifying only the method of material presentation to fit the child's strengths rather than attempting to remediate the underlying process deficiency. More typically, the distinction between these two approaches is not clearly drawn by the specialists, each seeming to have his/her own beliefs about how best to teach children.

Some programs are more oriented toward the broader strategy for the delivery of service rather than the specific theory upon which the remedial effort is based. Such an interest makes sense in terms of state level planning where the mechanisms for delivery of service are of most critical concern. For example, a state may adopt a resource room approach, creating a classroom where a child can receive supportive help from less than one to as many as ten hours per week in subjects in which he is deficient. Another state may utilize a consulting model in which learning specialists without specific caseloads are used to provide assistance to the regular classroom teachers in order that the disabled child can remain in the regular classroom and yet receive supportive services. Other states, where all personnel who carry the job title of teacher must have a caseload, may run a consulting model where the specialist teacher works directly with the child as well as with the child's classroom teacher. The varieties may appear somewhat limited but, in practice, almost every conceivable variant on the themes mentioned appears to be in practice. The pity of it all is that the data that could be collected to answer questions about the efficacy of these various intervention models will not be forthcoming because program evaluation has been centered within each project rather than allocated to a single evaluation research group which could then spend the sizeable sum to examine the efficacy of the various strategies.

A second major component of the programs besides child service is in-service training for teachers. The desire here is to create teaching personnel more attuned to the special needs of handicapped learning disabled children. These programs typically involve monthly or semi-monthly in-service workshops though some of the programs have more extensive teacher training components. One of the older programs, which had previously operated on other federal funds before becoming a VI-G program, offers internships for surrounding special education personnel so that they will become capable of training others just as they themselves have been trained at the parent center. This notion of the student immediately becoming the teacher of others has become quite popular in education, not only because it does have a logical ring to it but also quite obviously because it is efficient. There have been many complaints heard from many quarters about the inadequacy of university based training of teachers. The in-service effort is an attempt to fill the training gap purportedly left by university programs.

A third component, less frequently represented than the other two, concerns involvement of parents in the services to the learning disabled child. At the very least, parents are typically involved in the advisory committees to the projects. In some projects parents actually become involved as classroom aids or as paraprofessional assistants in the administration of screening instruments for child selection. In other cases the involvement is limited to becoming acquainted with the field of learning disabilities and becoming active in local chapters of the Association for Children with Learning Disabilities. Parent involvement is also stressed in a number of programs by dramatically increasing the number of conferences between the teacher and the parent concerning their child in the project. A number of the projects are also involved in creating parent handbooks on learning disabilities or in training parents how to aid in the child's education through activities at home.

### Leadership Training Institute in Learning Disabilities

By virtue of their being funded under VI-G, all forty-three CSDP's receive consulting services from the Leadership Training Institute in Learning Disabilities, itself a federal project funded under Title VI-G. Since its inception, the Leadership Training Institute (LTILD) has been based at the University of Arizona, College of Education, Department of Special Education with Dr. George Leshin, the Department of Special Education's Head being its principal investigator. The LTILD is presently in its third year of operation, its first year being devoted primarily to a survey of the field of learning disabilities and the resultant drafting of a number of state of the art papers. Dr. Dale Bryant of Teachers College, Columbia was the project director during that first year with Dr. Corine Kass of the University of Arizona being associate director.

The present year has been a continuation of the second year effort with twenty new programs being added to the funded list. In addition, however, the Leadership Training Institute has itself changed in a couple of basic ways. First, the Institute has increased in size in order to keep pace with the demands made upon it by the CSDP's. The second change involves the addition of two new LTILD functions: the most sizeable addition is the Evaluation Research Component which I direct while a small proportion of our resources is devoted to a Training Component.

The Training Component sponsored two courses offered last summer at the University of Arizona, one concerning administration of special education programs, the other diagnosis and remediation of learning disabilities. Other training component activities will involve one day workshops just prior to the ACLD and Council for Exceptional Children Conferences this winter and spring. These workshops will be for selected teacher trainers at colleges of education around the country and will concern relevant topics from related disciplines. One of the programs will involve recent research and theory in information processing, the second will involve psycholinguistics.

The Evaluation Research Component of the Leadership Training Institute has the central purpose of providing backup support to the technical assistance functions. It is more product oriented in its approach and hopes that its efforts will be disseminable beyond the needs and interests of the forty-three CSDP's.

The Evaluation Research Component has undertaken a number of projects. These include an examination of the characteristics of the children actually being served by the Child Service Demonstration Programs in an effort to provide feedback to states and federal government agencies about how the legislation for learning disability children is being operationalized. The Evaluation Research Component is also examining the screening methods used by the forty-three programs in an effort to evolve a summary statement of the various methods in use and the strengths and weaknesses of each of the procedures. Another project involves collecting data on all of the programs along a variety of dimensions interesting to practitioners and program initiators so that they will have some touchstone to use when planning new programs. Such a data base will hopefully have many other uses. Another project involves the creation of a file of assessment instruments useful for the screening and diagnosis of learning disabled children and for the evaluation of programs involving such children. Such a file would be useful in assisting programs who need such procedures recommended to them and will also be helpful to others through further dissemination in the form of packets of suggested tests to serve certain specific purposes such as preschool screening, the evaluation of in-service programs for teachers, the assessment of gains in school skills, and so forth. This project typifies the central theme of our Evaluation Research Component which is to assemble and disseminate those procedures that are already available, thereby making practice as up-to-date as possible. There are a variety of other projects such as an overview of secondary programs for learning disabled children at the secondary level and a manual for the projects and others to use for evaluating special education programs: the evaluation manual will provide a step by step set of procedures which a project director without previous experience can utilize to construct a credible and useful evaluation.

One final project that we are undertaking involves a study of the Child Service Demonstration Programs as new institutions. Viewed within an organizational psychology framework, these settings must be well administered and organized in order to be capable of providing the new kinds of services for which they were initiated. Our evaluation technical assistance found so often that the efficacy of the program was determined much less by the specific intervention strategy or theoretical model than by the organization and administrative aspects of the setting. The "setting study" as we have termed it is under the co-direction of Dr. Steven Reiss and myself, Reiss being a psychologist at the University of Illinois, Chicago. We hope this study will provide a framework for assessing the efficacy of settings independent of their specific educational focus.

I have only begun to tell you about the model centers and the Leadership Training Institute. It should be clear how far the field of learning disabilities has come in the last ten years. Those initially interested in minimal brain damage as an area of study must recognize that the new term, learning disability, can in no way be considered synonymous with MBD as addressed by the medically oriented Task Force a decade ago. As the field of Learning Disabilities strives to serve more and more underachieving children, the nature of the population we call "learning disabled" will continue to change. As I discuss in my other chapter on future research needs, it is critically important for the research effort to evolve their own taxonomic structures complete with specific measurement criteria for their study of these disabling problems.

## REFERENCES

Chalfant, J. C., and Scheffelin, M. A.: *Central processing dysfunctions in children: A review of research, phase three of a three-phase project,* NINDS Monograph No. 9, U.S. Department of Health, Education and Welfare, 1969.

Clements, S. D.: *Minimal brain dysfunction in children: Terminology and identification, phase one of a three-phase project.* Bulletin No. 1415, NINDS Monograph, No. 3, U. S. Department of Health, Education and Welfare, 1966.

Hallahan, D. P., and Cruickshank, W. M.: *Psychoeducational Foun-*

dations of *Learning Disabilities*. Englewood Cliff, Prentice Hall, 1973.

Haring, N. G., and Miller, C. A. (Eds.): *Minimal brain dysfunction in children. Educational, medical and health related services, phase two of a three-phase project*. N&SDCP Monograph, Public Health Publication No. 2015, U. S. Department of Health, Education and Welfare, 1969.

Kass, C. E.: *Final report U.S.O.E.*, Contract No. OEG-0-9-121013-3021 (031) Advanced Institute for Leadership Personnel in Learning Disabilities, 1970.

Kass, C. E., and Myklebust, H. R.: Learning disability: An educational definition. *Journal of Learning Disabilities*, 2:38-40, 1969.

Kephart, N. C.: *The Slow Learner in the Classroom*. Columbus, Ohio, Charles E. Merrill, 1960.

Kephart, N.: *The Brain-Injured Child in the Classroom*. National Society for Crippled Children and Adults, Inc., 1963.

Kirk, S. A.: Lecture in Kass, C. E. *Final report, U.S.O.E.* Contract No. OEG-0-9-121013-3021-(031). Advanced Institute for Leadership Personnel In Learning Disabilities, 1970.

McCarthy, J. M.: Education: The Base of the Triangle, Paper presented at Minimal Brain Dysfunction Conference, New York Academy of Sciences, New York City, March 22, 1972.

Morgan, W. P.: A case of congenital word blindness. *Br Med J*, 2:3178, 1869.

National Advisory Committee: Special Education for Handicapped Children. The first annual report of the National Advisory Committee on Handicapped Children. Washington, D.C. Office of Education, U.S. Department of Health, Education and Welfare, 1968.

Orton, S. T.: *Reading, Writing and Speech Problems in Children*. New York, Norton, 1937.

Senf, G. M.: Learning disabilities. In Grossman, H. J. (Ed.): *Learning Disorders. Pediatr Clin North Am*, 20:3. Philadelphia, Saunders, 1973.

Strauss, A., and Lehtinen, L.: *Psychopathology and Education of the Brain-Injured Child*. New York, Grune & Stratton, 1947, Vol. I.

Strauss, A., and Kephart, N. C.: *Psychopathology and Education of the Brain-Injured Child*. New York, Grune & Stratton, 1955, Vol. II.

Vandevoort, L., Senf, G. M., and Benton, A. L.: Development of audiovisual integration in normal and retarded readers. *Child Dev*, 43. No. 4, December, 1972.

―――Chapter III―――

# THE MBD PROBLEM: ATTENTION, INTENTION, AND INFORMATION PROCESSING

Roscoe A. Dykman, and Peggy T. Ackerman

## PROLOGUE AND OVERVIEW

### The Circular Nature Of Behavior And Occam's Razor

WE WERE ASKED TO review and reflect upon three lines of investigation in the domain of minimal brain dysfunction (MBD): attention, memory, and concept attainment. To no one's surprise, we found much to review: many findings and opinions but few definite conclusions. All of which goes to support the view that psychologists never really solve anything. They just get tired of pondering one problem and move on to another.

While trying to organize our thoughts, we were reminded of Captain Gulliver's stay among the Houyhnhnms. This noble breed of horses, rational beyond belief, always acted on the basis of knowledge rather than conjecture. In their language they needed no word for speculation just as they needed no words for lying and thievery. Recall, however, that Swift never let anyone off scot free. The rationality of the Houyhnhnms precluded their entertainment of novelty, and because Gulliver looked something like the brutish Yahoos and bore no physical resemblance to a horse, the Houyhnhnm assembly directed Gulliver's master either to treat Gulliver as a Yahoo (i.e. slave) or else to command him to swim back to the place from whence he came.

Obviously, the Houyhnhnm langauge would leave us short on words, and this chapter could be quite brief. Dr. Macdonald Critchley, however, has given us the courage to go ahead with what we wanted to do in the first place—and that is speculate. Critchley (1973) quoted Oscar Wilde, who said that there are words which one does not understand for a long time. The reason is that these words bring answers to questions that have not yet been raised. Thus, we researchers have our *raison d'être*. On such faith, we shall here attempt to sort out what is definitely known, but we shall also, through speculation, hope to raise some of the right questions.

We have elaborated elsewhere (Dykman, *et al.*, 1971) our belief that attentional deficits are a basic problem of children with minimal brain dysfunction (MBD). Now we wish to modify our position somewhat to incorporate the closely related concept of in-

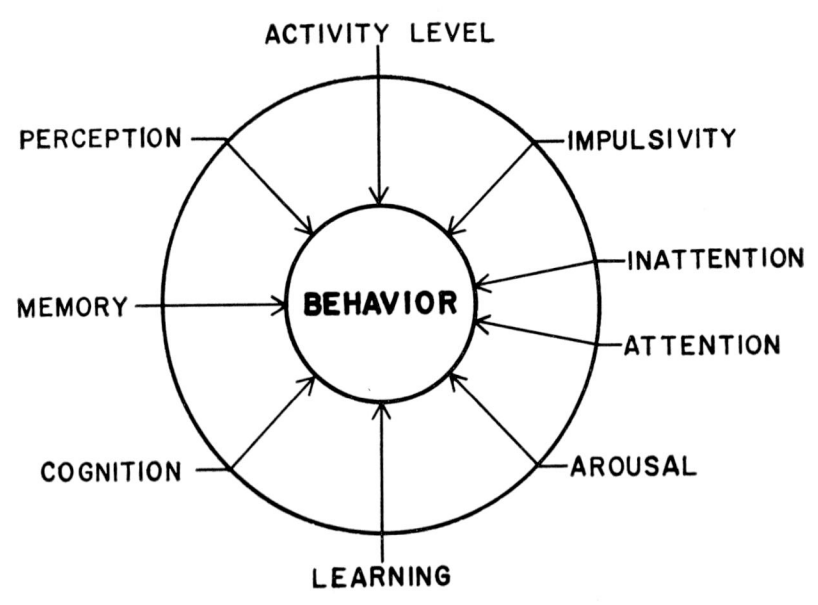

Figure III-1. The Circular Nature of Behavior. A given behavior can be the resultant of deficiencies in one or several basic processes. Moreover, a deficiency in one area can interfere with efficiency of another, as faulty attention, for example, hampers efficient encoding and memory.

tention. In so doing, we shall develop a more general model around information processing theory.

Though we still adhere to the thesis that faulty attention is at the root of most learning disabilities, we recognize the role of other factors. From a literature review, one can make a good case implicating any one or all of the following: arousal, short-term memory, long-term memory, problem solving strategies, developmental immaturity, and so on. The question is where best to enter the circle and explain a given set of behaviors (Fig. III-1). Since all explanatory concepts underlying behavior are interrelated— especially arousal, attention, and memory—a satisfactory theory of attentional deficits would undoubtedly be a satisfactory theory of other interdependent psychological processes.

Occam's Razor says that we should move from the simple to the complex in experimentation and interpretation. We should not look for a higher level explanation when a lower level explanation suffices. From this standpoint, the most parsimonious approach is to consider *arousal* as the basic defect in MBD. We have been down this road before, and for various reasons, which will become clear as we go along, it has not proved satisfactory. In 1971, therefore, we turned to *attention* as the next elementary phenomenon. Still dissatisfied, we now move to a considerable elaboration, adding *intention and other psychological processes* (Douglas, 1972). There are significant differences between the concepts of attention and intention, at least as we define them. Attention relates to the adequacy of one's informational gathering ability, focusing and stimulus selection (sampling the environment). Intention has more to do with the utilization of information, its implications and consequences (Shannon and Weaver, 1962). In a broader philosophical sense, intention connotes attitudes, values, will power, or sustained attention (James, 1890). The philosophical and neurophysiological question is the same: Is it that the MBD child cannot sustain his attention or will not?

## INTRODUCTION

### Description Of The Population

The papers in this session deal with various facets of information processing in mainly hyperactive and/or learning disabled

(LD) children. In general, a population of hyperactive children will contain a high proportion of children who are also LD, and the converse. Therefore, studies of children selected for hyperactivity or LD show a considerable amount of agreement. For convenience, we include both hyperactive and LD children under the MBD rubric.

There are no doubt many diagnostic subtypes within the MBD population. In our clinic, we regard MBD as suitable shorthand for a heterogeneous group of children who exhibit one but usually more than one of the following troubling traits: hyperactivity, hypoactivity, restlessness, excitability, impulsivity, faulty attention, motor incoordination, and/or specific learning deficits (a year or more behind expected grade level in reading, spelling, arithmetic, or handwriting). We generally exclude from the MBD category children whose learning deficits can be attributed to inadequate cultural stimulation, emotional upheaval in the home, definitive neurological damage, or low IQ (the child must have either a Verbal or Performance WISC IQ of at least 90).

We find MBD a useful organizing concept, for it serves to remind us that the brain can produce an array of specific kinds of learning deficits, and that we all experience some of these to some degree.

## Etiology

There is no one single etiologic explanation of MBD in our view, but some hypothesized causes seem more probable than others and more commonplace. MBD has been attributed to delayed neural maturation (Dykman, et al., 1971; Lucus, et al., 1965 and Solomons, 1965); delayed lateralization of the brain functions (Satz and Sparrow, 1970); chemical malfunctions of brain and/or brain stem (Shetty, 1971; Stewart, 1970; and Wender); heredity (Critchley, 1946); pre-, peri-, and postnatal insults (Rosenfeld and Bradley, 1948; Laufer and Denhoff, 1957); inadequate parenting (Bereiter and Engelman, 1966; Deutsch, 1964) and florescent lighting, radioactivity from television sets, as well as allergies to food additives.

There has been a great deal of serious theorizing concerning the brain mechanisms underlying MBD. Laufer and Denhoff

(1957) postulated what amounts to an attentional defect. They suspected a failure of some essential inhibitory control or filtering mechanism as well as a lack of coordination between cortical and subcortical structures, which would result in the cortex having insufficient control over lower regions. The reticular activation system has been implicated by several investigators, some theorizing that the MBD child is overaroused and some that he is underaroused (Laufer and Denhoff, 1957; Dykman, et al., 1971; Satterfield and Dawson, 1971; Stevens, et al., 1967; Stewart, 1970; Werry and Sprague, 1969).

Members of the McGill research team have failed to find any substantial evidence of brain damage in birth histories, electroencephalograms, or neurological examinations (Minde, et al., 1964, 1969). But, as Douglas (1972) says, these children do show many behavioral signs of neurological insufficiency: soft neurological signs, poor performance on the Wisconsin Card Sorting Test and the Porteus Mazes, which may reflect frontal lobe impairment.

In our 1971 paper, we said that a neurodevelopment lag could be the etiological explanation for most learning disabilities. This position came from the findings of such high incidence of so-called "soft signs" in our MBD study group. We went on to say that neurological immaturity could well explain the attentional deficits of LD or MBD children. Obviously, motor incoordination can be related to, and is correlated with, faulty attention; for attention is perfected, in part, through one's mechanical manipulations of the environment. While clumsiness and short attention spans are to be expected in preschoolers, the school age child should be well enough coordinated to learn to write, and he should be able to pay close enough attention to see and hear the differences between letters and sounds and to associate one with the other. We pointed out that a maturational lag theory is certainly a much more hopeful one than a theory of impaired neural structures. But we should have asked ourselves more about the etiology of a maturational lag, for it does little good to exchange one label for another.

Over the past two to three years, we have come to have other reservations *vis-a-vis* a maturational lag hypothesis. Follow-up study after follow-up study, including our own (Dykman, *et al.*, 1973), indicates that MBD children continue to lag at least into their mid teens. Though not illiterate, our MBD teenagers are relatively as far behind their age-mates scholastically as when they were seen initially (Dykman, *et al.*, 1973). Perhaps more disturbing, Mendelson and associates (1971) have reported a high incidence of antisocial behavior in teenagers whom they earlier diagnosed as hyperactive children. Thus, impulse control, or ability to foresee consequences, still appears to lag into the high school years. If one continues then to ascribe to a maturational lag viewpoint, he has to say that perhaps MBD children will overcome their handicaps at age 25 or 35 or 45. The only totally encouraging follow-up study is Margaret Rawson's (1968), and the language disabled children in her sample had very high IQs (a mean of 131) and came from upper-middle and upper-class families (see Herjanic and Penick's 1972 review of adult outcomes of disabled child readers).

What we now believe is that children have to discover, either on their own or with help from others, ways of working around their deficits. They must find or develop their own strategies for recognizing words and associating these words with their speaking and recognition vocabulary. A child who has limited ability to discriminate letters or to link sounds with letter units may eventually learn to read, perhaps by a strategy which allows him to identify words in much the same way you and I identify emblems or signs. We desperately need in-depth studies of those people who have successfully overcome severe reading disabilities as well as those who have overcome marked impulsivity and distractibility. Critchley (1973), drawing on almost 50 years experience with reading retarded youngsters, says that the usual adult "ex-dyslexic" will always be a reluctant reader and an even more reluctant writer. Critchley goes on to say that the most successful ex-dyslexics are those of higher intelligence who have what Americans refer to as ego-strength but what is called "guts" in Britain.

We have come more and more to Critchley's position that, at least for specific language disability, heredity is the main etiological factor. Bakwin (1973) recently reported 84 percent concordance for reading disability in monozygotic twins as opposed to 29 percent concordance in like sexed dizygotic pairs. Since heredity obviously is a major variable, then we should be asking such questions as: What aspects of mental ability and what traits of temperament are inherited? What is the mode of inheritance (one gene, a few genes, or many genes)? To what extent can inherited dispositions be shaped by life experiences? In view of the sex ratio of four or five boys to each girl in most LD or MBD samples, it would be instructive to determine the following conditional probabilities: What is the probability of a male sib being MBD given a sister who is MBD? What is the probability of a male sib being MBD given a brother who is MBD? If the first probability is higher than the second, we would have evidence of polygenic inheritance.

The best recent findings tangential to this question are in the Bakwin (1973) report. He found in monozygotic twin pairs no sex difference in concordance for reading disability. In the dizygotic like sexed twins, however, the concordance figure for males was 42 per cent and for females 8 percent. The severity and nature of the reading disabilities of these twins should be studied further. We would guess that severe dyslexia depends on a few major genes (perhaps only one), whereas hyperactivity and/or the attentional/intentional problem discussed above reflect polygenetic inheritance. Critchley (1964) favors a theory implicating a few major genes.

Whatever the mode, we are firmly convinced that children are not born with an equal potential for developing dyslexia or MBD, no more than infants are born with an equal potential for becoming schizophrenic (Meehl, 1972).

Many people react strongly against a genetic interpretation, saying this leads to a do nothing attitude on everyone's part. They generally fail to understand the concept of phenotype, which means genotype (what is inherited) shaped by experience (Falconer, 1960). To take a genetic point of view is not to play "wooden leg"; it is to recognize a child's limitations (genotype) and attempt to work around them to produce a productive citizen (phenotype). But to believe that any child can become, for example, a college professor, given appropriate experience, is a disservice to the child, his parents, and his teachers.

## THEORETICAL CONSIDERATIONS

A number of investigators have tried to pull together the diverse aspects of mental functioning in MBD children. One main theme recurs in all reviews and theoretical papers: MBD children are forever struggling with the problem of processing and storing information *at a rate acceptable to parents and teachers.* They are crippled in some of the most elementary mental abilities, and, though normally intelligent, cannot keep pace in school with age-mates. As already mentioned, we (Dykman, et al., 1971) have emphasized attentional deficits as basic to the problem. Virginia Douglas (1972;1973) considers the ability to sustain attention and to keep impulsive responding under control necessary not only to academic success but to social adjustment as well. Finding herself in the area of intention, she sought chapter and verse in William James. There she gained insight as to why such a high incidence of antisocial behavior is now being reported in follow-up studies of MBD children. James reasoned that moral or socially approved behavior is the result of an ideal plus effort. He said, "Moral action is action in the line of greatest resistance," and, "The essential achievement of will is to attend to a difficult object." Piaget (1932), too, leads us to the position that moral action is more a factor of ego strength than superego ideal, as does Kohlberg (1969).

Roessler (1973), in his presidential address to the Society for Psychophysiological Research, theorized in the Jamesian direction. In trying to synthesize recent research in the areas of personality, physiology and performance, he said that we must first know how a person perceives a stimulus before we can predict his response. Only if the stimulus is perceived (processed) correctly will a subject respond physiologically as we would expect. Roessler feels that the person who cannot correctly evaluate reality cannot cope with most life situations. Interpersonal coping depends on the ability to assess and respond appropriately to the behavior of others while at the same time maintaining one's ego. Ego strength as measured by the Minnesota Multiphasic Personality Inventory (MMPI) has proved to be more consistently related to physiological reactivity than any other personality variable, according to Roessler. Roessler says high ego strength subjects become more appropriately aroused physiologically than low ego strength subjects. They neither over or under react. Interestingly, de Hirsch and associates (1966), in their follow-up study of kindergarten children, found that the one measure which best predicted success in elementary school was the teacher's assessment of a maturity factor, which could well be labeled ego or coping strength. We have found in our follow-up study of MBD boys (Dykman, et al., 1973) that at age 14 a significant number score in the disturbed range on the Reality (ego strength) scale of the Minnesota Counseling Inventory.

From the standpoint of transactional analysis (TA) theory, many MBD children have a blocked out Parent and/or a blocked out Adult, leaving only the Child part of their personality free to function. The child with a blocked out Parent will show little concern for rules and implications, but the child with a blocked out Adult will have difficulty receiving, processing, storing, and acting upon information in a rational way. Generally such youngsters are labeled Adapted or Rebellious Children. The Adapted Child, the Little Professor, develops legal thinking in order to find ways to express his Natural or his Rebellious Child. He often sounds like a Philadelphia lawyer when he tries to justify (rationalize) some of his childish actions. His central concern is how to be naughty while seeming to be innocent of infractions of the laws of home, school, and society. Many Adapted Children wind up playing the game 'stupid' or 'wooden leg' in order to avoid taking responsibility for their own actions and to get even with their adult persecutors.

It is further intriguing that so many of the characteristics attributed to MBD children also describe Eysenck's (1967) extraverted type. Eysenck theorizes that extraverts (as identified by the Maudsley Personality Inventory) are less cortically aroused than introverts. He and his associates found that extraverts are more susceptible to an accumulation of inhibition than introverts and thus show more *involuntary* rest pauses (lapses of attention) on a vigilance or tapping task. Introverts, by contrast, condition more easily and are more tolerant of long conditions of the same, complex mental work. Extraverts are more tolerant of pain and therefore fail to learn from ordinary punishment. Extraverts are more affiliation oriented, whereas introverts are more achievement oriented, but introversion-extraversion is not correlated with IQ. Trauel (1961) reported that extraverts subjectively tolerated a sensory deprivation period better than introverts—*but only because they could not conform to the rules.* Subjects were instructed to lie quietly, which introverts did, but extraverts tapped, wiggled and squirmed and thus devised a way to endure the unpleasant situation.

We, and others, have speculated that MBD children constantly seek stimulation, thinking principally of the hyperactive-impulsive type. Earlier we (Dykman, et al., 1971) theorized that hypoactive children also seek stimulation but in order to stay alert, and that in so doing, some become quite restless. In all of our experiments, however, hypoactives are the least physiologically and motorically responsive to stimuli. Thus, hypoactives may seek some types of stimuli, but they appear to wish to avoid any type stimulation which they must process.

As an explanation for stimulus seeking behavior in MBD children, we theorized in our 1971 article that many of these youngsters may be cortically under-aroused (see also Boydstun, et al., 1968). Physiological and EEG studies point to that conclusion in hyperactives as well as nonhyperactive groups. Further evidence of cortical underarousal is the finding that stimulant drugs can improve attention in groups of MBD children (Douglas, 1972; Laufer, et al., 1957; Satterfield and Dawson, 1971). Paul Wender (1972) likewise contends that MBD children are deficient in arousal and has added one other speculation: that MBD children tend to have a higher pain-pleasure threshold than normal children, which would make it less likely that they (like Eysenck's extraverts) would respond to ordinary reward or punishment in a conditioning and learning situation.

Just as some puzzling findings begin to mesh, we remember two disquieting facts: In our clinical practice, we have seen children, albeit a small proportion, who are introverted as well as hyperactive and impulsive, those a teacher might label "nervous" or "high strung." Secondly, though usually introverted, hypoactives do not condition any better than hyperactives. Thus, the extraversion-introversion dimension, a really significant one in terms of MBD, may be orthogonal rather than isomorphic with the attention-intention dimension.

Still asking questions and seeking answers, we turn to more strictly neurophysiological research. Pribram's work with monkeys seems particularly relevant to our conceptualizing regarding attention and intention. Pribram (1960; 1967) found that monkeys with dorsolateral frontal lesions are not as concerned as normal animals with the immediate consequences of their actions. By contrast, animals with inferior temporal lesions do not differ from normal animals in this matter of implications. Rather, the inferior temporal animals show deficits in visual, auditory, and somesthetic choice behavior. These particular lesions lead to deficiencies in scanning and sampling the environment. When placed in a learning situation which forces responses to many cues, the inferior temporal lesion animals sample only a limited fraction of the cues available, and, as a consequence, do not learn as well as control animals.

Pribram (1960) utilized a modified Wisconsin Card Sort type task. The monkey first had to learn how to get a peanut by lifting one or two small objects. The objects could be moved to any one of twelve positions on a board (twelve peanut holes). After the monkey had chosen the correct object five times, the contingency of reward changed. The other object became "it" (a response reversal task), and the monkey had to learn to choose it. After making this correct choice for five consecutive trials, he was shown a three object display with each, in turn, becoming "it." Objects were progressively added until the monkey had to chose the one of twelve that covered the peanut. The position of the objects on the board changed in a predetermined random order on every trial. And, as with the simple task, after five consecutive correct trials the reinforced object (concept) changed. With each change in reward contingency, then, an animal "had to learn" which new object to select, and he had to refrain from responding to the previous positive cue ("unlearn what he had learned"). Pribram states that the solution to this problem is facilitated when a monkey attains two strategies: a set to keep sampling until the right object is discovered (search strategy), and a set to continue to choose the object which most recently brought reward until it no longer brings reward (after-search strategy). Clearly, the first strategy is related to selective attention (the process of acquiring information) and the second to implication (how to use the information).

Surprisingly, with up to five to six objects (cues), the monkeys with posterior lesions (inferotemporal region) made fewer errors than controls. Inferotemporal animals were, it appeared, restricted in the number of alternatives they could sample or handle at one time. This finding concurs with certain predictions made about error rate from mathematical learning theory: "the rapidity of increase in errors depends upon the sampling ratio—the fewer objects sampled, the more delayed the peak in recorded errors" (Pribram, 1960, p. 1329). The inferotemporal cortex determines the constant in the mathematical model (the ratio of the number of elements sampled to the total number that could be sampled).

Pribram's model of selective attention follows: First the posterior association cortex is modality specific, and the inferotemporal area, one part, subserves visual choice behavior. Second, the posterior association cortex partitions, or gates, events in the primary sensory receiving areas, the extrinsic cortex. We interpret partition to mean dividing the stream of information into meaningful units, but the term partition connotes more than this. The inferotemporal cortex also enhances the activity of cells in the primary sensory regions—potentiation of stimulation underway. Reserve capacity is adequate to allow each of a series of inputs to occupy a different set of cells since new inputs cannot occupy what is already occupied. The cells in primary sensory areas, still excited by the posterior cortex, act as a short-term memory against which correct input can be matched. Pribram says a match-mismatch operation of this sort is demanded by many models of recognition and selective attention (Bruner, 1957; Craik, 1943; MacKay, 1956; Sokolov, 1960).

Pribram emphasized that the *primary* function of the posterior association cortex is to partition events and not to act as an association or memory area. It is, to speak in analogies, a programming area which contains stored tapes on how to search and select stimuli. Continued activity of the posterior sector "results in a sequence of patterns of information (partitions) of increasing complexity, which in turn allows more and more release specification of particular elements in the set (or subsets) of events occurring in the extrinsic systems" (p. 1333, 1960). Here, the extrinsic system refers to the primary sensory areas. Through continued functioning of the posterior sector, more and more information can be conveyed by a given channel. Pribram assumes that the channels active and potentiated shape the pattern of potential information—the stimulus the organism will choose to attend to. But, where selective attention leaves off and intention begins is not clear.

According to Pribram, lesions in the frontolimbic sector interfere with "those aspects of intention that depend on an estimation of the effects that an outcome of an action has in terms of the total set of possible outcomes" (p. 1336, 1960). Frontal lesion animals also make a large number of errors on the task earlier described, but because they fail to choose the correct object again following initial reward. (Pribram simply tallied the number of errors made after one success, calling this "after-search" behavior). Error rate also varied as a function of the number of cues; frontal lesion animals made far more errors than controls or inferotemporal animals when they had to consider five or more objects. Frontal lesion animals invariably chose the novel cue immediately in the complex cue discrimination task.

Pribram (1961) trained some frontal lesion animals in an operant procedure. After many years of training them on mixed and multiple schedules, he ran four hours of extinction; reinforcement was omitted while other conditions remained the same. Whereas the control monkeys extinguished, frontal animals continued to respond. Even though they did not find the reward, they kept going back to look for it. Thus, they seemed not to be influenced by changed conditions of nonreward. These monkeys did not reprogram. Since the frontal lesion monkey had learned the operant procedure—that is, reacted to the reward conditions, why did they not adapt to nonreward? Pontius (1972) theorizes that the inability to switch from one principle of action to another when conditions change is a basis of delinquent behavior and the resultant of frontal lobe immaturity and/or neuropathology.

The model Pribram develops for intention parallels that of attention. The anterofrontal cortex (intrinsic cortex) partitions events in the extrinsic mediobasal forebrain (structures having to do with feeding, fleeing, mating, maternal behavior, duration of avoidance behavior to painful stimulation, reactions to frustration, etc.). The effect of continued activity of the intrinsic frontal cortex is "to allow more and more precise specification of intent that can be conveyed for any given outcome" (p. 1399, 1969). The frontal intrinsic sector "is a programming mechanism that maps intentions" (p. 1399, 1969).

To simplify, Pribram is talking about two kinds of mechanisms. One, located posteriorly, promotes differentiation and stimulus selection; the other, located frontally, subserves intention. Pribram admits that this distinction is not new. In both areas, increasingly complex neural events occur, which allow more and more precise differentiations and intentions. Ultimately one comes to more philosophical distinctions involving interest, value orientation, will power, implications—the bases of socially adaptive and acceptable behavior. Pribram's 1960 paper is a definitive statement, a brilliant chapter, and must reading for theoreticians and clinicians.

The kinds of behavorial deficiencies produced by injuries of the frontolimbic areas and associated cortex (Milner, 1963) are very similar to those seen in MBD children—hyperactivity, impulsivity, perseveration or inability to switch from one action to another, dissociation of action and verbalization, and disregard for rules and consequences. Clearly these behaviors tend to be associated more with intention then attention, *if there is a difference.* Perhaps, we are talking about two aspects of faulty attention—one a defect in the primary sensory pathways having to do with the reception and storage of information and the other with inattentiveness (intention) as a personality trait.

Distractibility is generally mentioned in the same breath with faulty attention. It is well to note there are two kinds of distractions. One meaning of distraction refers to the interfering effect of specific irrelevant stimuli and the other relates to the state of being dazed, scatterbrained, or day-dreaming. William James discussed the latter state of distraction as the opposite of attentiveness. Perhaps in the light of Pribram's model, we could consider specific distractors as allied with attention while nonspecific distractors are closely tied to intention.

The neurological evidence reviewed above, combined with research and clinical experience, points to at least two main types of MBD children: the first, the "frontal lobe type," is the one most commonly seen in clinical practice. He is hyperactive, impulsive, inattentive, careless of rules, and has little staying power (or task persistance). Since he has little concern for implications and consequences, he is generally poor in all school subjects and in interpersonal relations as well. In general, this type does well on the truly verbal tasks of the WISC (Information, Comprehension, Similarities, Vocabulary) but he is poor on Mental Arithmetic, Digit Span, Coding, and Mazes. Such a child could be expected to show a dissociation between verbalization and performance—he might say "Don't press" to a negative signal but go right ahead and do it. These frontal lobe types obviously manage to sample enough while "on the go" to learn a great deal—and this is not surprising considering the redundancy built into the elementary school curriculum. Such a child may even perform well on classwork when the teacher provides him continuous reinforcement.

We have one reservation in ascribing the above MBD constellation to frontal lobe dysfunction, for we do not know for certain the relation between sustained attention (one form of intention) and an inability to evaluate and weigh different alternatives (the implications and consequences aspect of intention). For now, we will assume that these two aspects of intention compose a unitary trait. If subsequent research indicates that they are, in fact, orthogonal, then we must think in terms of two hyperactive-impulsive subtypes.

The second major category of MBD children (really many different types) have a specific processing defect in visual, auditory, and/or other sensory areas. Though his senses are, medically speaking, intact, this type MBD child generally does not perceive (register) the salient or unique characteristics of letters, words, or sounds, or he does not fill in the Gestalt. He cannot look at letters or words and decide rapidly whether they are the same or different. Moreover, unlike normal learners, he cannot derive meaning from reading or speech by sampling only a fraction of the message.

A monkey can quickly discriminate p and q or b and d and without attaching any symbolic significance to these stimuli whatsoever. A young child with normal perceptual experience can do likewise. Why can some older MBD children not do this? In our previous paper (Dykman, et al., 1971). we speculated that such a child's basic defect is not so much misperception as faulty attention. Focusing requires that relevant inputs be selected, that there be a tuning of receptors, effectors, and brain mechanisms (appropriate arousal) for environmental inputs and input ideational transactions, as well as freedom from distractibility (James, 1890; Sokolov, 1690). We continue to contend that the defect is in attentional mechanisms rather than perception: perception is sensation plus meaning and discriminations can be made without attaching meaning to stimuli. Such a defect would seem to be in the primary sensory systems and in basic input mechanisms.

Before a child attaches any symbolic significance to letters whatsoever, he first has to distinguish them. He has to compare one with the other and decide same or different. The child who cannot easily make such simple discriminations (a child with a visual attention or object constancy problem) has to work around this recognition problem with other higher level processes. He requires a different learning strategy. Obviously, normal children, who can make relevant comparisons in a first-stage processor (attentional mechanisms), should have far less difficulty in attaching to letter groups the higher order symbolic and semantic meanings—the process we call learning to read.

As in the case of the frontal lobe type MBD child, there may be two varieties of posterior defect children. One could have inoperative or defective channels, making it almost impossible for him to differentiate (efficiently encode) similar symbols (e.g. b and d or saw and was). The other subtype may run into difficulty only when the number of elements to be sampled overloads his reserve capacity (as in the complex visual choice problems presented to Pribram's monkeys). For now, we shall assume this encoding inefficiency is a unitary trait; i.e. restriction in choice behavior automatically implies a confusion of inputs. The apprehension of *was* as was (not saw) requires a temporal ordering of inputs which must be matched with the *was* stored in permanent memory.

From another point of view, we are talking about focus and scan operations: focus has to do with the clearness of the image and scan relates to sampling. The best scanners should also be best

## ATTENTION

|  |  |
|---|---|
| IMPULSIVE BEHAVIOR PROBLEM NO LEARNING PROBLEM | ACADEMICALLY AND SOCIALLY SUCCESSFUL |
| IMPULSIVE BEHAVIOR PROBLEM GENERALIZED LEARNING PROBLEM | NICE CHILD SPECIFIC PROCESSING HANDICAP AND ASSOCIATED LEARNING PROBLEMS |

– _____ INTENTION +

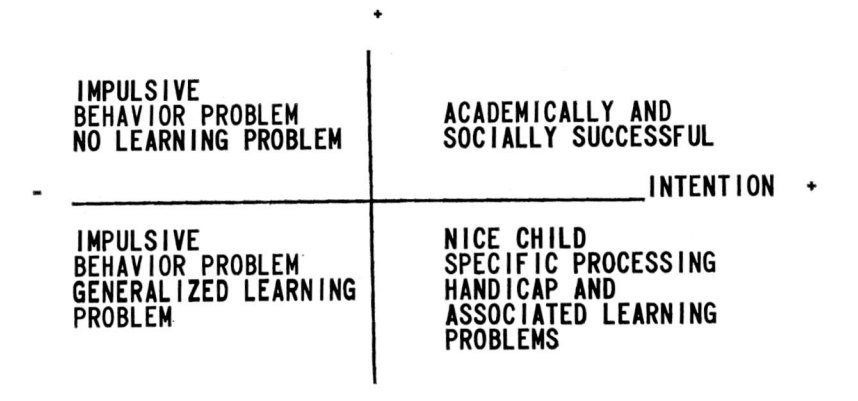

Figure III-2. The Attention-Intention Plane. MBD-LD subtypes suggested by the interaction and attentional and intentional deficits.

at focusing, but in some children these capabilities may not be in parallel. Future research could show that focusing and scanning are quite different aspects of attention. If we use the term "search strategy," as employed by Pribram, we can be reasonably certain that we are at least generically close to describing the learning disability of this type MBD child.

Figure III-2 is an attempt to position four main types of MBD children in two dimensional space. Attention is here considered to be orthogonal to the intention dimension. Since this lay-out ignores dimensions of temperament such as activity level and introversion-extraversion and does not entertain the possibility of the two aspects of attention and intention alluded to above, it should in no wise be considered anything other than food for thought.

In our earlier theoretical papers (Dykman, et al., 1970; Dykman, et al., 1971) we argued that organically based deficiencies in attention explain the poorer performance, the slower reaction times, the lower amplitude contingent negative variation wave, and the decreased physiological reactivity of learning disabled children on laboratory tasks and in the school room as well. Organic, in this particular context, referred to subtle changes in the wiring or the hook-up of neural connections in the brain.

Arousal is generally recognized as being closely related to attention. *But arousal supports all complex mental and informational processing* activities, including all motor activity. In this sense, arousal is no more related to attention than to any other action of the organism. The organism must be aroused to an appropriate level for behavior to be maximally efficient. We assume, with Hebb (1955) and Malmo (1959), an inverse U shaped relationship between arousal and the efficiency of attention or other psychological processes such that peak efficiency occurs in the mid range of the arousal continuum. This relationship is only part of the story, however. Probably of greater importance is the very qualitative nature of the arousal process itself. With attention turned in there are certain kinds of physiological changes, but with attention turned out, there are other kinds of physiological changes, two distinctive patterns (Boydstun, *et al.*, 1968; Lacey, *et al.*, 1963). And there are likely variations of attention-in and attention-out, so that other patterns of physiological responsivity remain to be identified. In any event, we suspect that the qualitative nature of the arousal process depends upon reverberating circuits between brain stem arousal mechanisms and diencephalic and cortical structures. It is said that by way of nerve fibers descending to the brainstem and the ascending system from the brainstem, the cortex is able to regulate its own arousal to a considerable extent. This arrangement constitutes a semi-independent generator or booster which must be intact for efficient attention and learning.

But the brain stem reticular formation is not, in and of itself, sufficient to explain the subtleties of arousal. Clemente (1968) has described a forebrain inhibitory system capable of controlling both somatic and visceral mechanisms. Electrical stimulation of this system suppresses movement, synchronizes electrical cortical activity, and produces sleep. The inhibitory effect is proportionate to the intensity of stimulation (hence, a weak stimulus might slow but not halt on-going behavior). Clemente proposes that his forebrain inhibitory system and the reticular formation act reciprocally, perhaps via relays in the limbic circuit and in the diffusely-projecting thalamic nuclei. We postulated that the brain stem reticular formation and the forebrain inhibitory system provided the neural energy invested in attending and in mediating specific patterns of autonomic and somatic (striated musculature) excitation. Then, following Penfield (1969), we envisioned a switching mechanism located in the diencephalon. This mechanism is programmed from above and determines whether attention will turn in or out. Such a switching mechanism can be inferred also from Russian experimentation into what they term mobility of central nervous system processes (Pavlov, 1928; Gray, 1964).

The motor restlessness of hyperactive MBD children is a red herring which has led many investigators to postulate overarousal. The weight of physiological evidence suggests, to the contrary, that MBD children are cortically underaroused (see research review). To explain excessive restlessness in the face of underarousal, we envisioned a shunting or divergence of excitation from structures essential to attention and learning to other brain structures, such as the extrapyramidal motor system. The opposite of focus is diffuseness, and we merely assumed that there are discrete and random processes within the nervous system which parallel external behavioral processes. Some hypoactive children become restless, and we postulated that their fidgety behavior stems likewise from an inability to focus on relevant stimuli. In their case, there is divergence from an inhibitory neural focus, whereas in hyperactive children there is divergence, or shunting, from excessive excitatory neural activity. There are inhibitory and excitatory neurons in the central nervous system, and activity in one is not basically different from activity in the other. Theoretically, in either case you could have an overflow effect. Suppose, as Pontius theorizes (1972), frontal-lobe myelinization is incomplete in some MBD children: inasmuch as this would spell "poor insulation," then more diffuse activity from neurons sounds quite plausible.

Borrowing again from Russian psychology, and particularly Luria (1959, 1969), we can postulate that the hyperactive child has an excess of excitation rather than inhibition, whereas, the reverse obtains for the hypoactive child. According to Luria, the end effect of excessive excitation or inhibition on school performance in the same; both hyperactive and hypoactive children fail to keep pace with their classmates.

If hyperactive children have an excess of excitation due to diffusion within the nervous system, then it follows that they will be overattentive to external events. The hyperactive child should be weakest in tasks requiring sustained attention-in (e.g. mental arithmetic). Because he is so distractible, the hyperactive reacts even to familiar irrelevant stimuli and "loses" his train of thought in problem solving. The hypoactive child also performs inadequately in mental arithmetic, but probably because he does not attend to full statement of the problem in the first place. With an excess and/or diffusion of inhibition, he does not encode all of the information needed to solve the problem. Hyperactives seem to favor the attention-out mode and hypoactives the attention-in mode of operation. This preference can be likened to a response set or even an enduring personality trait. Because of this "set," whatever the direction, all learning disabled children can be expected to exhibit considerable inertia in switching from attention-out to attention-in, or the reverse. Effective learning requires appropriate switching.

We are comfortable in reasoning that hyperactive children have a stimulus hunger. They are distractible even in a quiet environment and become very restless in search of stimuli. Hypoactive children are much more puzzling. We know that these usually slow moving children also tend to be flat or sluggish in emotional responses. In general, they are somewhat introverted and nonaffiliation oriented. As stated earlier, our impression is that hypoactives wish to avoid stimuli which must be processed. Though they seem to prefer attention-in, they are not proficient at problem solving (Gates, 1968). Unfortunately, very few investigators have studied hypoactive LD children. Doyle, et al. (1973) found that hypoactives unlike hyperactives were not attracted to a visual distractor in a vigilance task, but the performance of both types of children deteriorated with time. Possibly the hypoactives were distracted more by internal than external events (day dreaming). Perhaps when hypoactive children exhibit restless, fidgety behavior in our laboratory, we should read this as a sign that they would like to escape the almost incessant stimulation of a day of individual testing (i.e. as a defensive hyperactivity).

Both from a behavorial and neurophysiological standpoint, there appears to be a reciprocal relationship between attentiveness and motor restlessness. As one process becomes dominant, the other is suppressed. Reciprocal relationships of the nervous system are well recognized, particularly in Russian conditioning theories. Reciprocal inhibition could, for example, greatly increase the specificity and density of neural activity. Reciprocal inhibition could interdict attention-out as attention-in becomes dominant, and the converse. Perhaps the most important function of reciprocal inhibition is the delineation of active from inactive channels of communication. This action restricts the range of neural activity, narrowing the channel, and leaving other fibers available to receive other inputs. With a lack of reciprocal antagonism, the number of inputs which can be processed successively, or at the same time, is greatly reduced. In summary, reciprocal inhibition limits the number of stimuli the organism can attend to at any one time and it heightens arousal, thus helping to ensure that appropriate action is taken in the face of the most relevant stimuli.

In elaborating our earlier model, we felt an adequate explanation of attentional processes in man could not ignore the role of speech functions and language. Previously we said (Dykman, *et al.*, 1970, p. 779), "The impaired ability of CLD (children with learning disabilities) to abstract or devise sufficient rules for data processing and classification might explain their impairment in neglecting irrelevant information (faulty inhibition)." We hypothesized that mechanisms of speech control central inhibition, perhaps more effectively than any other mechanism. To respond rapidly and precisely, one must ignore (reciprocally inhibit) irrelevant information, whether environmentally or self-produced, and one must focus his excitation on specific stimuli. In our choice reaction time experiments, the child who verbalizes, explicitly or implicitly, "get ready; press to red; ignore green; release to white; ignore noise," should theoretically have a great advantage over one who has not acquired or fails to use verbal mediators. We shall presently review recent evidence upholding this point.

We followed Piaget (1959) and Luria (1961) in emphasizing inner speech as a mechanism nonpareil in the control of behavior. Luria (1961) reported that many children who were slow in conditioning and differentiation were helped by self induced speech commands. Vygotsky (1962) theorized that the egocentric speech of young children does not vanish at a certain age, as held by Piaget, but rather that such speech becomes *sotto voce* and continues to help the older child think through a problem. Inner speech likewise evolves and condenses until ultimately one needs only fragments to guide his thinking in ordinary circumstances. Extraordinary events can, however, elicit this inner speech, even from adults.

## AN INFORMATION PROCESSING MODEL

In an attempt to pull together our earlier and more recent thoughts regarding information processing in MBD children, we have devised the schema shown in Figure III-3. This model, which is in harmony with the theoretical positions of Simon (1972) and Kesner (1973), also permits a framework for the investigations to be reviewed. More importantly, the model points to practical research that needs to be done in order to answer the question of how best to teach each individual MBD-LD child.

The major structures in the model are arousal, short term memory (STM), long term memory (LTM), central processing units (CPs), and attention-out and attention-in registers. Though direct evidence and logic point to the existence of most of the parts, how they all work together remains elusive. Brain dysfunctions obviously can stem from a defect in any structure but from defects in the organization of, or connections between, centers as well. In the final analysis, speed of information processing, which may be the essence of intelligence, is a matter of innate neuronal organization, the intactness of the nervous system at a given point in development, and acquired habits and patterns for encoding and retrieval.

In our schema, attention-in (AI) and attention-out (AO) registers function as millisecond memories, a term borrowed from our friend and collaborator, Dr. John E. Peters. Attention-out registers, actually sensory registers for external events, are modality specific (i.e. a different register for each sensory system). The contents of an attention-out register may be brought into sharp focus and evaluated via the action of central processing units. If the information is wanted, it will be held in the register briefly, or else transferred to short term memory, and occasionally given sufficient rehearsal or impact, on to long term memory.

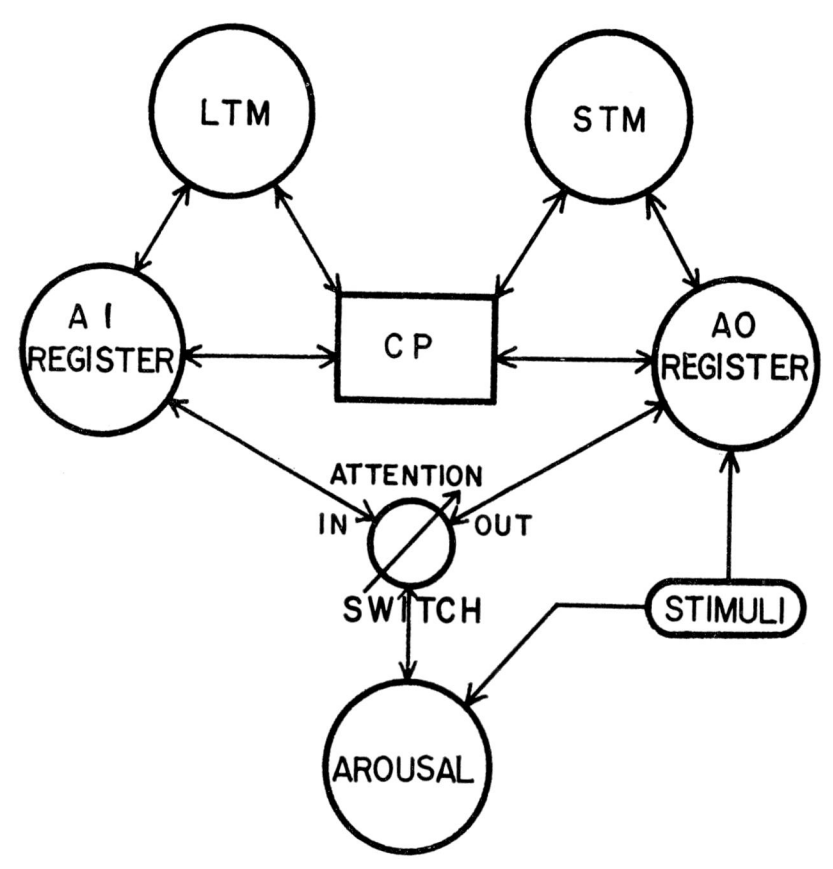

Figure III-3. Information Processing Model. In this diagram, STM = short term memory, LTM = long term memory, CP = central processing units, AO = attention out, and AI = attention in. Connections are assumed from arousal mechanisms to all other structures above.

Consider the role of attention-out registers in a nonsymbolic or nonsematic matching task, that is, one not involving long term memory (no familiar figures). The standard could, for example, be stored in short term memory. Then, other objects can be admitted to the attention-out register and matched via a central processing unit with the standard held in short term memory. A central processing unit can also compare information in different attention-out registers in a cross-modality matching of a tone sequence with a tactile or visual pattern. Attention-out registers also function in the clarification and consolidation of events in short term memory. That is, a central processing unit can withdraw a memory from short term memory and intensify it in the attention-out register either for the purpose of matching or rehearsal.

Attention-out registers are only under the partial control of central processing units, for a strong or novel stimulus can override any volition to ignore the outer world or to pay attention only to certain events. A major assumption is that attention-out registers have direct connections with movement and speech processes in LTM. Otherwise we cannot explain certain more or less automatic responses to external stimuli.

Attention-in registers operation in relation to long term memory in much the way that attention-out registers function in relation to short term memory. But, whereas attention-out registers and short term memory are modality specific, with a separate center for each sensory system, attention-in registers and long term memory are function specific. Function specific means that organization is in terms of major behaviorial categories such as search behavior, sequencing, concept formation, intentions, and implications.

For clarification purposes, contrast the matching of nonfamiliar figures (above) with matching involving familiar patterns which would be stored in long term memory. For example, in response to the Picture Completion cards of the WISC, a central processing unit is thought to withdraw a relevant image from long term memory and to intensify it in an attention-in register. This image can then be directly compared with the actual image in the visual attention-out register. Comparison of information in attention-out and attention-in registers is the route by which more accurate schemas of the external world are built into long term memory.

Matching may then occur between attention-out and attention-in registers as well as between different attention-out registers. Conceivably, all comparisons are made in registers; that is, images stored in short term memory may have to be placed in a register before the match can be made. An alternative hypothesis is that attention processes function to illuminate certain contents of memory. Thus, attention might be analagous to a beam of light shining now on this part of memory and then on another part. The focus could be either narrow or wide. The question is whether attention should be conceived as structural (attention registers under the control of central processing units) or whether attention is, in fact, a descriptive term for neural processes. According to Simon (1972), attention is the set of processes that filters information and determines what small part of it will occupy the central processor at any given time.

We think there is a process of attention as well as the structures for registering events. Thus, what one attends to may be in a register or in memory (short term memory or long term memory); this act of selective attention defines one's immediate state of consciousness. The concept attention implies all the neurophysiological mechanisms which determine our conscious awareness at a given point in time; awareness, in turn, is intimately related to and dependent upon our state of arousal.

*Arousal mechanisms,* involving the forebrain inhibitory system and the brain stem activating system, regulate the responsivity of all higher cerebral processes. Were our schema three-dimensional, arousal mechanisms would be drawn to project upwards and link with all other structures in the diagram. A main function of arousal centers is the sensitization of synapses, which, in turn, facilitates conduction and increases the probability that new information will be retained. Arousal is a relatively discriminant process, for the most facilitated parts of the CNS are those appropriate for the kind of information conveyed. At the same time, arousal is widespread, because even the simplest responses involve so much of the nervous system. In a sense, attention is the resultant of arousal, that is, the sensitization of certain neural pathways, either reflexly or volitionally.

At any given moment, attention is generally directed either in or out, with the other inhibited. William James observed that when attention is intently turned in and sustained, there is a diminution or partial inhibition of all incoming sensory stimuli. We even tend to roll our eyes upwards and backwards, and children sometimes shut their eyes when trying hard to think. We postulate an *attention switching mechanism,* perhaps located in the diencephalon, which controls the direction of focus.

Experiments by Lacey and associates (1963) and from our laboratory indicate that attention-in tasks produce cardiac acceleration and certain respiratory changes. But, with attention turned out, opposite kinds of physiological and skeletal motor adjustments occur. Although attention-out and attention-in usually have quite different concomitant arousal patterns, we probably must take into account also the degree of arousal. When engaged in very active attention-out processing, as in the case of a flight controller at a busy airport, the physiological arousal pattern may be unlike that evoked in a less active attention-out state, say, a simple reaction time procedure. Similarly, an active attention-in information processing task (mental arithmetic) may evoke quite a different physiological pattern than an attention-in state when processing is negligible or nil (reverie or wool gathering). With intense active processing, whether attention-out or attention-in, physiological levels may be so elevated as to obscure patterns easily demonstrated in less active states. Neither attention-in nor attention-out processing is likely efficient when one is overly excited, perhaps in part, because attention is adversely affected by inappropriate physiological activation.

Following William James, we postulate that when the switch is set to the out position, the attention-in registers are generally deactivitated, and that all neural processing is focused on external events. Attention-out involves in the main, the sensory registers, short term memory, central processing units, and the arousal mechanisms. Conversely, with the switch set to the in position, attention-out registers are not attended to. Thus, attention-in usually involves long term memory, central processing units, and the arousal system. However, short term memory can be utilized in some attention-in operations just as long term memory can be utilized in certain attention-out operations.

If there is a high predictability of attention-out input, requiring only minimal processing and overlearned responses, then attention-in and attention-out may occur more or less in parallel. For example, most of us can drive our cars safely through busy but familiar city streets while at the same time making future plans or rehearsing the events of the day. We may even engage in active learning (listening to a newscast or a tape cassette). Since neither attention-out nor attention-in dominates in such a situation, there perhaps is a neutral switch position which allows attention-in processing while performing principally attention-out tasks. We favor a simplifying supposition, however; at least for some kinds of attention-out operations, particularly those involving highly overlearned stimulus-response patterns such as movements and speech, the attention-out registers are directly connected to long term memory via programs in the central processing units. Since the usual attention-out-short term memory loop is by-passed in such instances, attention-in need not be inhibited.

The child must actively process more sensory stimuli than the adult. Because of limited experiences, he encounters more events that are unfamiliar or only vaguely familiar. He has built up fewer direct connections between attention-out and long term memory than the adult. Therefore, in most active transactions with the environment, he must rapidly switch attention from out to in and back. Many MBD children appear to be inefficient switchers. Attention may be out when it should be in, or the converse. In some children, the switch seems to stick in the out position (the stimulus distractible child), whereas in others the switch adheres to the in position (the daydreamer). The switch of the scatterbrained child seems to whip back and forth too rapidly to allow adequate processing and consolidation of information.

There are children who attend intently yet who cannot encode all needed information. Here we suspect problems with short term memory (STM). STM, also called scan-and-hold or new memory, presumably accepts information from attention-out registers. STM in the adult is usually limited in capacity to some seven chunks (Miller, 1956). STM is further limited in that it can retain information at best only a few seconds without rehearsal and then for no more than a few minutes. It operates almost exclusively on the principle of recency, then. Like the attention-out registers, STM is believed to be modality specific. STM is better able to store gestalt-type information than discrete bits; that is, most of us can remember a new face with much less effort than the name of the person. When the so-called magical limit of STM is exceeded, the only ways in which new information can be admitted are (1) by clearing out some or all of that present or (2) by chunking or consolidating several bits, as for example, to compress a telephone number into a triad and two dyads rather than try to hold seven digits. But, STM has no capacity within itself to chuck or reorganize information. Such strategies and programs are learned, either formally or by trial and error, and are utilized by the central processing units.

Some children can commit a set of facts to memory at night only to have lost them by morning. We suspect defect in long term memory (LTM) in such cases. LTM holds old rather than new information. Though huge, LTM is not infinite. There is an overload point such that if new information from STM is to be stored, some part of the old must be erased. That which is least used (or not overlearned) is generally the first to go. Thus, LTM consists of memories which persist from minutes to a near lifetime. Apart from rehearsal (or use), the major psychological principle involved is primacy. That is, first exposures and experiences are stored most efficiently—the first few letters of a word, the first lines of a poem or song, the first day in school, the honeymoon. Other factors which affect transfer of information to LTM are state of arousal, saliency of input cues, complexity of the stimulus pattern or material, and intervening or distracting events (Kesner, 1973). But the foremost element is rehearsal, for the other factors really influence how much the new information gets rehearsed.

As with STM, LTM appears to be more efficient with continous than discrete information. Visual recognition LTM is quite remarkable. Haber (1970) asked students to view 2560 photographic slides at the rate of one every ten seconds. Half the subjects had four one-hour sessions on consecutive days and the remainder had two-hour sessions, one day apart. An hour after each subject had seen the last group of slides, he was presented 280 pairs of pictures and asked to designate the one of each pair he had previously seen. Accuracy ranged from 85 to 95 percent, and length of viewing session was not critical. Haber maintains that accuracy in memory depends on whether material is pictorial or linguistic. Apparently a picture is indeed worth a thousand words, and the implication is that the better we pictorialize linguistic material, the better symbolic and semantic learning will be.

Encoding and retrieval from LTM are accomplished via the

*central processing units* (CPs). In a sense, CPs are the couriers of the informational processing system. While only one CP is shown in Figure III-3, we postulate many CPs, one subserving each major behavorial function. CPs can be activated singly or simultaneously in subgroups. The CP which serves the function of intention or implications is thought to be situated in the frontal lobes, while the CP which "manages" search behavior (or problem solving) possibly functions out of the inferotemporal lobe (Pribram, 1960). Still another CP subserves speech and most logically would be located in the temporal lobes of the left (or dominant) hemisphere. Other CPs are thought to subserve movement and motor patterns, emotional and social behaviors, sequencing, and conceptual thinking. Only by postulating multiple CPs, each with an adjacent LTM, can we explain the rapid access to certain kinds of information.

Though CPs are conceived to be innate, we do not believe they are fixed. The basic programs for encoding, retrieval, and response are contained in the CPs; but the data to be used in the programs is stored in LTM. Thus, our model is consistent with the speech model proposed by Chomsky (1968). That is, LTM contains the words (English, German, or whatever) used in speaking but not the programs used to acquire language and create units of speech (phrases and sentences).

Just how many CPs there are, we cannot say. For example, form recognition is presumably mediated by the CP for search behavior; however, it may be an entirely separate operation or else represent a combined operation of several CPs. Moreover, it may be that every CP has its own sequencer or that there is an independent CP for random accessing. On the other hand, some postulated CPs may not exist. Social behavior could be mediated by the strategies and programs of the intentions and implications CP, and this particular CP could well be the "head ganglion" of the entire brain.

A major function of CPs is to effect the transfer of new information from STM to LTM; the main psychological principle is rehearsal coupled with intent to retain. A single emotionally charged experience is readily stored in LTM, largely because arousal structures sensitize the CPs and LTM. That is, with appropriate arousal, the amount of rehearsal needed to make an engram in LTM is greatly reduced. Mundane experiences are not apt to get transferred to LTM because arousal is low and rehearsal is unlikely. Therefore, information which though potentially useful has little emotional charge (e.g. the multiplication tables) is stored in LTM only after intentional rehearsal (drill).

Some further examples of information processing may help to elucidate the model. Consider a "simple" reaction time task wherein the subject must press a key to one light and release it to a subsequent one. Such actions would involve mainly the visual attention-out register, STM, and rehearsal structures. CPs would call up from LTM appropriate programs for movements and search behavior. Once instructions are processed, the attention switch is set to "out." Within a constricted age range, speed of reaction should then be proportional to intensity of stimulation. But, in fact, reaction times will vary both between and within children of the same age, reflecting innate conduction differences *but also strength of intention.*

The model allows movement and speech CPs (and their respective areas of long term memory) to function in either attention-out or attention-in operations. Once a movement pattern is stored in LTM, it can be directly accessed and executed on command via the central processing unit-attention-out mechanism (perhaps located in the thalamus). For this reason, a complex motor movement, such as a golf swing, can be explained in essentially the same way as simple reaction time. However, whereas there are only a limited few ways one can press a key, one learns many different golf swings. Therefore, the pattern that is discharged is response to the image of the golf ball in the visual attention-out register may be quite variable (and surprising).

Subtraction by 7's from 100 is a good example of an essentially attention-in process. After attending out briefly to encode instructions, the subject then must shut out the outer environment. That is, the switch is set to attention-in and the attention-out mechanism is "turned off." The CP for language and cognition accesses the relevant program from LTM using only two factors from STM—the instructions to subtract by 7's and the starting number, 100. As indicated above, this type mental exercise is associated with increased heart rate and other physiological changes appropriate for the support of attention-in (Lacey, 1963). The WISC arithmetic subtest is also mainly an attention-in task, but demands more efficient encoding (an attention-out and STM operation) than the subtraction by 7's task.

Coding, block design, and digit span forward on the WISC are essentially attention-out operations, and the matching called for is presumed to occur in the attention-out registers and STM. Object assembly, picture completion, and picture arrangement, on the other hand, elicit material from LTM to achieve matchings isomorphic with past experiences. These latter tests require considerable switching from attention-out to attention-in and between the processors and STM and LTM. Information, comprehension, similarities, and vocabulary subtests assess primarily attention-in and the LTM side of our model. Digits backwards tests efficiency of scan-and-hold memory, which is accomplished through rehearsal (inner speech) for most subjects. Those with extraordinary memory spans probably have stored in CPs and LTM certain strategies which make rehearsal less necessary. Some perhaps pictorialize auditory stimuli, as was the case with the famous Russian mnemonist studied by Luria (1968).

From a developmental standpoint, we postulate a blank LTM at birth or at that moment during the prenatal period when the brain becomes sufficiently developed to register experiences. This is not to say that the brain is simply a *tabula rasa* which passively records experiences. Indeed, spurred by innately organized CPs, the organism actively seeks information (Piaget, 1959). Concrete thinking ability precedes conceptual development, but some individuals attain very little conceptual thinking skill. Conceptual ability possibly reflects the function of a CP (or several CPs) which perfects programs for comparing and categorizing information.

In harmony with Piagetian theory, we envisage a definite sequence of changes such that CPs would modify or update stored programs throughout life. Still following developmental theory, we would expect that movement CPs are the first to undergo organization, followed perhaps in order by CPs for search behavior, intentions, speech and random accessing (permutations and combinations). The speech CP could evolve, as Piaget (1959) and Vygotsky (1962) theorized, with egocentric speech (thinking aloud) preceding inner speech (socialized thought).

A learning disability can stem from defects in any major structure as well as from faulty or inadequate experiences and/or neurological defects in the organization of the brain. However, it is our belief that most learning disabilities result from poorly organized or defective CPs rather than defects in other structures. That is, the deficiency is in the organization of what is stored and retrieved, particularly strategies for relevant stimulus selection and chunking. Obviously, the more CPs that are defective, the more severe the learning disability. The poor reader may be so because of his hyperactivity-impulsivity (defective CP for intentions) and inadequate strategies for search, chunking, and organization. On the other hand, since the brain functions as a unit, deficiencies in just one part (e.g. implications) can well interfere with efficiency of other parts (search behavior). Our challenge is to design experiments that will focus in on the specific structures in our model. Unfortunately, most investigations to date leave us still up in the air. We in the area of MBD-LD research must get on with the business of finding out what is in that black box.

## REVIEW OF RECENT RESEARCH ON MENTAL PROCESSES OF MBD CHILDREN

Having elaborated a model by which to explain breakdowns in informational processing of MBD children, we now may test some aspects of this model against recent research findings.

### Simple and Choice Reaction Time to Sensory Stimuli

Simple reaction time is the measure *par excellence* of attention-out, unconfounded by other higher order processes (James, 1890). Pressing a key to a single stimulus and releasing it to a subsequent one requires little in the way of long term memory or learning strategies.

Several studies have shown that reaction time is slower in MBD than in academically adequate children. Two explanations are offered: MBD children cannot or do not sustain their attention (intention) as well as controls, or their central processing time is slower under most conditions. Motor coordination has been ruled out as a contributing factor by most investigators, not via research but on the basis of speculation that a simple act, such as pressing a key, requires little in the way of eye-hand coordination.

Douglas (1972, 1973) and associates at McGill (Cohen, et al., 1971; Parry, 1973; Sykes, et al., 1971, 1972) have demonstrated that hyperactive MBDs can respond as fast as controls when their attention is engaged. In one such experiment, the child was told to get ready to respond and was not given a stimulus unless he appeared to be ready. In another, a serial reaction time task, the child controlled the appearance of the stimuli. Reaction time was not significantly different in hyperactive and controls on either task. By contrast, in experimeter-paced, vigilance type tasks, the McGill group found highly significant differences between hyperactive subjects and controls. Thus, Douglas (1972, 1973) favors a theory of impairment in sustained attention over a central processing deficit. The McGill group have not studied hypoactive or normoactive MBD children, however, and it may well be that in the nonhyperactive types, slowness of central processing is the major problem. In order to shed light on this point, we should like to review next our reaction time experiments with hyperactive, normoactive, and hypoactive MBD subjects (Dykman, et al., 1970, 1971).

For our simplest procedure, the child was told to press a telegraph key as rapidly as possible when the red light came on and to release it rapidly when the subsequent white light appeared (10 trials). The differentiation procedure was similar except that on half the trials (5) a green light was given, the child having been instructed to disregard it (no white light followed a green light). This procedure was followed by a distraction phase in which a very loud hooter (90 decibels and lasting one second) sounded before or during the initial (red or green) light (20 times). In all three procedures, the interval between the red warning light and the white light was four seconds. The intertrial interval was ten seconds.

We found in these three reaction time experiments that no MBD groups (hyperactive, hypoactive, or normoactive) responded as rapidly as controls to the red warning lights (press latencies) and that hypoactives were significantly slower than hyperactives. The only statistically significant difference with *release* latencies, however, came in the distraction phase, this involving the total MBD sample versus controls. One could argue from these data that the slower mean reaction time of MBD subjects to the red warning light reflects failure to sustain attention during the ten second intertrial interval. Attention was aided, in a sense, for the release response (the key was depressed), and no differences emerged except when a loud distractor was added.

We have some evidence of slower central processing, however, and particularly in younger hypoactive MBD subjects. When we divided our sample into two age groups (those eight to ten years and those ten to twelve years), we found that release as well as press latencies discriminated the younger hypoactives in the three procedures described above (Dykman, *et al.*, 1971). This difference could not be demonstrated in the older subjects, but, even with attention aided, the young hypoactives could not respond as fast as controls and other young MBD children.

Figure III-4 shows data from a later phase in which differentiation was reversed; that is, the children were told to press to the green light, which they had previously ignored, and to ignore

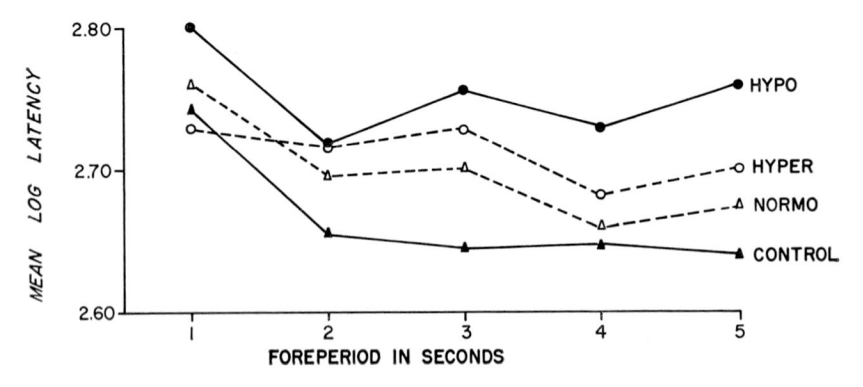

Figure III-4. Mean Log Latencies in Relation to Foreperiod, and Time from Onset of Stimulus One (Colored Light) to Onset of Stimulus Two (White Light). Three MBD-LD groups were studied: hyperactive, normoactive and hypoactive boys, ages 8 to 11 years.

the red light to which they had previously responded. Control and MBD children performed this simple reverse mobility exercise with equal success so far as errors were concerned, but the MBD group could not match the controls in release speed.

As an added wrinkle, in this particular procedure we varied the interval between the warning light and white light (the foreperiod). Our concern was whether a four or five second foreperiod was too long to be an effective preparatory interval. Given that long, the child might start looking around the room before the release signal light occurred. The data revealed that MBD groups were not as quick (ready) to respond at any interval as controls, a finding supported by the delayed reaction time experiments of Douglas and associates (1972). Controls reached a maximum readiness to respond in about two seconds and sustained this readiness. Hyperactive and normoactive MBD subjects did not achieve their maximum readiness until four seconds after the warning light. Hypoactives were as ready at two seconds as at four seconds, but were abnormally slow whatever the foreperiod. The finding that controls were ready to respond (release) sooner than the MBD groups could be taken as support for the slower central processing theory.

Another possible explanation of our press-release latency findings should be mentioned. The press response, which is sustained throughout the preparatory interval, interferes with the subsequent antagonistic release response to some degree. This interference effect could be greater in younger MBD children, particularly hypoactives, and could explain their significantly slower release times. Given all these considerations, however, we are more inclined to favor an attentional focus hypothesis, which postulates that the speed of reaction is proportional to the intensity of the attentional focus. The warning light in our experiments was not nearly as effective an aid to focus as Douglas's methods (i.e. waiting until the child appeared ready or letting him pace himself). Still there seems to be little doubt that attention was better engaged for the release than the press task.

In our experiments (Dykman, *et al.*, 1971) the various independent variables we introduced had mainly an additive effect on reaction time. That is, reaction time in a simple "go-no go" decision process increased over the "go" alone situation. But, there was no interaction effect: the controls slowed about as much as MBD children. The distracting stimulus contributed another substantially additive increment with no interaction. Thus, a simple nondiscriminatory reaction time task is about as good as a discrimination situation compounded with noise in separating subgroups of MBD children (hyperactive, normoactive and hypoactive) from controls. This conclusion holds only, however, for the simplest kinds of choices. Nora Jacobs (1972), contrasting hyperactives and controls, reported data suggesting an interaction effect as a function of task complexity. Perhaps we have to get somewhere beyond two choices to get a clear interactive effect (see below).

The most surprising finding in our experiments was that release latencies of controls and MBD children showed the same kind of general additive shifts with complexity and distraction as did press latencies (Fig. III-5). Once the key was down in the differentiation tasks the discrimination was made. No decision was required to release at the appearance of the white light. Why then did release latencies increase so dramatically and after only ten trials? Certainly fatigue effects had not set in so soon. And the child's attention was engaged. Our guess is that there was interference in the attention-out loop. The child had to hold an additional instruction in mind, and in order to press to red but not to green, some inhibition was necessary. Thus, the CP making the go or no-go decision may have caused sufficient diversion to slow down the well practiced release response.

Another very interesting effect seen in our differentiation data was what we referred to as an induction phenomenon (Dykman, et al., 1970). This effect was noted in the press latencies of MBD children but not in controls. It was found that a negative (no go) stimulus facilitated reaction time to a subsequent positive (go) stimulus. But, a positive response slowed reaction time to a subsequent positive stimulus, again in MBD children but not in controls. Because we had only ten trials (5 positive and 5 negative) to look at, these phenomena may have been chance occurrences,

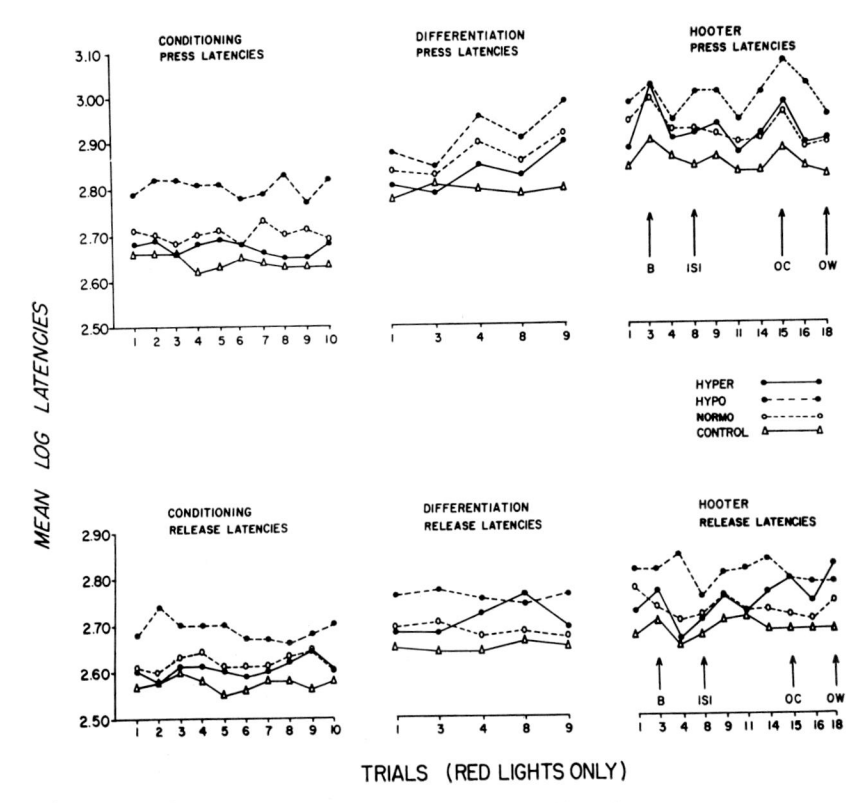

Figure III-5. Log Press and Release Latencies for Each Red Light Trial in the First Three Reaction Time Procedures. In the right-hand figure, B denotes a hooter noise given 1.5 seconds before a red light, ISI a noise given 1.5 seconds after onset of a red light, OC a noise overlapping the white light (came on 0.5 seconds before the light), and OW a noise overlapping the white light (came on 0.5 seconds before the white light). The hooter noise lasted one second. Missing numbers on the abscissa denote green lights (no latencies for no go signals).

but we don't think so. This kind of stimulus interaction, or response interaction, deserves further study in MBD children.

## REACTION TIME TO SYMBOLIC MATERIAL

Carl Spring and associates (1971; 1973) have studied reaction time and sustained attention in retarded readers and hyperactive boys. Two adjacent, upper-case letters were projected and the subject was instructed to press a switch in the dominant hand if the letters were the same and to press the switch in the non-dominant hand if the letters were different. Each session was divided into six blocks of twenty trials each, preceded by a practice block. The sound of the projector provided a ready signal (fixed foreperiod of one second). The intertrial interval was five seconds. Poor readers had significantly slower reaction times in every block and deteriorated more with time than controls, despite a ten minute break between Blocks 4 and 5. Spring concluded that the central processing time was much longer for poor readers than for normal readers. Central processing speed was estimated from the differences between time required to discriminate two highly dissimilar letters and time required to discriminate two highly similar letters.

In a follow-up experiment, Spring, *et al.*, (1973) contrasted twenty hyperactive boys taking methylphenidate, nineteen hyperactive boys whose medication was temporarily discontinued, and nineteen normal boys. Both hyperactive groups were slower on the symbolic reaction time test (described above) than controls, but were not significantly different from each other on the early trials. However, as testing progressed, the performance of hyperactives off medication declined, and by the sixth block the decrement was markedly greater than in the medicated boys and controls. Methylphenidate did not eliminate the difference in initial reaction time but rather prevented excessive performance decrement. Spring contends that the stimulant drug does enhance sustained attention but does not increase encoding speed (initial reaction time). Thus, he says, his findings may explain the clinical observation that stimulant drugs often result in dramatic improvement in the restless behavior of hyperactive children without producing comparable gains in school achievement.

Spring and associates did not look separately at the fastest reaction times of each hyperactive boy. The control group-hyperactive group mean difference in initial reaction time may stem from *greater variability* in the hyperactives' performance, even in the early trials. Though attention was aided in Spring's experiments via a click from the slide projector, it was not aided in the same significant way as in the experiments by Douglas and associates. Obviously, his results can be interpreted in a strictly intentional framework: we need assume only that poor readers and hyperactives did not pay close attention. However, the information processing was more complex than in simple reaction time studies, not only from the standpoint of stimuli and response (both hands) but from the standpoint of the known handicaps of the subjects. Encoding time could be slowed either because of attentional or perceptual deficiency or both, not to mention right-left confusion, which we (Peters, *et al.*, in press) found highly discriminative of MBD and control children. There is also the question of response selection as will be seen next.

Katz and Wicklund (1969, 1971, 1972) have done a series of investigations of reaction time to letters and words in good and poor grade school students. In their 1969 study, they presented 5th graders with a memory set of two, three or five words, followed by a single target word. The expected result of a linear increase in reaction time with increases in memory set did not occur, but overall the good readers reacted 250 msec faster than poor readers. Next they studied word scanning rate by presenting a key word followed by a target row or two or three words. The children had to scan the target row and respond orally "yes" or "no" depending on the presence or absence of the key word. Poor readers were overall 250 msec slower than good readers *but the increase in reaction time for three word targets was the same (100 msec) for both groups*. Hence, the difference was not in scan rate but apparently in response selection (retrieval from short term memory). In their third investigation, Katz and Wicklund (1972) utilized letters instead of words and the response was manual rather than oral. The child had to press a "yes" or "no" labeled telegraph key depending on whether the key letter was in the target row (one to four letters). Good and poor readers responded equally fast in this test. The failure to obtain a difference possibly resulted from the short scan length. Four letters should be in the span of apprehension of good and poor readers alike. But Katz and Wicklund also contend that their response retrieval hypothesis was not discredited. Words, they say, are not overlearned as well as letters; and if in responding to a target row of words, the subject tried to retrieve the name of the key word, the poor reader will retrieve slower than the good reader.

## VIGILANCE TASKS

Dr. Robert Anderson and associates (1973) have demonstrated in a pilot study that a simple vigilance task reliably separates age matched LD children and controls. The child was asked to attend to two flashing lights. When a red-green combination appeared he was to press a button mounted on a bicycle handle-bar grip, but he was to refrain from pressing to green-green or red-red presentations. The test was thirty minutes long; sixty positive patterns were interspersed among a total of 900 stimuli. Stimulus duration was .2 second and the interstimulus interval was two seconds. Controls made significantly more correct detections and fewer false alarms than LD children. Anderson, *et al.*, also reported several revealing observations on their subjects: the hyperactives performed less well than normoactives, the LD children taking stimulant drugs performed better than those not on medication, and nonhyperactives moved about without a decrement in performance. Dr. Robert Doyle will report further investigations with this promising laboratory procedure which provides an excellent assessment of attention-out.

Atkinson and Seunath (1973) also used a vigilance-type task to contrast LD children and controls. They projected a three by four rectangular matrix with five colored and seven white squares. In the constant condition, the colored squares (one each of red, orange, green, yellow, and blue) appeared at the same matrix position at each presentation. In the stimulus change condition, the colored square positions were randomly changed on each trial. The child was told to press a button whenever a small dark dot appeared on the red square. The dot was presented on twenty-seven of the 138 slides. Dot duration was randomly varied (seven durations ranging from 1.4 to 4.1 seconds). Errors of omission and commission were tallied, along with visual fixations away from the screen. LD subjects in the stimulus change condition made siginificantly more errors of omission than controls. The constant condition did not elicit a group difference, and errors of commission and visual inattentiveness failed to yield differences in either condition. The LD children must have got caught attending to the irrelevant aspects of the tasks (positions of the colored squares) rather than to the relevant aspect (dot on red). Or they may not have been able to search quickly enough on the short duration trails. The investigators, unfortunately, did not graph errors against dot duration.

## MEMORY TASKS

The heading of this section is somewhat arbitrary. Though memory processes have been tapped in all investigations described below, other processes have been tapped as well.

Dr. Gerald Senf has conducted a number of studies of short term memory in normal and retarded children. In earlier experiments, he utilized a bisensory memory test whereby a visual and a different auditory signal are presented at the same time. Each stimulus card contains three visual and three auditory digits (a total recall of six chunks). A Bell and Howell Language Master is programmed to present the digits at varying interpair intervals. The subject then recalls the digits in any order he can. With no set, the child may prefer to say the visual triad first or the auditory triad first. Very few children, either controls or retarded readers, recalled the digits as audiovisual pairs, that is, in the order in which they are presented. The majority of retarded readers prefer to recall auditory stimuli first, while controls are about equally divided (Senf, 1969). Further, LD children are deficient in total recall compared to controls.

Senf later studied the effect of a perceptual set to "see" the stimuli as audiovisual pairs rather than as separate visual and auditory stimuli. Normal readers were found to be significantly more sensitive to the pair-set induction than retarded readers, with the older controls accepting the set much better than the younger controls. By contrast, older retarded readers accepted the set little better than younger ones. Nor could the retarded readers perform well with a "set" to recall by modality—either with short or long interdigit intervals.

Senf (1971) next explored presenting the auditory and visual stimuli in alternating order to obviate the masking effects of one stimulus on the other. Two directed recall (instructional sets) conditions were utilized: to recall audiovisual pairs in the order of arrival, or to recall all visual items before recalling auditory items. In all conditions, LD children performed poorer than controls. Since the children performed no better in the alternating than in the simultaneous presentation condition, there was no evidence that sensory masking accounted for the LD children's inability to recall the digits. Having shown the sensory masking hypothesis to be invalid, Senf then inferred a deficit in higher order mental processes. He implicated four possible areas: auditory dominance, auditory distraction, deficient visual information processing and/or deficient informational organizational processes. The auditory dominance and distraction hypotheses say that MBD children may overreact to auditory stimuli and, as a consequence, pay less attention to visual stimuli. Senf's other two hypotheses are congruent with the information model which we have previously elaborated.

In a more recent study, Vandevoort, Senf, and Benton (1972) contrasted younger and older retarded and normal readers on three matching tests: visual-visual, auditory-auditory, and auditory-visual. The subject simply had to judge whether the second stimulus was the same as the first. Auditory signals were standard 1,000 Hz tones, and the visual stimuli were dot patterns typed on onion skin paper. The purpose of this study was to test the hypothesis of Birch and Belmont (1964) that one possible cause for reading failure "could be a primary inadequacy in the ability to integrate visual and auditory stimuli." Birch and associates emphasized in a number of papers that one of the significant aspects of human development is that of the elaboration of sensory integrative functions—coordination between sensory modalities. This sort of theorizing plays a prominent role in the Piagetian school, too.

In the Vandevoort, *et al.* study, *retarded readers were inferior performers on all three matching tasks,* and at that juncture the investigators hypothesized that the root of the problem was either encoding or short-term memory rather than a cross-modality deficit. That is, they found the Birch hypothesis invalid. Half the subjects in each group had a three second interstimulus interval and half had a six second interstimulus interval. On the cross modality task, older controls performed better with the longer interstimulus interval than younger controls, but this age interaction did not hold for retarded readers. Even with simultaneous presentation of the auditory-visual stimuli, the retarded readers performed significantly poorer than controls. Hence, memory would seem to be less a factor than immediate stimulus encoding (registration) of all the relationships of the configuration so that the decision "match or no-match" can be made. This immediate encoding operation is exactly what we have implied by focus or selective attention in our model above. We judge that Senf has come to the conclusion on the basis of these last results that faulty attention may be at the root of memory deficiencies.

Selective attention has been implicated in numerous studies of reflection-impulsivity. When LD or hyperactive children are tested on the Matching Familiar Figures (MFF) test, the findings are remarkably consistent—that is, these youngsters respond too quickly, before they consider all elements, and thus make more errors than normal children. For example, Keogh and Donlon (1972) recently reported that a group of severely reading disabled boys, whose mean age was ten years five months, had MFF scores comparable to average first graders. Poor MFF performance in hyperactives has been interpreted by Douglas and associates (1972, 1973) to reflect an incapacity to stop, look and listen before acting.

When studying either short- or long-term memory deficits, it is difficult or impossible to pin down just where the process breaks down—whether in encoding or storage or retrieval or in the initial recognition process. Quite obviously the apprehension span of many LD children is restricted. Mean WISC profiles of LD, MBD or hyperactive children consistently show a depression on Digit Span. We have looked separately at digit span forward and backwards of a group of fourteen year olds, earlier categorized as either LD (N=31) or normal achieving (N=22). In these teenage LD boys, digits backwards mainly accounts for the depressed digit span scale score. The mean forward span of the fourteen year old controls was 6.3 as opposed to 6.1 for LD boys. However, the mean backwards span was 4.1 for LD boys as opposed to 5.0 for controls (Chi square=5.30, p<.05). We think that this finding points to a problem in the organization of short-term memory by a central processor (a reversible scan-hold operation). Some younger LD children simply do not understand the concept 'backwards' as opposed to 'forward' but many who do understand cannot give the numbers backwards.

Korsakoff patients, for whatever the observation is worth, do much better on digits forward than digits backward (Wechsler, 1958). Jensen (1973) says that whereas digit span is an almost pure measure of association or rote learning ability (what he terms Level I) that digits backward involves some Level II ability (i.e conceptual or abstractual skill). Digits backwards involves a transformation of input. Jensen has found that forward digit span correlates higher with the WISC information subtest than with arithmetic whereas the opposite holds for digit span backwards.

Even in a one-to-one testing situation, where most MBD children try to pay attention, they reach sensory overload very quickly. We have noted this problem with the (mental) arithmetic subtest of the WISC as well as on digit span (Dykman, et al., 1971). MBD children ask to have questions repeated more often than control children, and especially when several elements have to be recognized. Consider this item from the WISC: "If you buy three dozen oranges at 30¢ a dozen, how much change should you get back from a dollar?" By the time we read "If you buy three dozen oranges at 30¢ a dozen," the control child has anticipated the rest of the question and has a dime in his pocket. Not so with most MBD children. The Detroit Learning Aptitude Test contains a number of subtests assessing auditory and visual apprehension or attention span. LD children are poor on nearly all of these. Myklebust, et al. (1971) found eight selected subtests from the Detroit battery to be highly discriminative of LD and matched control children.

Kleuver (1971) used Guilford's model to investigate the structure of memory in reading disabled youngsters and matched controls. He administered tests to get at sixteen hypothesized memory factors. Kleuver found normal readers scored higher than retarded readers on all tests except digit span forward. The memory skills which were more difficult for his reading retarded boys involved transformations and implications. As an example of a symbolic transformation task, the experimenter first showed the subject a list of misspelled words. Then the list was removed and the subject was given a page where the same words were spelled correctly. His task was to recall the exact misspellings of each word. To get at semantic transformation ability, the subject was asked to study sentences containing a word of a homonym pair. The meanings of the homonyms must be identified on the test page. As an example of an implications task, the child was shown a list of names of people and their occupations. Subsequently, he was asked to study the names and identify some aspect of each person's occupation from a four choice set.

When Kleuver divided these memory tasks into visual or auditory input/output, he found that the auditory tasks did not discriminate, whereas on nine of twelve visual intrasensory tasks, the normal readers were superior to retarded ones. There were few significant intercorrelations of memory factors in either group, supporting Guilford's theory. An exception was memory for sentences and memory for digits. Kleuver concluded that normal readers are more successful than poor readers as material progresses from nonmeaningful (figural) to meaningful (semantic) and that this is especially true for the more complex memory tasks. It should be noted that Kleuver's groups were matched for Full Scale WISC IQ, and, as has happened for so many of us, he then found the normal readers significantly higher than retarded readers on the verbal scale.

In this same general line of investigation, Myklebust, *et al.* (1971) found that intercorrelations among WISC subtests were quite different in LD groups (moderate and severe) as contrasted with normal achievers. Of principal interest to Myklebust, there were many more significant intercorrelations for the controls, indicating that the G factor is less intact for LD children and that the structure of intellect is different in these children. He further showed that whereas WISC subtests are consistently related to academic achievement in controls, comparable analyses for LD children yield fewer and lower correlation coefficients. Performance subtest scores, except Coding, correlated with many measures of school success in normal achievers but with only a few in LD children. Myklebust concluded that in LD youngsters what is learned nonverbally is not easily converted to verbal meaning and vice versa and that the teacher must help these children in "generalizations" and "transformations." It is as if the CPs of LD children do not communicate and hence do not update programs and strategies.

Dr. Phillip Marshall, who will report to this conference his work on memory, has found that MBD children as a group do not differ markedly from controls on a free-recall task. However, when age was taken into account his analyses revealed that with increasing age, MBD children show an improvement in STM but not in LTM. Just the opposite was observed with normal controls. Marshall suggested that MBD children may even catch up with normals in terms of LTM. We need to know whether this finding would still stand up given a different set of instructions, or search strategies, or direct aids to attention. Kesner (1973) says that information processed under low arousal is retained well in STM but not LTM and that information processed under high arousal is better retained in LTM than STM. Thus, the LD child might master a spelling assignment at home (low arousal) but fail a test on the next day. The words he did recall correctly, by this theory, should be the more emotionally charged ones. We are reminded of the MR child whose teacher had worked for weeks to teach him to spell his first name. One day he came in excitedly saying "I can spell a word! I can spell a word." And he then printed very carefuly his first mastered word, "SHIT."

## CONCEPT IDENTIFICATION OR ATTAINMENT

Dr. Mary Parucka will present in this session her work in concept attainment, which complements similar investigations begun by Douglas and associates. Freibergs and Douglas (1969) used a concept learning apparatus developed by Osler (Osler and Finel, 1961). The machine delivers two pictures at a time, one being the exemplar of a concept such as "flower" and the other a non-exemplar of the concept. The child is given only vague instructions: "Look carefully and you will find that there is something in the pictures, like an idea, which will tell you which one to choose. If you choose the right one, the machine will give you a marble." Number of errors and trials to criterion are used as measures of learning efficiency. The experiments of Douglas and associates, as well as those to be reported by Parucka, indicate that with continuous reward hyperactives attain simple concepts as well as controls. Partial reward is less efficacious than no reward, however. Level of IQ seems to be unrelated to simple concept formation (Parucka, 1973).

To repeat ourselves, it is difficult to say where one line of investigation leaves off and another logically begins. Our dilemma is especially difficult in the face of the wide ranging studies of Penny Parry (1973), a student of Virginia Douglas. We shall discuss her design and aims in a subsequent section. Suffice it to say here, that in the absence of continuous reward Parry's hyperactive subjects not only experienced greater difficulty than controls in concept attainment, once they reached criterion many could not verbalize the contingency for reward. Though twenty-eight of thirty hyperactives eventually reached criterion on the first problem, only sixteen could verbalize the solution; twenty-nine of thirty controls were able to do so. Thus, Parry elicited the problem with nonverbal to verbal transformation alluded to by Myklebust (see above). Parry's hyperactives also performed poorly on another concept attainment task, the Wisconsin Card Sort. Effect of reward was not studied on this test. Given standard instructions, hyperactive children made fewer correct matches, more perseverative errors, and more unique responses than did controls. The groups did not differ on number of nonperseverative errors. One third of the hyperative children were able to discover only two of the three response categories. Excluding those children who did not discover all three response dimensions, hyperactives differed from controls only in number of unique, or illogical, responses. Parry included the Wisconsin Card Sort mainly to test the suggestion of frontal lobe involvement in hyperactive children

(Douglas, 1972; Lytton and Knobel, 1958; Milner, 1963, 1964). Parry interprets her results (the high number of illogical matches made by hyperactives) as more suggestive of attentional and impulse control difficulties than cortical impairment. Of course, illogical matching can also be produced by damage to the frontal lobe.

Gates (1969) compared hyperactive and hypoactive LD children on the Vygotsky Block Test of Concept Formation. Both groups were markedly but equally deficient at this task.

An earlier study from our laboratory (Boydstun, *et al.*, 1968) could be considered a concept attainment task. The MBD children had to discover when to pull a cord to receive a penny reward. Stimuli were a high (positive) and low (negative) tone. Criterion was defined as five successive correct responses (i.e. pulls during the action of the higher tone and refrains from pulling to the lower tone). If the child had not caught on after twenty-five tones, he was given a clue (told the tones were different and that pulling to one would result in reward). The experiment was terminated at fifty trials. Whereas 92 percent of controls reached criterion only 61 percent of the MBD children did.

In summary, MBD/LD children as a group encounter great difficulty with more complex concept attainment tasks but are able to match the performance of controls on simpler tasks under continuous reward conditions. The question of "why" remains unanswered. We suspect that such higher level mental operations require intactness of the entire information processing system plus appropriate life experiences.

## PHYSIOLOGICAL AROUSAL AND ATTENTION MEASURES

There have been a number of studies in this area, and most point to the general conclusion that MBD children are cortically *underaroused* as compared to controls. Our own studies show that while controls and MBDs have comparable resting autonomic levels, controls become more physiologically reactive than MBDs in simple conditioning and discrimination tasks (Boydstun, *et al.*, 1968; Dykman, *et al.*, 1971). This finding has also been true for orienting response and reaction time experiments (Cohen and Douglas, 1972; Hunter and Johnson, 1971; Hunter, Johnson and Keefe, 1972; and Hunter and Lewis, 1973).

Sroufe and associates (1973) at the University of Minnesota studied anticipatory heart rate (HR) deceleration and reaction time (RT) in learning disabled boys. A warning tone sounded five seconds prior to the light, and the subject was told to press a switch as fast as possible when the light appeared. The intertrial interval was 20 seconds in order to allow HR to recover. Only fifteen trials were given. The LD boys showed a significantly greater *variability* of RT and significantly less HR deceleration to the warning tone than age-matched controls. Subsequently, in a double-blind experiment to assess the effects of methylphenidate, clinic children on medication decelerated significantly more to HR to the warning tone than those given placebo. The on-drug children also had significantly faster median RT than the placebo group. There was a significant correlation between RT and HR deceleration for control children (–.52) and for clinic children on medication (–.56); the nonmedicated clinic group did not exhibit a significant coupling. Sroufe interprets these findings to support the position that LD children cannot maintain a set to respond (attention-out) as well as their normal-achieving agemates.

Hunter, Johnson and Keefe (1972) studied reaction time and autonomic response pattern of twenty male nonreaders, ages eight to eleven. Fifteen orienting tones were followed by five signal tones. Compared with matched controls, the nonreaders were found to have significantly lower skin conductance levels on no-task and task trials and to give fewer electrodermal and HR anticipatory responses on task trials. Moreover, they had slower reaction times. These investigators concluded that nonreaders are less physiologically mature, unable to maintain a constant attentional level, and slower in "simple" learning as measured by reaction time to an auditory stimulus.

The literature on the orienting response is somewhat confusing. There are apparently differences between controls and MBD children when tones are given *through a loud speaker* (Cohen and Douglas, 1972; Dykman, *et al.*, 1971) but not when the tones are presented through earphones. In HR there is an initial deceleration followed by acceleration, and it seems to be the latter component which most clearly separates controls from MBDs (Dykman, *et al.*, 1971). We regard the orienting response as a two-phase response: first, attention-out, and then a switch to attention-in. Cardiac deceleration in the first phase reflects the attention-out, anticipatory or tensing component and cardiac acceleration in the second phase reflects the attention-in evaluating process. Giving credence to this interpretation is the finding by Sroufe and others that a warning signal nearly always produces cardiac deceleration in anticipation of the imperative stimulus.

In our orienting response experiments, the skin resistance habituation curve of MBD children was different from that of cotrols in rather surprising ways. To the first tone (the most novel stimulus) a larger percentage of MBDs than controls showed a drop of at least 600 ohms (88% versus 71%). However, the controls who did respond tended to drop more than 5,000 ohms, whereas the MBD responders showed a less marked drop. Further, a greater proportion of MBD children continued to respond to the subsequent tones, whereas controls quickly habituated in skin resistance. The failure of MBD children to exhibit a smooth habituration curve may be related to their lability, for our subjects had significantly more intervals of nonstimulus coupled background activity in the basal period before orienting tones began.

Physiological arousal in MBD children is also being studied via EEG measures—contingency negative variation (Cohen, 1970) and average evoked responses. Conners (1972) has conducted auditory (AER) and visual (VER) studies on three different groups of children with reading disorders. Consistent significant relations with reading and spelling were found only with VER, left parietal amplitude. One of Conner's groups was selected for large WISC Verbal-Performance IQ differences. The children with markedly lower performance IQs had significantly lower latencies on VERs from the right side.

Conners (1972) went on to ask the question of whether stimulant drugs would effect the evoked response of LD children.

Contrasting Dexedrine-®Ritalin-®placebo, he found no changes in amplitudes, but highly significant drug effects on the latencies were seen—again primarily in the VER. Other investigators have reported lower amplitude electrocortical activity in MBD children and subsequent enhancement by drugs (Cohen, 1970; Satterfield, *et al.*, 1973).

Shields (1973) studied average visual evoked response (VER) in a group of ten LD children who had visual processing deficits. These children matched their controls in Verbal IQ (WISC) but had depressed scores on block design, object assembly, coding and other measures of visual-motor integration (hence were similar to Conner's low Performance IQ group). Shield's stimuli were light flashes, pictures, designs, words, and nonsense words (twenty of each). Mean latencies of each of the five components of the VER were significantly slower in the LD children, *but* the amplitudes of the $P_1$ and $P_3$ components were *greater* than in the controls. Shields concluded that while her LD subjects must be slower at processing visual stimuli, they might actually be trying harder to attend. Larger amplitudes of evoked response components have been reported by most investigators to accompany greater attention to stimuli (Spong, *et al.*, 1965; Satterfield, 1971). Shields did not report data separately for the right and left hemisphere. Her results obviously do not concord entirely with those reported by Conners or Satterfield.

Conners (1972) has characterized seven different subgroups within the general LD population—this on the basis of a factor analysis of test scores and teacher and parent ratings. He reports that post-stimulant changes in test performance and in evoked responses can be reliably predicted from these pre-drug profiles. Additionally, Conners has found that his seven groups differ markedly on two measures of hemisphere dominance: the left/right ratio of amplitudes of waves V and VI from the parietal areas.

One of the more intriguing reports in the arousal area has to do with catecholamine output in Swedish school children (Johansson, *et al.*, 1973). These investigators studied the excretion of two catecholamines, adrenalin and nonadrenalin, in 240 children sampled from a longitudinal study. During a passive period, the children viewed a film, and in a subsequent active period, they performed on an arithmetic test. In the boys, the mean adrenalin excretion increased significantly during the active as compared with the passive period. In both sexes, those who had increased adrenalin output during the arithmetic test performed better on the test, in terms of speed and endurance, than did children who did not respond to mental work by adrenalin increase. These investigators concluded that the excretion of catecholamines increased as concentration (attention-in) improved and as activity and aggressive behavior decreased.

Several authors have speculated that MBD children have some kind of biochemical defect, usually implicating catecholamines (Shetty, 1971; Silver, 1971; Stewart, 1970; and Wender, 1972). The agents useful in treating MBDs, stimulant drugs, affect the central metabolism of serotonin, dopamine and norepinephrine. These substances are presumed to function as neurotransmitters in certain parts of the nervous system. Wender (1972) speculates that MBD children have a generalized dysfunction of norepinephrine metabolism, although he would not rule out abnormalities of serotonin and dopamine. He assumes that the abnormality associated with these neurotransmitters, particularly norepinephrine, results in decreased arousal and diminished sensitivity of the reinforcement systems of the brain.

## MODIFICATION OF LEARNING PERFORMANCE AND ATTENTIVE BEHAVIOR IN MBD CHILDREN

The first group of studies we shall review in this section deal with reinforcement and conditioning and these may be conceived as another type of attentional aid. Freibergs and Douglas (1969) utilized two reward conditions in a concept attainment task—100 percent or 50 percent reward. They found that hyperactive children had no difficulty solving the problem under continuous reinforcement and that they showed good transfer. But with partial reinforcement, many hyperactives failed to reach criterion, even after dozens of trials.

Penny Parry (1973) recently cross-validated many of Douglas's findings and has added important new information about the effects of reward on learning patterns of hyperactive children. She studied both simple and delayed reaction time (RT) under different reward conditions. In the simple RT task, the reinforcers were black and white marbles which could be exchanged for money at the end of the experiment. One third of the subjects were on 100 percent reinforcement schedule, one third on a 50 percent schedule, and the remainder on a 30 percent schedule. Hyperactive children performed as well as controls with continuous reinforcement, but under partial reward conditions were significantly slower and more variable. In Parry's delayed RT task, the reinforcement was verbal. The experimenter said "good" when the subject improved on his average base line response speed. One third got 50 percent feedback, and the remainder received 50 percent noncontingent reward. Several major differences emerged. Controls improved under all reward schedules, and even though RT slowed in extinction, it remained significantly faster than in the base line period. Hyperactive children improved with 100 and 50 percent schedules, but deteriorated in the noncontingent condition. Also, during extinction, hyperactive children did not maintain the speed gained under reward but slowed back to the base line level.

Douglas (1972) has said that with generalized, noncontingent reinforcement, hyperactive children may become overly excited and focus on the reinforcement rather than the task. The reinforcement must be tied to that aspect of the task to be learned. Further, reward may not be effective unless the task to be learned is within the child's comfortable acquisition range. That is, the learning task must be carefully programmed so that the child experiences a minimum of failure, for frustration on difficult problems could result in an inability to learn even simple problems which had previously been easily solved (Zeaman and House, 1963). There remains also the problem of reverting to baseline whenever reward is withdrawn. In line with Parry's finding on this point, Quay, et al. (1966) earlier reported that performance of MBD children deteriorates when rewards are withdrawn. Parry has shown that partial reward is not the answer, and Parucka will report that partial reinforcement can interfere with retention and generalization of training (at least concept attainment).

To mention a few examples of behavior modification applications, Quay and associates (1966) found that flashing lights to reward a child for paying attention helped to reduce hyperactive, impulsive behavior in the classroom. Other studies show that contingency management is effective in decreasing hyperactivity (Patterson, et al., 1965; Pihl, 1967). A token economy conditioning procedure also can be used to improve reading (Bijou, et al., 1965; Birnbrauer, 1965; and Camp, 1973).

Of course, many studies show that stimulant drugs reduce activity and impulsivity, improve sustained attention, and hence result in better performance. The combination of drugs and conditioning seems to be better than either alone. Christensen and Sprague (1973) played the "sit in your seat" game with twelve hyperactive subjects. Each session lasted about twenty minutes during which four subjects at a time viewed a film strip, had a discussion with the experimenter, and then took a multiple choice quiz. Half the boys received .30 m/Kg of methylphenidate 1.5 hours prior to each experimental session; the other half received placebo. Seat movements were obtained from a stabilimetric cushion in base line, drug only, drug plus reinforcement, and extinction sessions. In the conditioning sessions, the children received two cents for each minute wherein their seat movements did not exceed their average number of movements as established in base line sessions. A white light flashed at the end of each minute in which the subject moved less than or equal to his base line level; a red light flashed if he moved a greater amount than during base line. There was a significant drug effect, a significant reward effect, and a significant interaction. Moreover, in the first extinction session, where reward was dropped but medication continued, the placebo group showed an increase in seat movement but the drug group did not. We hope Christensen and Sprague will later publish results relating to the quiz the children took.

Pilot studies from the University of Washington (Lovitt, 1973) indicate that impulsive children can be trained to chart their own behavior, and that self-charting results in the elimination of undesirable behaviors (speaking out, moving about). Self-charting of work accomplished per unit of time (e.g. number of math problems solved) also results in improved performance. For those who have serious reservations about the use of stimulant drugs with MBD children, these studies must offer encouragement.

One last approach to the modification of hyperactive behavior, and one that we speculated about previously and which relates to our present model, is that of direct verbal control. Hyperactive children can be trained to talk themselves into less impulsive responding (Meichenbaum and Goodman, 1969; Palkes, et al., 1968; Santosphano and Stayton, 1967). The verbalization of strategies and search techniques is very helpful (Meichenbaum, 1971), but modeling or reinforcement without specific verbal commands or directions may not be effective (Debus, 1970; Kagan, et al., 1964, 1966; Yando and Kagan, 1968).

## THE EFFECTS OF SUPERIOR ATTENTION

In concluding this review, we should mention that excellent powers of attention and concentration seem to account for statistical "overachievement," just as attentional deficits are the key to learning disabilities. We shall discuss only three studies, though many others could be cited. One group of children with superior attention has been labeled "pseudogifted" (Namy, 1967). Namy found that among children recommended by classroom teachers for special classes for the gifted, there were a number who had Full Scale WISC IQs below 120 and who were below the 90th percentile on the California Test of Mental Maturity. These pseudogifted children were significantly lower than a group of bona fide gifted children on all WISC subtests except two: coding and arithmetic. The implication is that these children rely, for the most part, on associative memory, attention, and concentration to attain knowledge, and that in elementary school they make as good grades as students with IQs in the very superior or genius range. Interestingly, Hunter, et al. (1973) found in a two year follow-up of poor readers that those who had made the greatest gains had high WISC coding and arithmetic scores.

A second group of good attenders are children with retinoblastoma. For years there has been voiced the clinical impression that these bilaterally blind children show signs of genius. Witkin and associates (1971) contrasted a group of congenitally blind children and children with retinoblastoma with a group of gifted controls. The blind children were superior to the gifted children on two WISC subtests, digit span and arithmetic. Levitt, et al. (1972) cross-validated this finding pointing to superior auditory attention.

Lastly, there have been many reports in the literature of the superior rote recall capacities of certain groups of mentally retarded children. As one example, Spitz and LaFontaine (1973) studied eight idiot savants. These subjects had a mean IQ of 48, yet all had a forward digit span in the normal range of five to nine. Their digit span was much better than that of other retarded subjects of higher overall intellectual ability. There are, of course, isolated reports in the literature of idiot savants who memorize perpetual calendars or who can stand along side the railroad tracks and remember the numbers on boxcars that have just passed—feats which could never be accomplished by the average person. It is almost as if the gates to long-term memory were wide open and everything that entered from attention-out passed directly to long-term memory with little or no programming on the part of the central processing unit. Such seems to have been the case with Luria's (1968) mnemonist. Moreover, he never forgot what he committed to memory unless he deliberately concentrated on wiping it out.

## CRITICAL AFTERTHOUGHTS

In summary, it appears that a good deal of the MBD research points, as Douglas (1972, 1973) and we (Dykman, et al., 1971) have said, to defects in attention and impulse control. However, we cannot rule out other aspects of nervous system dysfunctioning. Nor do we expect all MBD children to exhibit the same pattern of deficits. We must keep our minds open to all possibilities, but our priority list will push us to pursue vigorously research into the basic areas of information processing.

We promised some answers but anticipated that the few known facts could do little more than point to the sea of unknowns. As we see it, though, the weight of evidence is on the side of the following postulates:

1. Sensorially intact children of normal intelligence and advantage who exhibit learning deficits or classroom management problems have a more basic informational processing deficiency. Normal advantage implies social and emotional nutriment.

2. Since the brain is the organ which processes information, it is logical to speak of minimal brain dysfunction in these children.

3. Brain dysfunction can be generalized (if arousal, neurotransmitters, or myelinization are implicated), or specific to areas and hence to modalities.

4. Groups of MBD children, whether identified as language disabled or hyperactive, normoactive, or hypoactive, include many children who, by physiological measures, are cortically underaroused.

5. Groups of MBD children include a majority who are less attentive than normal achieving age mates. Purer measures of sustained attentiveness, such as simple and choice reaction time and signal detection (vigilance), as well as more complex measures (scan rate) elicit major and consistent differences in favor of normal achievers.

6. Faced with sensory overload, MBD children tend to respond impulsively and hence commit many more errors than controls (e.g. on the Matching Familiar Figures Test).

7. MBD children as a rule are particularly poor on tasks involving scan-hold memory (e.g. digit span backwards and mental arithmetic problems).

8. MBD children can perform as well as controls on some tasks when attention is aided via warning signals, continuous reinforcement, or stimulant drugs (e.g. on simple reaction time and simple concept attainment tasks).

9. When reward is withdrawn, MBD children tend to lose gains and to revert to pre-reward levels.

10. MBD children have great difficulty with more complex concept attainment tasks such as the Wisconsin Card Sort and the Vygotsky Block Test. They appear to have trouble catching on

and reprogramming when instructions are purposefully vague. Partial reward conditions hamper concept attainment, retention and generalization.

11. MBD children do not outgrow their difficulties, as a rule. But the brighter and emotionally stronger (guttsier) ones learn ways of coping, either through unique strategies or ingenious circumventions. Once away from formal education demands, they may function quite well indeed. The less bright and less secure ones become society's misfits. Parents who are not upward mobile or determined that their children must go to college tend to provide a more secure homebase for MBD children.

We would now like to reveal some of the questions which have been raised in our minds as we wrote this paper. We hope they are the right questions.

1. Can we sort out of the MBD population several more homogeneous sub types? For example, are there significant numbers of "true" dyslexics who agree to attend (have good intentions) but who focus on irrevelant aspects of a stimulus complex or else scramble it in some way? Are there children *who want to but cannot* sustain attention no matter what aids are employed? Are there children who "perversely" choose not to attend to what adult society labels relevant? Can we identify introverted and extraverted subtypes who have differing patterns of basic skill deficits or informational processing styles or strategies?

2. What strategies can we provide children who do not learn with ordinary instruction? Are there short-cuts, or must children with such difficulties be resigned to working harder? What can be learned from those who have devised (or lucked onto) ways around their handicaps—particularly the blind, deaf, and frankly brain damaged? How can "ordinary" instruction be modified to preclude problems for non-ordinary learners?

3. What do cultural differences tell us? Why do Oriental school children rarely exhibit hyperactivity (Willerman, 1973) and why do they have fewer problems learning to read? Why are lower social class children with IQs around 80 better on rote learning tasks than middle class children with the same IQ level (Jensen, 1973)? Why are MBD boys three to four four times more prevalent than MBD girls?

4. Given that true dyslexia is probably inherited, what evidence do we have with regard to heritibility of attentional (and intentional) defects which result in more generalized learning problems? Can we pin down the mode of inheritance?

5. Can we follow leads from neurophysiological studies of lesioned animals to arrive at a better understanding of informational processing in the human brain?

6. Do subtypes of MBD children lag in moral development? If so, is their amoral or immoral behavior a reflection of lack of ideal or lack of effort or both? Can the methods of the ethologists help us to a better understanding in this area? Can we show a connection between operant conditioning performance (including an extinction phase) and moral behavior? Is the child who requires continuous reinforcement in order to improve more apt to go astray in the real world where such feedback is rarely totally consistent? On the other side of the coin, do MBD children who present behavioral management problems have a higher threshold for aversive stimuli (punishment and threat of punishment)? Can operant conditioning techniques be used to train MBD children in more efficient and acceptable ways of behaving?

7. Do all MBD children given stimulant drugs perform better on laboratory tasks, such as those reviewed in this paper, than they do in the non-drug state? Are gains with drugs circumscribed or more general, both from the point of the type child and the type task? What drugs (or other aids to attention) are most efficacious with the various MBD subtypes?

As our list of questions reveals, we are still circling round and round. The interrelatedness of behaviors within an organism is as real as the interrelatedness of that organism with the rest of the natural world. "Not man apart," wrote the poet Robinson Jeffers. "Not attention, or memory, or strategies apart," we would echo. And, if all of this sounds like nothing, recall what the ancients said, "Nothing is at least an object of conjecture."

## REFERENCES

Anderson, R. P., Halcomb, C. G., and Doyle, R. B.: The measurement of attentional deficits. *Except Child, 39*:539, 1973.
Atkinson, B. R., and Seunath, O. H. M.: The effect of stimulus change

on attending behavior in normal children and children with learning disorders. *Journal of Learning Disabilities, 6*:569-573, 1973.

Bakwin, H.: Reading disability in twins. *Dev Med Child Neurol, 15*: 184-187, 1973.

Bereiter, C., and Englemann, S.: *Teaching Disadvantaged Children in the Preschool.* Englewood Cliffs, Prentice-Hall, 1966.

Bijou, S. W.: Experimental studies of child behavior, normal and deviant. In Krasner, L., and Ullman, L. P. (Eds.): *Research in Behavior Modification.* New York, H R & W, 1965, p. 56-81.

Birch, H. C., and Belmont, L.: Auditory-visual integration in normal and retarded readers. *Am J Orthopsychiatry, 34*:853-861, 1964.

Birnbrauer, J. S., Bijou, S. W., Wolf, M. M., and Kidder, J. D.: Programmed instruction in the classroom. In Ullman, L. P., and Krasner, L. (Eds.): *Case Studies in Behavior Modification.* New York, H R & W, 1965, p. 358-363.

Boydstun, J. A., Ackerman, P. T., Stevens, D. A., Clements, S. D., and Dykman, R. A.: Physiological and motor conditioning and generalization in children with minimal brain dysfunction. *Cond Reflex, 3*:81-104, 1968.

Bruner, J. S.: On perceptual readiness. *Psychol Rev, 64*:123-152, 1957.

Camp, B. W.: Learning rate and retention in retarded readers. *Journal of Learning Disabilities, 6*:65-71, 1973.

Chomsky, N.: *Learning and Mind.* New York, Harcourt, Brace and World, 1968.

Christensen, D. E., and Sprague, R. L.: Reduction of hyperactive behavior by conditioning procedures alone and combined with methylphenidate (Ritalin). *Behav Res Ther, 11*:331-334, 1973.

Clemente, C.: Forebrain mechanisms related to internal inhibition and sleep. *Cond Reflex, 3*:145-174, 1968.

Cohen, N. J., and Douglas, V. I.: Characteristics of the orienting response in hyperactive and normal children. *Psychophysiology, 9*: 238-245, 1972.

Cohen, N. J., Douglas, V. I., and Morgenstern, G.: The effect of methylphenidate on attentive behavior and automatic activity in hyperactive children. *Psychopharmacologia, 22*:282-294, 1971.

Conners, C. K.: Stimulant drugs and cortical evoked responses in learning and behavior disorders in children. In Smith, W. L. (Ed.): *Drugs, Development and Cerebral Function.* Springfield, Thomas, 1972, p. 179-199.

Craik, K. J. W.: *The Nature of Explanation.* London, Cambridge U Pr, 1943.

Critchley, M.: *Developmental Dyslexia.* London, Heinemann, 1964.

Critchley, M.: Some problems of the ex-dyslexic. *Bulletin Orton Society, 23*:7-14, 1973.

Debus, R.: Effects of brief observation of modeling behavior or conceptual tempo of impulsive children. *Dev Psychol, 2*:22-32, 1970.

deHirsch, K., Jansky, J., and Langford, W.: *Predicting Reading Failure.* New York, Harper and Row, 1966.

Deutsch, M.: Early social environment: Its influence on school adaptation. In Schreiber, D. (Ed.): *The School Dropout.* Washington, National Education Association, 1964.

Douglas, V. I.: Stop, look and listen: The problem of sustained attention and impulse control in hyperactive and normal children. *Canadian Journal of Behavorial Sciences, 4*:259-281, 1972.

Douglas, V. I.: Sustained attention and impulse control: Implications for the handicapped child. In Swets, J. A., and Elliott, L. L. (Eds.): *Psychology and the Handicapped Child.* Washington, Office of Education, 1973.

Doyle, R. B., Anderson, R. P., and Halcomb, C. G.: Attention deficits and the effect of visual distraction. *Journal of Learning Disabilities,* In press.

Dykman, R. A., Ackerman, P. T., Clements, S. D., and Peters, J. E.: Specific learning disabilities: An attentional deficit syndrome. In Myklebust, H. R. (Ed.): *Progress in Learning Disabilities.* New York, Grune and Stratton, 1971, Vol. II, p. 56-93.

Dykman, R. A., Ackerman, P. T., Galbrecht, C. R., and Reese, W. G.: Psychological reactivity to different stressors and methods of evaluation. *Psychosom Med, 25*:37-59, 1963.

Dykman, R. A., Peters, J. E., and Ackerman, P. T.: Experimental approaches to the study of minimal brain dysfunction: A follow-up study. *Ann N Y Aca Sci, 205*:93-108, 1973.

Dykman, R. A., Reese, W. G., Galbrecht, C. R., Ackerman, P. T., and Sundermann, R.: Automatic responses in psychiatric patients. *Ann N Y Aca Sci, 147*:237-303, 1968.

Dykman, R. A., Walls, R. C., Suzuki, R., Ackerman, P. T., and Peters, J. E.: Children with learning disabilities: Conditioning, differentiation, and the effect of distraction. *Am J Orthopsychiatry, 40*: 766-782, 1970.

Eysenck, H. J.: *The Biological Basis of Personality.* Springfield, Thomas, 1967.

Falconer, D. S.: *Introduction to Quantitative Inheritance.* Edinburgh, Oliver Boyd, 1960.

Farnham-Diggory, S.: The development of equivalence systems. In Farnham-Diggory, S. (Ed.): *Information Processing in Children.* New York, Academic Press, 1972, p. 43-64.

Freibergs, V., and Douglas, V. I.: Concept learning in hyperactive and normal children. *J Abnorm Psychol, 74*:388-395, 1969.

Gates, M. F.: *A comparison of the learning characteristics of hyperactive children with related central nervous system dysfunctions,* doctoral dissertation, Ohio State University, 1968.

Gray, J. A.: Strength of the nervous system as a dimension of personality in man: A review of work from the laboratory of B. M. Teplov. In Gray, J. A. (Ed.): *Pavlov's Typology.* New York, Pergamon, 1964, p. 157-287.

Haber, R. N.: How we remember what we see. *Sci Am, 222*:104-112, 1970.

Hebb, D. O.: Drives and the C.N.S. (conceptual nervous system). *Psychol Rev, 62*:243-254, 1955.

Herjanic, B. M., and Penick, E. C.: Adult outcomes of disabled child readers. *Journal Special Education, 6*:397-410, 1972.

Hunter, E. J., and Johnson, L. C.: Developmental and psychological differences between readers and nonreaders. *Journal Learning Disabilities, 4*:527-577, 1971.

Hunter, Edna J. Johnson, L. C., and Keefe, F. B.: Electrodermal and cardiovascular responses in nonreaders. *Journal Learning Disabilities, 5*:187-197, 1972.

Hunter, E. J., and Lewis, H. M.: The dyslexic child—two years later. *J Psychol, 83*:163-170, 1973.

Jacobs, N. T.: A comparison of hyperactive and normal boys in terms of reaction time, motor time, and decision-making time, under conditions of increasing task complexity. *Dissertation Abstracts Int, 33* (3-A): 1045, 1972.

James, W.: *The Principles of Psychology (1890).* London, Dover, 1950.

Jansky, J., and deHirsch, K.: *Preventing Reading Failure: Prediction, Diagnosis, Intervention.* New York, Harper and Row, 1972.

Jensen, A. R.: *Genetics and Education.* New York, Harper and Row, 1973.

Johansson, G., Frankenhaeuser, M., and Magnusson, D.: Catecholamine output in school children as related to performance and adjustment. *Scand J Psychol, 14*:20-28, 1973.

Johnson, E. G., and Lyle, J. C.: Analysis of WISC coding: 1. Figural reversibility. *Percept Mot Skills, 34*:195-198, 1972.

Johnson, E. G., and Lyle, J. C.: Analysis of WISC coding: 2. Memory and verbal mediation. *Percept Mot Skills, 34*:659-662, 1972.

Johnson, E. G., and Lyle, J. C.: Analysis of WISC coding: 3. Writing and copying speed and motivation. *Percept Mot Skills, 36*:211-124, 1973.

Kagan, J., Pearson, L., and Welch, L.: Modifiability of an impulsive tempo. *J Educ Psychol, 57*:359-365, 1966.

Kagan, J., Rosman, B., Day, D., Albert, J., and Phillips, W.: Information processing in the child: Significance of analytic and reflective attitude. *Psychol Monogr, 78*: Whole No. 578, 1964.

Katz, L., and Wicklund, D. A.: *Perception and retention in children's reading.* National Institute of Child Health and Human Development Progress Report, 1969.

Katz, L., and Wicklund, D. A.: Word scanning rate for good and poor readers. *J Educ Psychol, 68*:138-140, 1971.

Katz, L., and Wicklund, D. A.: Letter scanning rate for good and poor readers in grades two and six. *J Educ Psychol, 63*:363-367, 1972.

Keogh, B., and Donlon, G. M.: Field dependence, impulsivity, and learning disabilities. *Journal Learning Disabilities, 5*:331-336, 1972.

Kesner, R.: A neural system analysis of memory storage and retrieval *Psychol Bull, 80*:177-203, 1973.

Kleuver, R.: Mental abilities and disorders of learning. In Myklebust, H. R. (Ed.): *Progress in Learning Disabilities.* New York, Grune and Stratton, 1971, p. 196-212.

Kohlberg, L.: Stage and sequence: The cognitive-developmental approach to socialization. In Goslin, D. (Ed.): *Handbook of Socialization Theory*, New York, Rand McNally, 1969.

Lacey, J. I., Kagan, J., Lacey, B. C., and Moss, H. A.: The visceral levels: Situational determinants and behaviorial correlates of autonomic response patterns. In Knapp, P. H. (Ed.): *Expression of the Emotions in Man.* New York, International University Press, 1963.

Laufer, M. W., and Denhoff, E.: Hyperkinetic behavior syndrome in children. *J Pediatr, 50*:463-473, 1957.

Levitt, E. A., Rosebaum, A. L., Willerman, L., and Levitt, M.: Intelligence of retinoblastoma patients and their siblings. *Child Devel, 43*:939-948, 1972.

Lovitt, T. C.: Self management with children with behaviorial disabilities. *Journal Learning Disabilities, 6*:138-150, 1973.

Lucas, A. R., Rodin, E. A., and Simson, C. B.: Neurological assessment of children with early school problems. *Dev Med Child Neurol, 7*:145-156, 1965.

Luria, A. R.: Experimental study of the higher nervous activity of the abnormal child. *J Ment Defic Res, 3*:1-22, 1959.

Luria, A. R.: *The Role of Speech in the Regulation of Normal and Abnormal Behavior.* New York, Liveright, 1961. (J. Tizard, Ed.).

Luria, A. R.: *The Mind of a Mnemonist.* New York, Basic Books, 1968.

Luria, A. R.: The functional organization of the brain. *Sci Am, 222*:66-78, 1970.

Lytton, G. J., and Knobel, M.: Diagnosis and treatment of behavior disorders in children. *Dis Nerv Syst, 20*:5-11, 1958.

MacKay, D. M.: The epistemological problem for automata. In Shannon, C. E., and McCarthy, J. (Eds.): *Automata Studies.* Princeton, Princeton U Pr, 1956, p. 235-251.

Malmo, R.: Activation: A neurological dimension. *Psychol Rev, 66*:367-386, 1959.

Marshall, P.: Memory analysis. In Anderson, R. P., and Halcomb, C. G.: *Learning Disability/Minimal Brain Dysfunction Syndrome.* Springfield, Thomas, 1975.

Meehl, P. E.: A critical afterword. In Gottesman, I., and Shields, J. (Eds.): *Schizophrenia and Genetics.* New York, Academic Press, 1972, p. 367-415.

Meichenbaum, D. H.: The nature and modification of impulsive children: Training impulsive children to talk to themselves. *J Abnorm Psychol, 77*:115-126, 1971.

Mendelson, W., Johnson, N., and Stewart, M. A.: Hyperactive children as teenagers: A follow-up study. *J Nerv Ment Dis, 153*:273-279, 1971.

Miller, G. A.: The magical number seven, plus-or-minus two: Some limits on our capacity for processing information. *Psychol Rev, 63*:81-97, 1956.

Milner, B.: Effects of different brain lesions on card sorting. *Arch Neurol, 9*:90-100, 1963.

Milner, B.: Some effects of frontal lobectomy in man. In Warren, J. M., and Akert, K. (Eds.): *Frontal Glanular Cortex and Behavior; A Symposium.* New York, McGraw-Hill, 1964.

Minde, K., Webb, G., and Sykes, D.: Studies on the hyperactive child. VI. Prenatal and paranatal factors associated with hyperactivity. *Dev Med Child Neurol, 10*:355-363, 1968.

Myklebust, H. R., Bannochie, N. M., and Killen, J. R.: Learning disabilities and cognitive processes. In Myklebust, H. R. (Ed.): *Progress in Learning Disabilities.* New York, Grune and Stratton, 1971, Vol. II, p. 213-252.

Namy, E.: Intellectual and academic characteristics of fourth grade gifted and pseudogifted students. *Except Child, 34*:15-20, 1967.

Osler, S. F., and Fivel, M. W.: Concept attainment: I. The role of age and intelligence in concept attainment by induction. *J Exp Psychol, 62*:1-8, 1961.

Parry, P.: *The effect of reward on the performance of hyperactive children,* unpublished dissertation, McGill University, Montreal, 1973.

Parucka, M. R.: *Concept formation in children with learning disabilities,* presented Southwestern Psychological Association, Dallas, Texas, 1973.

Patterson, G. R.: An application of conditioning techniques to the control of the hyperactive child. In Ullman, L. P., and Krasner, L.

(Eds.): *Case Studies in Behavior Modification.* New York, H, R & W, 1965.
Pavlov, I. P.: *Lectures on Conditional Reflexes.* Translated by W. H. Gantt. New York, International Publishers, 1928.
Penfield, W.: Consciousness, memory and man's conditional reflexes. In Pribram, K. (Ed.): *On the Biology of Learning.* New York, Harcourt, Brace and World, 1969, p. 127-168.
Peters, J. E., Romine, J. S., and Dykman, R. A.: Neurological findings in children with learning disabilities (Minimal brain dysfunction). *Devel Med Child Neurol,* accepted for publication.
Piaget, J.: *The Moral Judgment of the Child.* London, Kegan Paul, Trench, Trubner & Co., 1932.
Piaget, J.: *The Langage and Thought of the Child.* New York, Humanities, 1959.
Pihl, R. O.: Conditioning procedures with hyperactive children. *Neurology, 17*:421-423, 1967.
Pontius, A.: Neurological aspects in some types of delinquency especially among juveniles. *Adolescence, 7*:289-308, 1972.
Pribram, K. H.: The intrinsic systems of the forebrain. In Field, J. (Ed.): *Handbook of Physiology.* Washington, American Physiological Society, 1960, Vol. II, p. 1323-1344.
Pribram, K. H.: Memory and the organization of attention. In Lindsley, O. B., and Lumsdaine, A. A. (Eds.): *Brain Function and Learning.* Berkeley, U of Cal Pr, 1967, p. 79-122.
Quay, H., Sprague, R., Werry, J., and McQueen, M.: Conditioning visual orientation of conduct problem children in the classroom. *J Exp Child Psychol, 5*:512-517, 1966.
Rawson, M. G.: *Developmental Language Disability: Adult Accomplishments of Dyslexic Boys.* Baltimore, Johns Hopkins Press, 1968.
Roessler, R.: Personality, physiology and performance. *Psychopsysiology, 10*:315-327, 1973.
Rosenfield, G. B., and Bradley, C.: Childhood behavior sequelae of asphyxia neonatorum. *Pediatics, 2*:74-83, 1948.
Santostephano, S., and Stayton, S.: Training the preschool retarded child in focusing attention: A program for parents. *Am J Orthopsychiatry, 37*:732-743, 1967.
Satterfield, J. H.: Auditory evoked responses in hyperkinetic children. *EEG and Clinical Neurophysiology, 31*:291, 1971.
Satterfield, J. H., and Dawson, M. E.: Electrodermal correlates of hyperactivity in children. *Psychophysiology, 8*:191-197, 1971.
Satterfield, J. H., Lesser, L. I., Saul, R. E., and Cantwell, D. P.: EEG aspects in the diagnosis and treatment of minimal brain dysfunction. *Ann N Y Acad Sci, 205*:274-282, 1973.
Satz, P. and Sparrow, S. S.: Specific developmental dyslexia: A the-

oretical formulation. In Bakker, D. J., and Satz, P. (Eds.): *Specific Reading Disability: Advances in Theory and Method*. Rotterdam, Rotterdam University Press, 1970.

Senf, G. M.: Development of immediate memory for bisensory stimuli in normal children and children with learning disorders. *Devel Psychol, 1*: 1969.

Senf, G. M., and Fishback, S.: Development of bisensory memory in culturally deprived, dyslexic, and normal readers. *J Educ Psychol, 61*:461-470, 1970.

Senf, G. M., and Freundl, P.: Memory and attention in specific learning disabilities: *Journal of Learning Disabilities, 4*:94-106, 1971.

Shannon, C. E., and Weaver, W.: *The Mathematical Theory of Communication*. Urbana, U of Ill Pr, 1962.

Shetty, T.: Photic responses in hyperkinesis of childhood. *Science, 174*:1356-1357, 1971.

Shields, Diarre T.: Brain responses to stimuli in disorders of information processing. *Journal of Learning Disabilities, 6*:501-505, 1973.

Silver, L. B.: Familial pattern in children with neurologically-based learning disabilities. *Journal of Learning Disabilities, 4*:349-358, 1971.

Simon, H. H.: On the development of the processor. In Farnham-Diggory, S. (Ed.): *Information Processing in Children*. New York, Academic Press, 1973, p. 3-22.

Sokolov, E.: Neuronal models and the orienting reflex. In Brazier, M. (Ed.): *Central Nervous System and Behavior*. New York, Josiah Macey Jr. Foundation, 1960, p. 187-226.

Solomons, G.: The hyperactive child. *J Iowa Med Soc, 55*:464-469, 1965.

Spitz, H. H., and LaFontaine, L.: The digit span of idiots savants. *Am J Men Defic, 77*:757, 1973.

Spong, P., Haider, M., and Lindsley, D. B.: Selective attentiveness and cortical evoked responses to visual and auditory stimuli. *Science, 148*:359-397, 1965.

Sprague, R. L.: Minimal brain dysfunction from a behavioral viewpoint. *An NY Acad Sci, 205*:349-361, 1973.

Spring, C.: Perceptual speed in poor readers. *J Educ Psychol, 62*:492-500, 1971.

Spring, C., Greenberg, L., Scott, J., and Hopwood, J.: Reaction time and effect of Ritalin on children with learning problems. *Percept Mot Skills, 36*:75-82, 1973.

Sroufe, L. A. Sonies, B. C., West, W. D., and Wright, F. S.: Anticipatory heart rate deceleration and reaction time in children with and without referral for learning disability. *Child Devel, 44*:267-273, 1973.

Stevens, D. A., Boydstun, J. S., Dykman, R. A., Peters, J. E., and Sinton,

D. W.: Presumed minimal brain dysfunction in children: Relationship to performance on selected behavioral tests. *Arch Gen Psychiatry, 16*:281-285, 1967.

Stewart, M. A.: Hyperactive children. *Sci Am, 222*:94-98, 1970.

Sykes, D. H., Douglas, V. I., and Morgenstern, G.: The effect of methylphenidate (Ritalin) on sustained attention in hyperactive children. *Psychopharmacologia, 25*:262-274, 1972.

Sykes, D. H., Douglas, V. I., Weiss, G., and Minde, K.: Attention in hyperactive children and the effect of methylphenidate (Ritalin). *J Child Psychol Psychiatry, 12*:129-139, 1971.

Trauel, N. N.: *The effects of perceptual isolation on introverts and extraverts*, unpublished Ph. D. thesis, Washington State University, 1961.

Vandevoort, L., Senf, G. M., and Benton, A. L.: Development of audiovisual integration in normal and retarded readers. *Child Devel, 43*:1260-1272, 1972.

Vygotsky, L.: *Thought and Language*. Translated by E. Hantmann and Q. Vakar. New York, Wiley, 1962.

Warrington, E. K.: Neurological disorders of memory. *Br Med Bull, 27*:243-247, 1971.

Wechsler, D.: *The Measurement and Appraisal of Adult Intelligence*, 4th ed. Baltimore, Williams and Wilkins, 1958.

Wender, P.: The minimal brain dysfunction syndrome in children. *J Nerv Ment Dis, 155*:55-71, 1972.

Werry, J. S., and Sprague ,R. L.: Hyperactivity. In Bostello, C. G. (Ed.): *Symptoms of Psychopathology*. New York, John Wiley, 1969.

Werry, J. Weiss, G., Kogan, K., Minde, K., and Douglas, V. I.: Studies of the hyperactive child, VII. Comparison of neurological findings between hyperactive, normal and neurotic children, paper read at the Canadian Psychiatric Association Annual Meeting, Toronto, June, 1969.

Werry, J., Weiss, G., and Douglas, V.: Studies on the hyperactive child. I: Some preliminary findings. *Can Psychiatr Assoc J, 9*:120-130, 1964.

Willerman, L.: Social aspect of minimal brain dysfunction. *Ann NY Acad Sci, 205*:164-172, 1973.

Witkin, H. A., Oltman, P. K., Chase, J. B., and Friedman, F.: Cognitive patterning in the blind. In Hellmuth, J. (Ed.): *Cognitive Studies: Defects in Cognition*. New York, Bruner-Mazel, 1971, Vol. II, p. 16-46.

Yando, R. M., and Kagan, J.: The effect of teacher tempo on the child. *Child Devel, 39*:27-34, 1968.

Zeaman, D., and House, B. J.: The role of attention in retardate discrimination learning. In Ellis, N. R. (Ed.): *Handbook on Mental Deficiency: Psychological Theory and Research*. New York, McGraw-Hill, 1963.

## Chapter IV

# COUNTING JARS OF RASPBERRY JAM

Robert L. Sprague

"Counting Jars of Raspberry Jam" sounds like a crazy title, and it is. But as you read further the implications of this title will become quite clear.

This may be my Great Pumpkin Speech. As some of you may know, Linus, from the Peanuts comic strip, was running for president of his class. All the members of his class were enthusiastically supporting him in this political endeavor, and his heart warmed within him as he basked in their compliments and praise. The culmination of the campaign was the speech to be given before the class immediately prior to the voting. Well, Linus was feeling so good in the midst of all of this praise and the almost certain probability of winning the election that he could not resist talking about the Great Pumpkin. For those of you with small children who watched Peanuts on television, you know the moans, groans, and cries of anguish that accompany presentation of the Great Pumpkin speech of Linus. Sure enough, the Great Pumpkin Speech disappointed, irritated, and angered every member of the class. When the vote was taken, Linus received no votes at all. Perhaps when I am finished with these critical comments about developments and programs generated by bureaucracies to deal with the problems of children with learning disabilities, I may have convinced you that this is a Great Pumpkin Speech.

In spite of this danger, I will proceed because I think it will be informative and perhaps useful to outline some of the misconceptions and fallacies which are abroad in the general area of learning disabilities (LD) or minimal brain dysfunction (MBD).

The general theme of this presentation is how traditionally held concepts often overlook the actual behavior of the child and, consequently, may do as much harm as good from the standpoint of the lifelong welfare of the child. Now, how in the world did "Counting Jars of Raspberry Jam" become connected with this theme? Occasionally, one finds outstanding letters from history that are excellent commentaries on the current scene. Recently I heard Dr. Iverson Riddle (1973) make a speech in which he read a letter from the Duke of Wellington to the British Foreign Office in 1812 during the Napoleonic wars in Europe. It went as follows:

Gentlemen:

Whilst marching to Portugal to a position which commands the approach to Madrid and the French forces, my officers have been diligently complying with your requests which have been sent by H.M. ship from London to Lisbon and then by dispatch rider to our headquarters.

We have enumerated our saddles, bridles, tents and tent poles, and all manner of sundry items for which His Majesty's Government holds me accountable. I have dispatched reports on the character, wit and spleen of every officer. Each item and every farthing has been accounted for, with two regrettable exceptions for which I beg your indulgence.

Unfortunately the sum of one shilling and ninepence remains unaccounted for in one infantry battalion's petty cash and there has been a hideous confusion as to the number of jars of raspberry jam issued to one cavalry regiment during a sandstorm in western Spain. This reprehensive carelessness may be related to the pressure of circumstance since we are at war with France, a fact which may come as a bit of a surprise to you gentlemen in Whitehall.

This brings me to my present purpose, which is to request elucidation of my instructions from His Majesty's Government, so that I may better understand why I am dragging an army over these barren plains. I construe that perforce it must be one of two alternative duties, as given below. I shall pursue either one with the best of my ability but I cannot do both:

1. To train an army of uniformed British clerks in Spain for

the benefit of the accountant and copy-boys in London or perchance.
2. To see to it that the forces of Napoleon are driven out of Spain.

Your most obedient servant,<br>Wellington

Now perhaps the title is clear. The Duke of Wellington was distraught to say the least that the accountants and copy boys in London were more concerned about counting jars of raspberry jam issued to one cavalry regiment during the sandstorm than getting on with the real business at hand, namely fighting a war against Napoleon.

Organizations or bureaucracies — bureaucracy is the name of an organization which we do not like — have the habit of losing sight of their goals for which they were created and becoming enmeshed in self-serving ends (Levine and Levine, 1970). This habit is particularly troublesome when the organizations deal with children, because children do not have any effective lobby to speak for them as teachers have educational associations or teachers unions, as doctors have the American Medical Association or County Medical Society, or as the truck driver has the Teamsters Union.

If you will indulge me some personal experiences with a bureaucracy, it will help to clarify this point.

Several years ago my wife and I decided to put our actions where our mouths were and made application for and became foster parents for a state Department of Children and Family Services which is the official title for the branch of state government concerned with the social welfare of children. Most of you know that it is exceptionally rare to find families with a professional background engaging in foster care. Most foster parents come from the blue collar segment of our society and should be praised for their awareness of the social needs of children and their attempts to meet these needs. Actually, this was not a particularly big step for us because we had adopted our two fine daughters and were aware of foster care and its implications. Since my wife was particularly interested in infants, we became licensed as a foster home for infants. Over a two year period of time, she took care of six infants who were brought to our home directly from the maternity ward of a hospital. I deliberately said "she took care of the infants" because the overwhelming burden of foster care is on the wife with the husband bearing only a small share of the responsibility. This is particularly true in our case, since I tend to be running around the country making Great Pumpkin Speeches.

Insofar as we could, we tried to accept these infants as members of the family. She and I stayed up nights at the hospital as some of the infants underwent surgery or were hospitalized. Certainly, our daughters accepted them as full members of the family because our youngest daughter, Lisa, willingly shared her bedroom with each of these children.

The Department was moving to specialized foster homes, and we gradually became somewhat of a specialized foster home for the care of infants with severe problems. At this point Bethy came along. Bethy is not her real name, but Bethy is the name that we selected for this cute little blond-headed girl who came to our home four days after her birth. A little background might put her situation in better perspective. Her mother was a fifteen year old girl who had one previous child, a boy. Since the mother did not want Bethy, apparently she tried to abort herself and was unsuccessful, although the record is not clear. She apparently tried to conceal her pregnancy from her family and her brother had to forcibly take her to the hospital for delivery of Bethy. It may be surmised that Bethy did not receive the best prenatal care.

At any rate, Bethy arrived in our home, and we gladly accepted her as a newborn infant. However, problems soon arose. My wife quickly noticed that Bethy had extreme difficulty taking her bottle. It appeared to me that there was some neurological problems related to the sucking and swallowing reflex. Rather than taking the bottle normally, she ordinarily would not suck unless stimulated greatly with the nipple, and when she did suck, she often could not swallow but rather collected the milk in her mouth or gagged. All of this would bring on a crying and screaming episode with movement of the arms and legs. Nursing the bottle created so much difficulty that my wife switched over to baby food at about four weeks of age because we were very much concerned that she was not getting sufficient nourishment. My wife went through a living hell to feed this child during her first year of life. It was not uncommon for her to spend 1 to 1.5 hours per feeding.

It was soon apparent that she also had another problem, namely that she had a convulsive disorder or epilepsy. Soon after she arrived she began to have seizures, and as could be expected, the pediatrician placed her on anticonvulsant medication. For some reason, riding in a car seemed to aggravate and precipitate seizures, so that it was quite difficult for my wife to take her anywhere with the rest of the children. In fact, my wife was almost incarcerated at home with Bethy. But fortunately the Department provided Sue, a homemaker, to give my wife relief.

Several months after Bethy came into our home, summer arrived and it was time for our vacation. The social worker at the Department assured us that arrangements could be made for Bethy's care during our vacation time because it would have been impossible to take this child on a long automobile trip, the type of vacation that we often take. Perhaps I should change the wording from "assured us" to "lied to us" about the vacation.

Now let's get down to the nitty gritty of what organizations do to people with exceptional children. As I said, vacation time arrived and it seemed impossible to take Bethy on an extended auto trip. At this point, the social worker was completely silent about our request for some kind of alternative care for two to three weeks. We then approached a neighboring mental health facility that proudly proclaimed the availability of respite care for parents, that is, care of children during vacations and other times for the parents. We applied to this facility, and after we completed the twenty-five to thirty page application form (for those of you who are trying to figure this out, that is about two pages per day of vacation given a two week vacation), we were then turned down, and one of the reasons was that we were foster parents and not real parents. Now that is an interesting policy. Certainly, I have no objection to respite care for biological parents, but why reject a foster family when they have voluntarily accepted the care and responsibility of an exceptional child.

Now let us go back a sentence or two for more about filling out forms. Forms are extremely important to organizations, and if you want to get along with the bureaucracy, you ought to take the matter of filling out forms seriously, perhaps. The Department had a regulation that all members of a prospective foster family had to have a physical examination. A family who were close friends to us rebelled at this requirement because of the cost to the family, because of the apparent lack of use of this information by the Department, and because there was almost no medical information available about the child who was coming to their home. Rather than flatly refusing to do this, the mother was ingenious. She listed her name at the top of the application, went down the application and marked "yes" to the question of whether there were mental disorders in the family, marked "yes" to the question of whether there was venereal disease in the family, marked "yes" to the question of whether they had had tuberculosis, and so on marking "yes" to every single item that indicated a medical problem. Then at the end of the form, she signed her name exactly as she did on the beginning of the application right before the MD initials at the end of the line. Now, what happened when this form was submitted to the Department? You guessed it. Exactly nothing! The form was filed in the proper file with the other physical examination forms without anybody anywhere bothering to read it. Do you get the message? The message is that the filling of the piece of paper is far more important than any information the paper may contain.

Considering the fact that Bethy did not walk until she was two years of age, that she did not talk in sentences until she was about four years of age, and that she had seizures, I think we can safely assume that she had learning problems. Now we were informed that children with LD or MBD often have perceptual motor difficulties and these difficulties lead to slowness in learning to read. Maybe so, but let me examine Bethy's behavior a little more, particularly in light of the work of Marc Gold which will be mentioned later in this chapter. We lived in a bilevel house which had seven steps from the lobby up to the main level and eight steps from the lobby down to the lower level. Unlike other homes in that subdivision, our house was not carpeted. One of Bethy's favorite pasttimes was deliberately crawling from the living room to the steps and rolling head first, head over feet, thumping down these steps. That habit frightened my wife and I, but Bethy enjoyed it, laughed about it, and would do it every time she got a chance. All of my behavior modification, and all of our efforts were to no avail in stopping her from tumbling down those steps. Finally, I put up a gate and carpeted the steps to provide some cushion for her.

The carpeting showed an interesting aspect in her behavior. My wife likes long shag carpeting. If any of you have shap carpeting, you know it is very easy to lose items like hair pins in it. My wife sews, and a number of pins were lost in the carpet. Another one of Bethy's favorite pasttimes was putting pins in her mouth. As you might expect, we kept the house free of pins except those that accidentally fell into the carpet around the sewing area and could not be found. Even though I had perceptual motor difficulty in locating pins in the carpeting, it was no problem for Bethy who could find them readily, put them in her mouth, and enjoy beating us at our game.

Now for the culmination of the ancedotes about Bethy. We moved to a farm with an old farm house. This old farm house did not have any fence around the yard, and it had a fifteen step narrow, high-riser stairwell to the bedrooms upstairs. Bethy was almost three years of age and not only walking, but running. Whenever we visited the farm prior to moving out there, we literally had to tie Bethy to a dog stake or to a tree to prevent her from running down the busy county highway and possible consequences therefrom. We had no viable plan for preventing her from going head first down the long stairs. Thus, we presented this problem to the Department, and the solution was simple. The solution was to move Bethy to another foster home and remove the foster care license from us because we were trouble makers anyway, always complaining about something and in the words of one social worker, "professionals don't make good foster parents anyway.'

That is exactly what happened. My wife has cried a lot about this official rejection particularly after putting hundreds of hours of care into this child, but I have always thought it was a backhanded compliment of this fouled-up bureaucracy.

Now these previous stories may appear as the jaundiced view of a person who has a sour grapes attitude of being expelled officially from the organization. Perhaps such an evaluation is correct. But before you make this evaluation, let me read to you a few paragraphs from an article in a paper last week.

> Lawyers for the . . . Department of Children and Family Services have told the disbelieving Circuit Court judge they don't know the whereabouts of fifty-five children who are wards of the state.
>
> Judge . . . angrily replied Tuesday that "This has reached crisis proportions . . . Your agency is responsible for children who have been removed from homes the court has found inadequate, and you tell me you don't know where they are!"
>
> The attorney for the Department, told the judge, "There is no excuse, but we have had some major reorganizational problems in our office."
>
> . . . "This is only the tip of the iceberg," Judge . . . said. "We only know about the missing children who are parties to this suit, but how many others are missing that we don't know about (Anon, 1973)?"

This is not the entire article, for I have quoted parts of it which seem pertinent to this discussion. Some of the children are apparently lost in private institutions in another state.

The point is that the state Department of Children and Family Services was counting jars of raspberry jam (filing medical reports) while ignoring the war with Napoleon (losing track of children who were their wards).

You may be thinking to yourselves that such glaring examples of mismanagement of children, for example, actually losing children for which you are responsible, could not happen in the area of LD or MBD. I sincerely hope that such thinking is correct. But we all know that there are a variety of theories about treating LD and that these theories run the gamut from those bordering on charlatanism to those substantiated with considerable empirical data. It is our duty and obligation as people interested in children, particularly children with LD or MBD, that we do our best to minimize the influence of some of our colleagues with their far out ideas. For example, in one city there has been a team of an optometrist and a physician who treat children by making them crawl on the floor on all fours. This was apparently quite embarassing for the older boys who refused to do it. So to entice them to make the crawling motion with their four limbs, they set up a tube for them to crawl through, and poke them with a long stick to encourage them to crawl through the tube.

Last year at a meeting sponsored by the National Institute of Child Health and Human Development, the National Institute of Neurological Disease and Blindness, the New York Academy of Sciences, and CIBA-Geigy a number of people were requested to present papers on MBD. I was fortunate enough to be one of those individuals, and I would like to present again some of the material given there (Sprague, 1973).

## TRAINING OF THE RETARDED ON A COMPLEX ASSEMBLY TASK

### Subjects

The subjects in Gold's (1972) original study were sixty-four retarded adolescents enrolled in four sheltered workshops in the greater Chicago metropolitan area. It is particularly interesting to note how these retarded subjects were selected. The workshop directors were asked to select the eighteen to twenty lowest performing clients, excluding from selection clients with severe sensorial or physical handicaps and clients with Full Scale or Performance IQ's of above 60. Following selection, sixteen subjects from each workshop were randomly assigned to groups, with the restriction that four subjects from each workshop were placed in each group.

The mean IQ of the sixty-four was 47. It is interesting to note that all the workshop directors indicated to Gold that their best clients would be unable to do the task. Several of the directors laughed when he requested the lowest performing clients.

## Materials

The training task was the assembly of a Bendix, RB-2 coaster bicycle brake consisting of fifteen parts. Each subject was required to learn to assemble the brake by himself, not as a part of an assembly line operation in which each person puts on only one part of the brake. As should be ascertainable from an inspection of Figure IV-1, this is a formidable task. In informal settings, I have not found one faculty member or research assistant in the university who could assemble the brake when the pieces are placed in a pile before him.

A simple programming board was built to hold the parts for sequential assembly by the subjects. It consisted of a tray containing fifteen compartments for the transfer task, which was an Oxford No. 584 men's lightweight rear caliper brake consisting of twenty-four parts (Fig. IV-2). A divider ran parallel to the front of the tray to separate the parts from the brake being assembled.

Two groups of subjects worked with the parts as they came from the factory (Form-Only Groups). The other two groups worked with the parts that were color coded (Color-Form Groups).

Figure IV-1. Coaster brake.

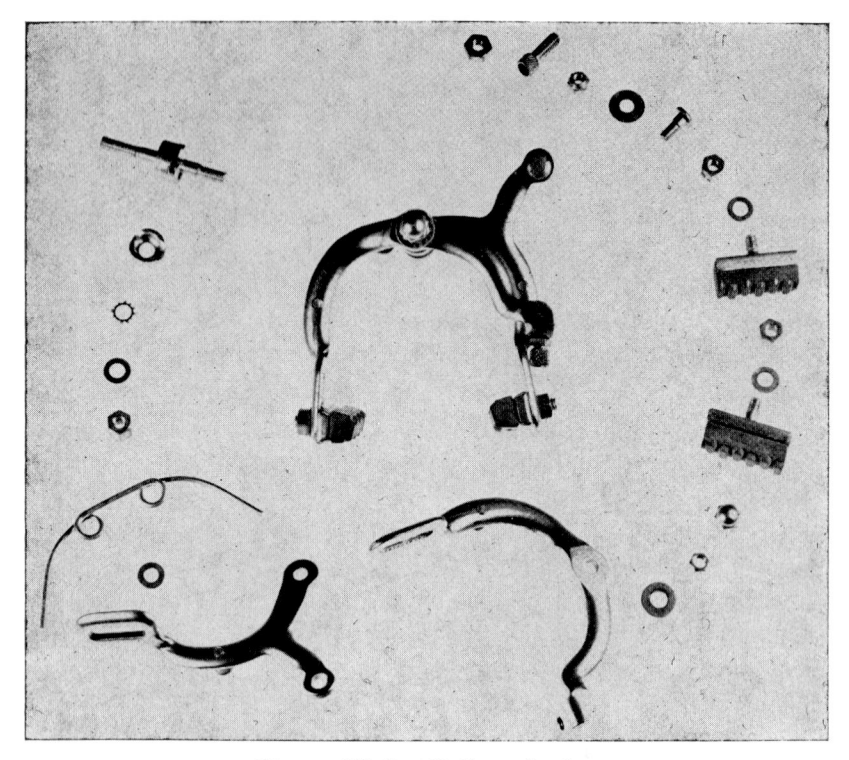

Figure IV-2. Caliper brake.

Coding consisted of painting red that surface of each part that is facing the subject when it is placed in the proper position for assembly. All groups worked with the parts of the transfer assembly as they came from the factory (Form-Only). A quantity of each part was placed in the proper compartment, so as to further approximate workshop conditions and so that there was no interruption for disassembly within trial blocks.

## Experimenters

The experimenters who actually trained the retarded subjects were recruited from among volunteers in the workshops and acquaintances of the workshop directors. Previous experience in training included some business schooling for all experimenters, and some volunteer work with retarded children for two of them.

None of the experimenters had specific training for work with the retarded.

Four experimenters were used in the experiment, one at each workshop. Four subjects from each workshop were in each group.

The training period for experimenters consisted of six half-day sessions. Training included the assembly and disassembly of the brakes, demonstration procedures, and recording the correction procedures. To test interexperimenter reliability, the experimenters judged five trials on the training test brake performed by a retardate not being used in the study. Of a total of 500 judgments (trial x steps x experimenters), there were twelve disagreements. A judgment was considered a disagreement if it contrasted with the judgments of the other experimenters.

## Procedure

The subject was seated at a table on which the tray was placed, with four disassembled brakes in the compartments. The experimenter was seated beside him. Before the subject's first trial on the training task and before the subject's first trial on the transfer task, the entire procedure was demonstrated once only by the experimenter. The demonstration consisted of the experimenter bringing one of each part forward, in front of the compartment divider, so that one set of parts was in position, then assembling the unit. Errors were made according to standardized demonstration format, and verbal cues that would be given when the subject made an error were used. The most frequently used cue was, "Try another way." The purpose of the demonstration was to show the subject how to respond to the few verbal cues used, not to teach the task.

The first day of the experiment for each subject consisted of one trial performed by the experimenter (demonstration) and three trials by the subject. On all subsequent days, the subject had four trials. Each subject began the transfer task on the day following criterion, or overlearning on the training task. Overlearning consisted of twenty additional training trials after the subject reached criterion.

Subjects failing to reach criterion by fifty-five trials were stopped and given a score of fifty-five. This happened with one subject only on the transfer task.

## Results

A 2 x 2 x 2 x 4 (Stage by Number of Relevant Dimensions by Amount of Learning by Experimenter) factorial analysis of variance was performed on each of the following dependent variables: trials to criterion, manipulation errors to criterion, and discrimination errors to criterion. The confounded effects of experimenter and workshop were included as a variable in the analysis; no main effects or interaction with this variable were found and are therefore not discussed any further.

Reliable effects for the Trials to Criterion dependent variable included main effects due to Number of Relevant Dimensions ($F=9.84$, $df=1,.48$, $p < .01$), Stage ($F=8.56$, $df=1,.48$, $p < .01$), and Number of Relevant Dimensions by Stage interaction ($F=54.48$, $df=1.48$, $p < .01$). The interaction is shown in Figure IV-3. The Form-Only Group required significantly more trials on the training task than on the transfer task. These subjects also re-

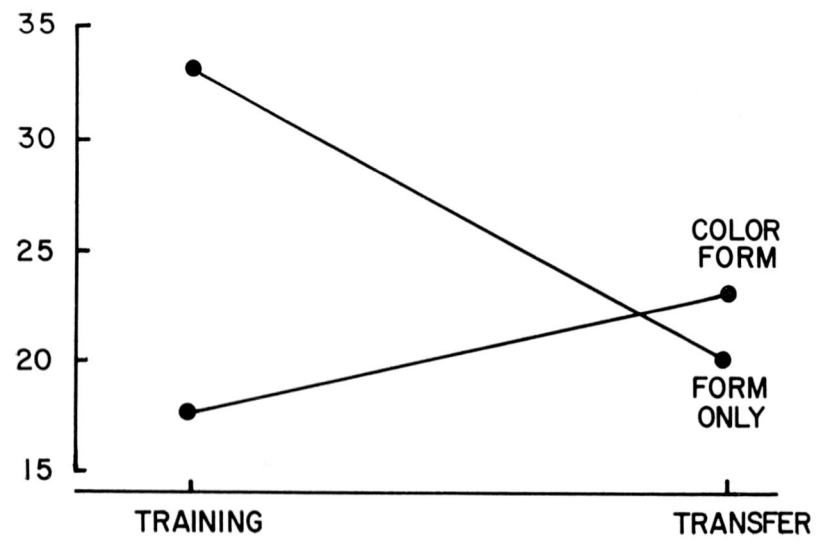

Figure IV-3. Trials to criterion on training and transfer.

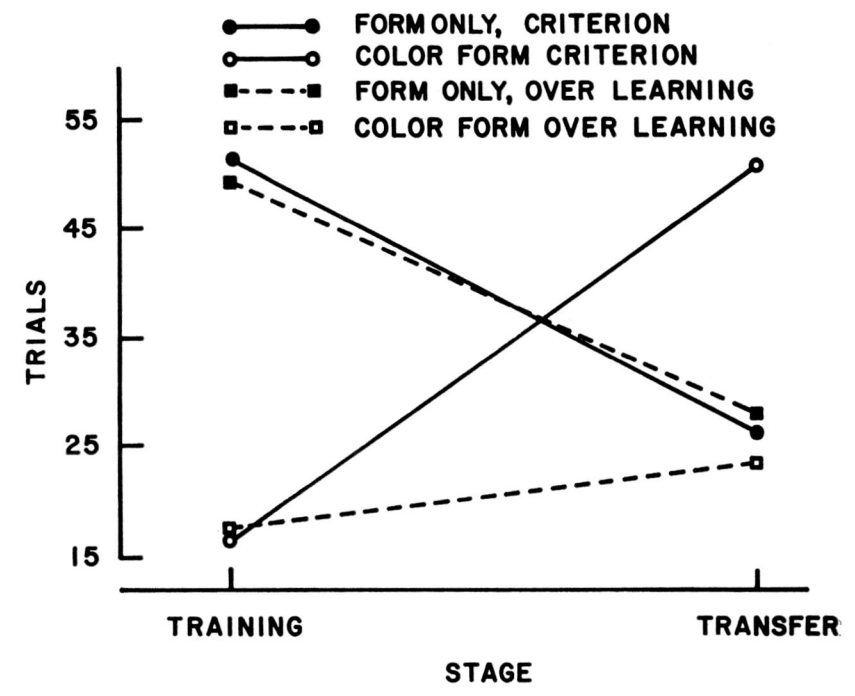

Figure IV-4. Discrimination errors to criterion.

quired significantly more trials on the training task than the Color-Form Group.

Reliable effects for Discrimination Errors to Criterion were obtained for a Number of Relevant Dimensions (F=8.74, df=1,.48, p <.01), Number of Relevant Dimensions by Stage (F=51.96, df=1.48, p <.01). The means comprising the triple interaction are shown in Figure IV-4. The interaction reflects the fact that overlearning affected only the number of discrimination errors made by the Color-Form Group on the transfer task (t=4.88, p <.01).

## Retention Study

The retention interval was one year. The same independent and dependent variables were used. In addition, Order of Presentation was included as an independent variable. That is, half the subjects started with the caliper brake (transfer task in the original study), so that an unconfounded retention measure could be obtained for both tasks.

## Subjects

Subjects were fifty-three (83%) of the original sixty-four subjects used in the acquisition and transfer study.

## Procedure

The same apparatus, task and experimenters were used. The procedure was the same, except that no demonstration and no overlearning trials were given, and half the subjects were started on the caliper brake.

## Results

A 2 x 2 x 2 x 2 (Number of Relevant Dimensions by Amount of Learning by Order of Presentation by Learning/Retention) analysis of variance, incorporating original learning and retention was performed. Highly significant main effects on retention were found for all dependent measures. In addition, many significant interactions were found. Because all of these interactions were functions of the large between-group differences in original learning, it was decided to not report the overall retention effects, but analyze the retention data separately. Table IV-1 shows the main effects for six dependent measures.

## Discussion

The results of this two-part study have dramatic implications, I believe, for the area of mental retardation and also for LD and

TABLE IV-I

MEANS AND F RATIOS FOR ORIGINAL LEARNING AND RETENTION USING THE COMBINED DATA

|  | Original Learning | Retention | F |
|---|---|---|---|
| Trials to criterion—Coaster brake | 26.09 | 14.31 | 66.55 |
| Trials to criterion—Caliper brake | 21.75 | 16.88 | 14.71 |
| Manipulation errors—Coaster brake | 33.47 | 6.18 | 66.16 |
| Manipulation errors—Caliper brake | 10.98 | 4.48 | 90.14 |
| Discrimination—Coaster brake | 35.05 | 9.21 | 95.53 |
| Discrimination—Caliper brake | 32.67 | 17.74 | 40.18 |

MBD. If you will recall, all of the workshop directors predicted that none of their best subjects could learn to assemble this complex task by themselves. In spite of the predictions of these very knowledgeable people, sixty-four of the original sixty-four subjects learned the fifteen piece task by fifty-five trials, the figure set as a maximum allowable number of trials, and sixty-three of the sixty-four subjects learned the twenty-four piece task within this arbitrary limit. Thus, an important outcome of this study is the wide discrepancy between the capabilities demonstrated by moderately and severely retarded individuals and what is presently expected of them in sheltered workshops. Expectancies held by workshop personnel, by educational personnel, and other professional personnel are a result of their academic training and experience with the clientele with whom they are working. These very expectancies can often seriously interfere with trying new procedures that may have rather dramatic effects. I believe this is the major contribution of this study, and it is from it that I want to draw an important analogy for MBD.

Besides the fact that these severely limited subjects learned the complex task, they remembered what they learned for more than a year, if F-test scores in the sixty to ninty range are accepted as a reasonably valid indicator of statistical significance. It is commonly believed that the mentally retarded cannot retain skills learned in training for long durations, although there is evidence that this belief has not been empirically verified (Belmont, 1966). So on two counts this study strongly indicates that the expectancies of experienced personnel seriously underestimate the ability of handicapped children.

Since his original work, Gold (1973) has conducted a number of other studies and demonstrations as to the effectiveness of his technique. One final example from the population of institutionalized retardates will amply illustrate the potential of these individuals. In a recent paper Gold (1973) reported that he had trained a group of institutionalized retardates to assemble a complex printed circuit board with resistors, transistors, capacitors and a transformer in an average time of 170 minutes. Let me repeat the time again — an average of 170 minutes for all subjects participating in the study. Surely the fact that one can teach institutionalized retardates to assemble a complex electronic circuit board should indicate that we ought to be more concerned about the behavior of the retardates, training them, than speculations about the reasons for their deficiencies.

An important lesson can be learned from this series of research. Vocational rehabilitation personnel have long been enamored of diagnosis of their clients' abilities, almost to the exclusion of their training, a trend that I perceive to be, unfortunately, similar to the trend in MBD. Gold has stated, "The extensive literature on vocational evaluation and prediction is full of statistical significance but devoid of practical significance (Gold, 1973)." The emphasis on diagnosis and prediction in this area has turned people's interests, energy, time, and money away from training or treatment per se, which is most unfortunate. To use a trite phrase, what is needed is a reordering of the priorties, so that the lion's share of the time, energy, and money is not devoted to diagnosis and prediction but ample recources are made available for the main job at hand, namely the training of children (Gold and Scott, 1971; Mann, 1970).

## MBD AND HYPERACTIVITY

Earlier workers in the field of minimal brain dysfunction, particularly Strauss, have emphasized hyperactivity as one of the very common symptoms associated with damage to the central nervous system (Strauss and Lehtinen, 1947; Strauss and Kephart, 1955). Following the early trends, considerable confusion currently surrounds the diagnosis of and treatment of hyperactivity and MBD. In a recent review, Werry has concluded after surveying pertinent literature in the area that hyperactivity is not a necessary or even a very common symptom associated with brain damage (Werry, 1972).

Werry's conclusion about the relationship between MBD and hyperactivity may not be shared by many, but it is based upon a series of studies by Werry and his co-workers in Montreal. Werry (1968) was able to obtain from the literature 140 different tests aimed at evoking both major and minor neurological signs; because of redundancy or exceptionally low frequency, he reduced them to sixty-seven items. A total of 103 chronically hyperactive children were examined with this battery, and the resulting data were factor analyzed. His conclusions were in consonance with the thesis of this paper. He stated, "It is my impression that the medical examinations lead to conclusions about cerebral status (MBD) or remote etiology (mostly perinatal) which usually have little direct relevance to what the teacher or parent is trying to do in academic or behavorial training (Werry, 1968)."

Few of the studies in this area make use of control groups with which one can compare the prevalence of neurological signs in the hyperactive or MBD group with the prevalence of the same signs in the presumed normal population. One of the few studies to use this kind of control was the experiment reported by Minde and colleagues. They examined the birth records of fifty-six hyperactive children and a like number of control children who were the next born children from the same hospital, matched for sex and socioeconomic status of the families at the time of birth. Their conclusion was, "The most striking finding of this study is the great similarity between the two groups and the incidence of severe prenatal and perinatal (sic) difficulties (Minde, Webb and Sykes, 1968)."

## BEHAVORIAL APPROACHES TO TREATING HYPERACTIVITY

In a previous chapter (Werry and Sprague, 1970), we have discussed the relationship between learning and hyperactivity in children. It was proposed that there might be an inverse relationship between learning and hyperactivity; that is, as the child becomes more active above an optimum level, he may learn less in a structured setting. Although the evidence was not very clear-cut at the time that the chapter was written, there are now more empirical data to support the hypothesis. An interesting aspect of this presumed relationship is the question of whether a basic attentional deficit results in both the hyperactivity and the poor performance rather than the overactivity, per se, leading to the poor learning. We lean towards the hypothesis that there is a basic attentional deficit that results in both learning difficulties and hyperactivity as has been argued convincingly by Douglas (1972).

In the first of our series of studies, the relationships between activity level and learning a very simple two-choice discrimination problem in trainable mentally retarded children was investigated (Sprague and Toppe, 1966). The two-choice learning situation required the child to select one of two objects in an attempt to gain reinforcement, in this case M&M® candies. The experimenter arbitrarily selected one of the objects as correct, usually reinforcing the selection of that object with candy or some other positive condition such as money. The trainable retardates were divided into three groups on the basis of the level on a stabilimetric cushion during the learning sessions. The hyperactive group and the low active group did not differ in IQ or MA; thus, there would appear to be no intellectual differences that could explain differences in learning. However, there was a statistically significant interaction between the high activity and low activity groups over trials, indicating that the low activity group learned the problem, whereas the high activity group remained at the chance, or 50 percent level.

Since that study, technology has progressed. The stabilimetric cushion now contains a small FM transmitter that is turned on whenever the child sits in the seat. Its signal is briefly interrupted whenever the child wiggles. The monitoring equipment can thus record the total time the child is actually seated on the cushion and the amount of activity he engaged in while seated there. This device has certain advantages for the normal classroom because it does not interrupt the classroom procedure. There are no wires hanging from the desk. The child cannot detect when the equipment is being operated because the radio transmission is silent.

After it was established that there was some relationship between activity level and learning, a series of studies were done to investigate whether activity in a classroom situation could be experimentally manipulated, using behavior modification techniques. Again, the subjects were mentally retarded children (Edelson and Sprague, (1974). An experimental classroom was arranged so that four children at a time could participate. They sat

Counting Jars of Raspberry Jam 113

at desks containing the stabilimetric cushion; to the top of each desk was attached a small box with a light on it that occasionally flashed. They were facing a screen on which audiovisual material of an educational nature was presented to them. At the end of

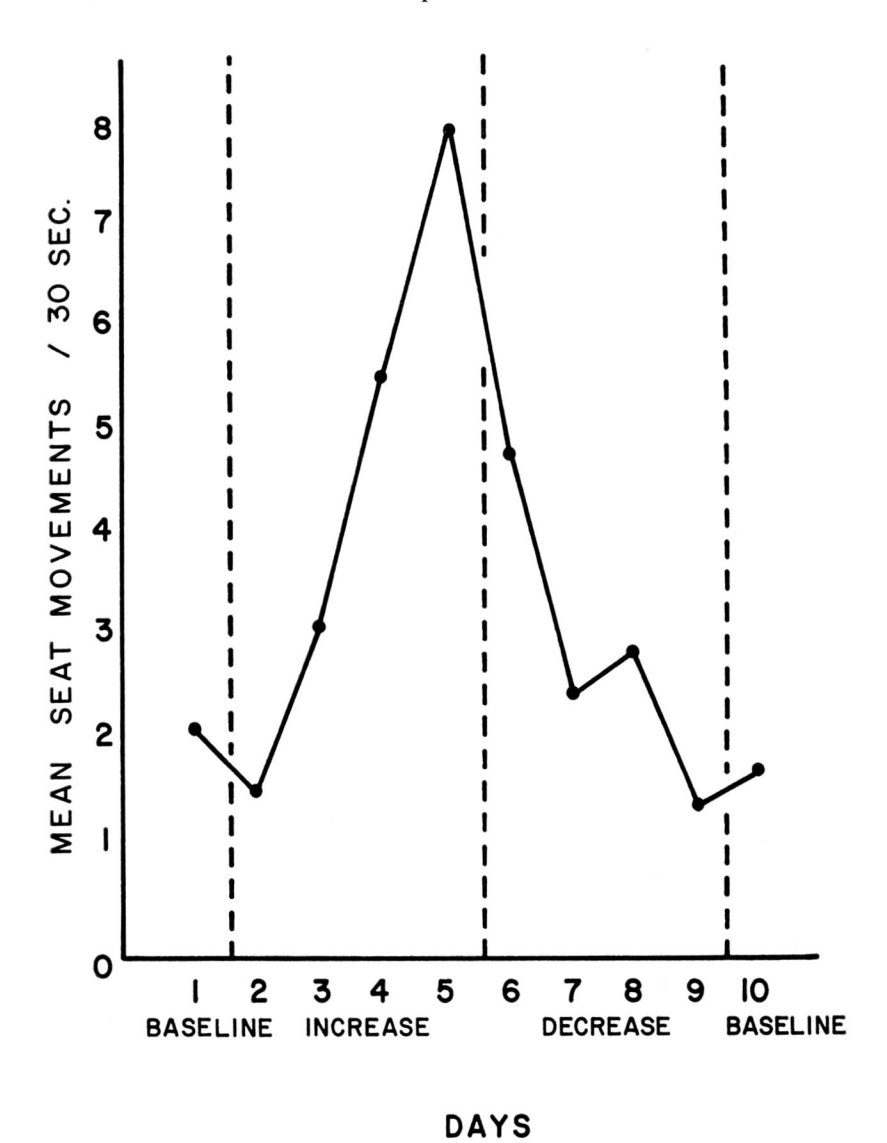

Figure IV-5. Mean seat movements/30 seconds.

each presentation, the children were given a multiple choice examination. Their only instructions were that this was the "sit-in-your-seat game" and that if they played the game correctly the light would blink on. Each blink of the light was worth a penny.

A contingency was established between each subject's activity level and the reinforcing condition. For example, if the child was placed on an increasing contingency, in a thirty second block of time, each time he moved as much or more than his baseline level of movement, the equipment automatically detected it and automatically flashed a light on his desk at the end of thirty seconds. On the other hand, if he was in the decreasing contingency, each time he moved less than his baseline level, the light was flashed. Half the subjects were assigned to a decreasing contingency after a baseline was established, and the other half were assigned to an increasing contingency. The contingencies were reversed after four sessions, although the subjects were not informed of this switch.

The effects of this procedure were statistically significant, as can be ascertained from Figure IV-5, which combines the data from the two orders in which the contingencies were applied. The analysis of variance for the interaction of Order by Session was significant ($F=2.72$, $df=11,143$, $p<.05$).

Although the index of academic learning was reasonably crude in this study, the results were interesting. The individual correlations between mean seat movement and number correct on the quiz were computed. These raw correlations $= -.45$.) This result just misses being significant at the .05 level for sixteen subjects.

In a very closely related study, Christensen investigated the effects of both behavior modification procedures and methylphenidate on the hyperactivity level of emotionally disturbed boys in an experimental classroom situation (Christensen and Sprague, 1973). The main findings of this study are shown in Figure IV-6 which displays the means and standard deviations of the two groups for the entire experiment. A statistically significant Treatments factor ($F=8.82$, $df=1,10$, $p<.05$) was obtained, indicating that placebo subjects were significantly more active than the drug subjects.

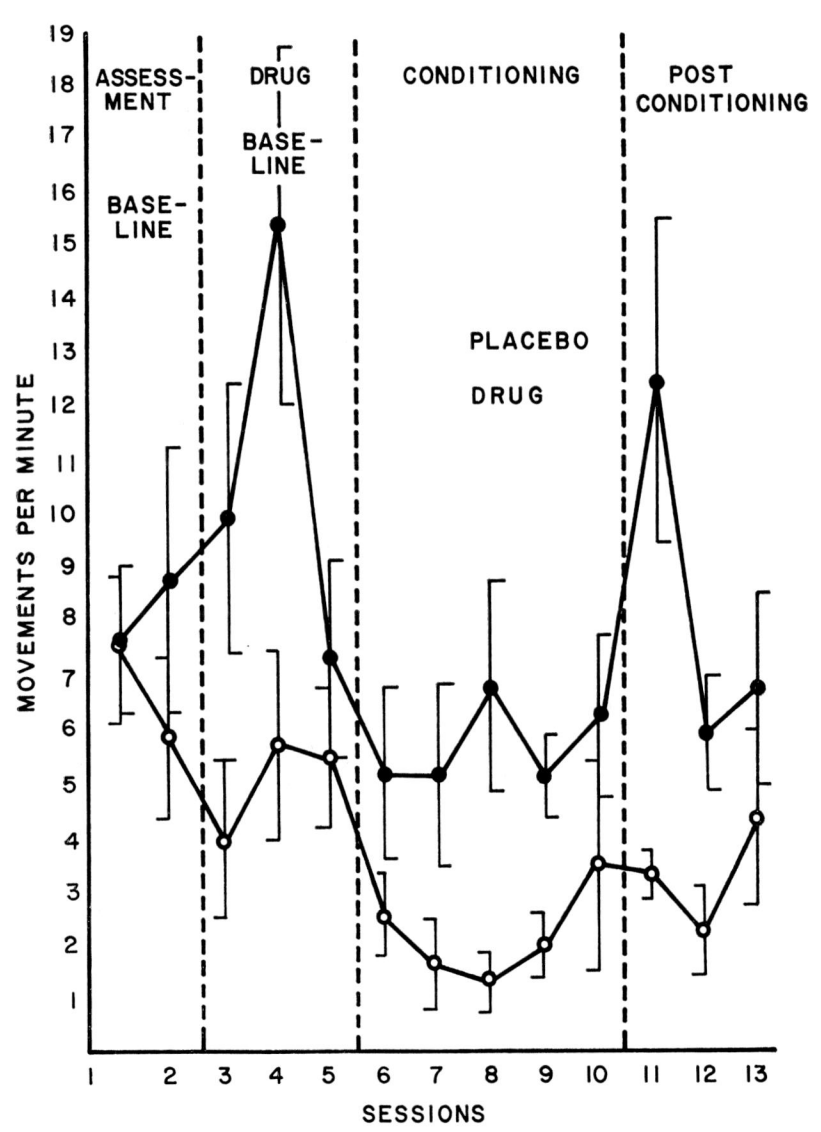

Figure IV-6. Mean seat movements for treatment groups.

Findings very similar to this were reported by Sprague and colleagues (Sprague, Barnes and Werry, 1970). While emotionally disturbed hyperactive boys were engaged in a recognition memory study, their stabilimetric seat activity was significantly reduced by the administration of methylphenidate in comparison to placebo but not altered by the administration of thioridazine. Concurrently, their learning performance was significantly improved. The number of correct responses increased significantly, and the latency, or speed of their responses was significantly reduced.

## COMBINATION OF DRUG AND BEHAVORIAL TREATMENTS

Stimulant drug treatment for hyperactivity is probably the most common form of treatment for this disorder (Sprague and Werry, in press). Behavior modification has been shown to have powerful effects on the behavior of children and is commonly used with exceptional children. But there has been almost no systematic investigation of the combined effects of these two powerful treatment procedures (Sprague and Werry, 1971; Sprague and Werry, 1974). Due to this lack of information, we supported Christensen's doctoral dissertation in this area (Christensen, 1973).

### Subjects

Sixteen hyperactive institutionalized retarded youngsters were selected. All were students of special education classes at Lincoln State School, Lincoln, Illinois. Children were referred by school personnel who were familiar with them, but the final selection was made on the basis of the assessment scores obtained on the Conners' Teaching Rating Scale (Conners, 1969) as well as other practical considerations, such as whether or not withdrawal from current medication was feasible. Ten of the subjects were males, six were females with a mean age of eleven years and ten months. Their mean IQ was 51.

### Design

The experiment utilized a within-group design with each subject serving as his own control. Although there were two experimental classes, each with different subjects, all experimental conditions were established and changed simultaneously in both classes. The study consisted of four major stages: baseline lasting for two weeks, and initial instatement of behavior modification conditions lasting for four weeks, a two week reversal back to baseline conditions, and a reinstatement of behavior modification procedures lasting another four weeks.

Drug trials were nested within the behavior modification stages so that medication was administered only while behavioral manipulations were also in effect. Drug trials were two weeks in length, with a subject receiving either active medication or placebo for that time. Subjects were randomly assigned to one of two counterbalanced drug schedules which called for them to receive either drug first then placebo or vice versa. Double blind conditions were maintained throughout.

### Classroom Conditions and Baseline Procedures

There were eight subjects in each of the two classes. The classes met five times each week for fifty minutes during successive hours in the morning. The classes were formed and in operation for five weeks before any baseline data was collected.

The two classes were nearly alike in as many aspects as possible. Both classes met in the same classroom. The same teacher, hired specifically for this project, taught both classes. Arithmetic was the only subject area covered in the classes. The class period always began with a fifteen to twenty minute group lesson. The remaining class time was spent on individual seat work, with a subject working on assigned academic material distributed daily by the teacher. At least one page of work, usually consisting of ten arithmetic problems, was required from them. After a subject's assigned work was completed and corrected he was either given supplemental work until the end of the period or allowed to use academic games.

During baseline conditions, the teacher was told to handle discipline as she saw fit. Verbal discipline, e.g. reprimands, were used most frequently during baseline.

### Behavior Modification Procedures

The behavior modification program was modeled after that reported by O'Leary and Becker (1967) and O'Leary, Becker, Evans and Saudergas (1969). It consisted of several distinct management procedures including the token reinforcement system, contingent teacher attention praise, rules and educational class structure. The major element of the program was the token reinforcement system. The tokens were delivered in the form of checks marked on a point sheet taped to the top of each subjects desk. There were six target behaviors for each subject, and four of these applied to the whole class: paying attention during the group lesson, working hard, completing assigned work and doing work correctly.

In addition to the point system, the teacher was instructed to systematically use praise and attention to reinforce appropriate behaviors.

## Drug Conditions

Methylphenidate was administered in the standardized dosages of 0.3 mg/kg adjusted to the nearest 2.5 mg. Both placebo and methylphenidate were packaged in 0-size orange opaque capsules. Envelopes were marked with the subject's name and the date the capsule was to be administered was given to the cottage personnel. Medication was dispensed approximately 1.5 hours before the beginning of each class by mental health technicians.

## Measures

A variety of assessment instruments and techniques were utilized to measure behavior change associated with the treatment. Seat activity was measured by the previously described stabilimetric cushion. Teacher ratings on the Conners' Teacher Rating Scale were obtained weekly. The longer, thirty-nine item instrument, was completed biweekly, and the shortened ten item Conners' Abbreviated Teacher Rating Scale was completed on alternate weeks. Two measures of academic performance were employed. Academic productivity was calculated by dividing the number of items a subject completed by the number of items included in his assignment, and the result was expressed in percentage terms. Academic accuracy was calculated by dividing the number of items done correctly by the number of items attempted. Time sampling observations by an independent observer were made of the classroom behavior according to an observation instrument described by Werry and Quay (1969). Inter-rater reliability checks were made on each subject at least once during each of the four stages of study. The average reliability for each category of the study was 95.4 per cent.

## RESULTS

Complete data were obtained from only thirteen subjects due to a variety of reasons such as hospitalization during the study, discharge from the institution, etc.

Data for each subject, summarized in two week time blocks, came from several sources: six observations, six academic assignments, ten days of seat activity, two administrations of the Conners' Abbreviated Teacher Rating Scale, and one administration of the Conners' Teacher Rating Scale, the thirty-nine item version.

These data were subjected to analysis of variance and eleven measures showed significant effects due to treatment. Rather than discussing these in detail, these findings will be summarized. The

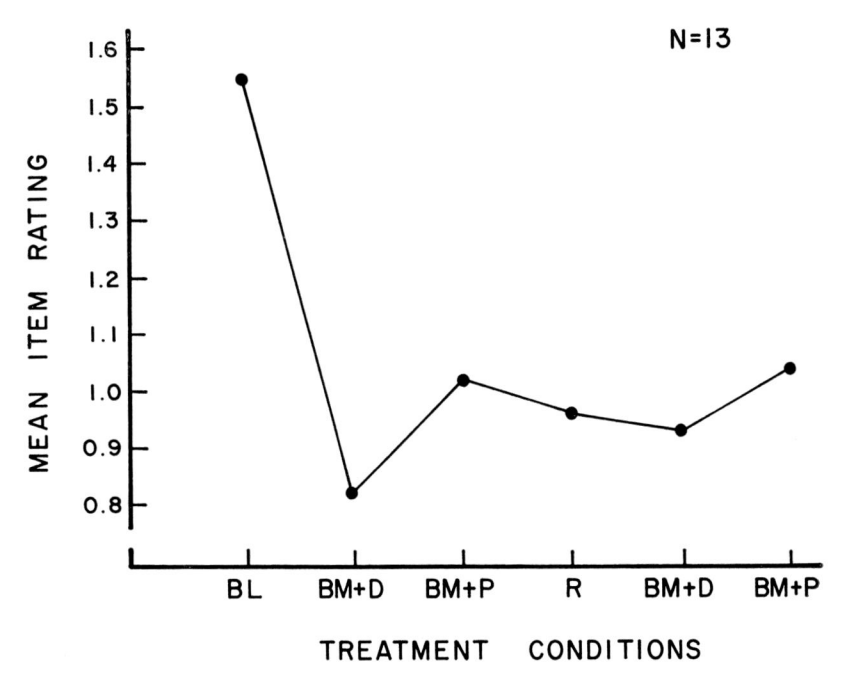

Figure IV-7. Mean item ratings on the abbreviated Teacher Rating Scale.

most consistent finding was showing significant difference in the direction of improvement between baseline conditions (that is baseline and/or reversal) and both stages of behavior modification (Fig. IV-7).

Observational measures indicated that the behavior modification program was very effective increasing attending, on-task behaviors, and, conversely, decreasing the percentage of total deviant behavior (Fig. IV-8).

With regard to comparisons between drug and placebo conditions, post hoc tests of significance showed differences on only two observation categories. These were "non-deviant" behaviors during the first regimen of behavior modification and deviant "vocalization" (speaking out of turn) during the second regimen of behavior modification. It should be noted in both instances, the significant differences between drug and placebo conditions seemed to be due to a weak effect of environmental program on these measures rather than a strong drug effect. The percentage of non-deviant behaviors observed in the first regimen of behavior modification with presence of active medication did not differ

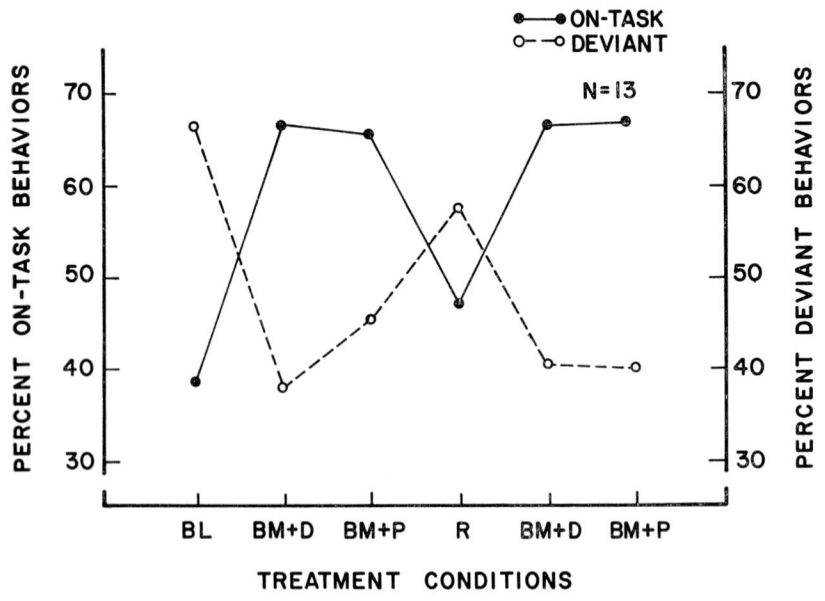

Figure IV–8. Percentage of on-task and deviant behaviors.

from the percentage of such behaviors observed during the second regimen of behavior modification in the presence of either placebo or active medication. The same pattern was evident with deviant vocalizations.

Interesting results were obtained from one subject who was surreptitiously placed on chlorpromazine during reversal. The administration of chlorpromazine reduced seat activity. (Fig. IV-9) but seriously reduced academic accuracy (Fig. IV-10).

The results of this study showed that the effects of methylphenidate were minimal in reducing hyperactivity and other disruptive behaviors compared to those of a behavioral modification program and related techniques. Most of the behavioral improvements were found to be attributed to the behavioral management procedures. The drug effects were essentially obscured by the relatively more powerful effects of the environmental treatment, and the addition of active medication produced little enhancement of the environmental procedures. The findings suggest that the methylphenidate

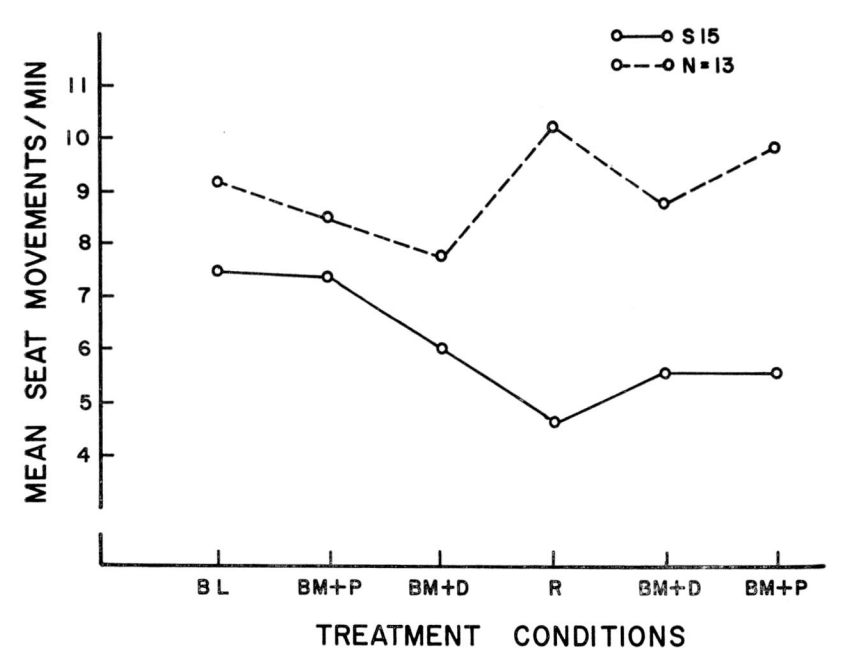

Figure IV-9. Seat movement data from a subject administered chlorpromazine during reversal conditions.

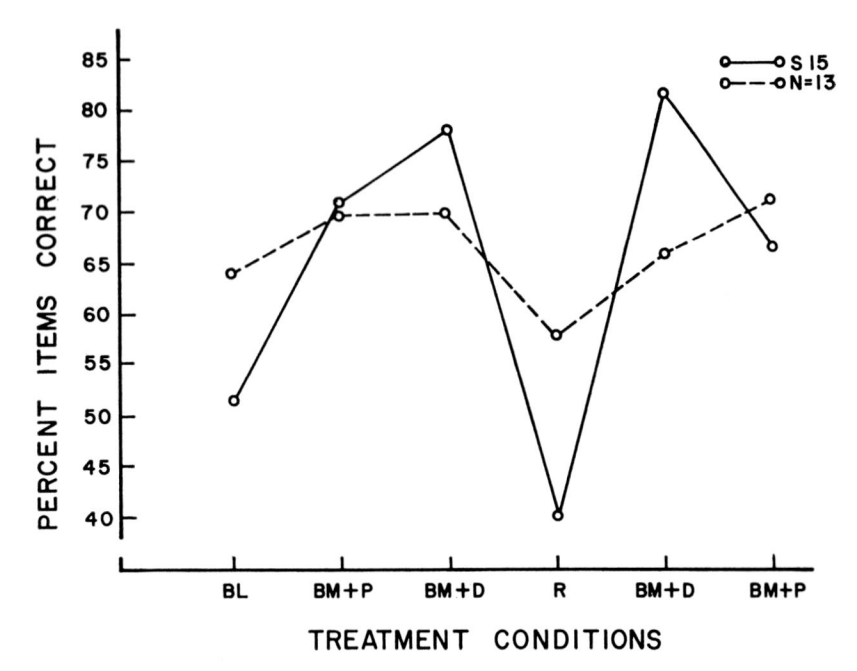

Figure IV-10. Academic accuracy data from a subject administered chlorpromazine during reversal conditions.

prescribed to control hyperactive disruptive and acting-out behavior in mentally retarded children may not be needed if a sound behavioral management program is utilized to control the same behaviors.

## SUMMARY

In summary, the main points of this presentation are: (1) Established organizations or bureaucracies often forget the reasons for their existence or the populations which they are supposed to serve. In other words they forget that there is a war with Napoleon, and spend most of their energies serving their own ends or counting jars of raspberry jam. An attempt was made to give blatant examples of this from my home state. (2) Since this trend seems to be universal in organizations of man, the same tendency is present in the area of LD or MBD. It may be debatable whether organizations serving MBD or LD children have rigidified to the point of serving their own ends, but trends are certainly present.

The heavy emphasis on theory and speculation about the cause of MBD as opposed to actually working with the behavior of the children involved was cited as a possible example of such bureaucratic self-serving tendencies. (3) When the actual behavior of the child and his ability to learn are examined, it may be seen that even children with rather severe impairments, such as the moderately retarded that Gold used in his experiments, are capable of performing at a much higher level than is expected of them. Certainly a few years ago no one in their right mind would have predicted that moderately retarded institutionalized children could learn to assemble complicated electronic circuit boards completely by themselves in less than three hours. (4) Considerable data have been presented here that hyperactivity, the most common complaint in the area of MBD or LD, can be handled behaviorally and, in fact, may be more efficiently treated behaviorally than with psychotropic drugs, the most common treatment form currently used.

And what does all of this mean for you, the typical person working with such children? It means that every person working with such children should maintain a broad perspective, listen closely to what the parents and child say about themselves, observe very closely what the child is capable of doing, and keep a very healthy skepticism for fads or strongly held theoretical viewpoints. Above all, make sure your major time and energy is devoted to fighting Napoleon, not counting jars of raspberry jam.

## REFERENCES

Anon, Agency 'loses' 55 wards of the state. *The Courier of Champaign-Urbana,* Illinois, October 10, 1973.

Belmont, J. M.: Long-term memory in mental retardation. In Ellis, N. R. (Ed.): *International Review of Research in Mental Retardation.* New York, Academic Press, 1966, Vol. 1, p. 219-255.

Christensen, D. E.: *The combined effects of methyphenidate* (Ritalin) *and a classroom behavior modification program in reducing the hyperkinetic behavior of institutionalized mental retardates,* unpublished doctoral dissertation, University of Illinois, 1973.

Christensen, D. E., and Sprague, R. L.: Reduction of hyperactive behaviors by conditioning procedures alone and combined with methylphenidate (Ritalin). *Behav Res Ther, 11*:331-334, 1973.

Conners, C. K.: A teacher rating scale for use in drug studies with children. *Am J Psychiatry, 126*:884-888, 1969.

Douglas, V. I.: Stop, look, and listen: The problem of sustained attention and impulse control in hyperactive and normal children. *Can J Behav Sci, 4*:259-282, 1972.

Edelson, R. I., and Sprague, R. L.: Conditioning of activity in a classroom with institutionalized retardates. *Am J Ment Defic,* 78:384-388, 1974.

Gold, M. W.: Stimulus factors in skill training of the retarded on a complex assembly task: Acquisition, transfer and retention. *Am J Ment Defic, 76*:517-526, 1972.

Gold, M. W.: Research on the vocational habilitation of the retarded: The present, the future. In Ellis, N. R. (Ed.), *International Review of Research in Mental Retardation,* New York, Academic Press, 1973, Vol. 6, p. 97-147. (a)

Gold, M. W., and Scott, K. G.: Discrimination learning. In Stephens, W. B. (Ed.): *Training the Developmentally Young.* New York, John Day, 1971, p. 420-444.

Levine, M., and Levine, A.: *A Social History of Helping Services.* New York, Appleton-Century, 1970.

Mann, L.: Perceptual training: Misdirections and redirections. *Am J Orthopsychiatry, 40*:30-38, 1970.

Minde, K., Webb, G., and Sykes, D.: Studies on the hyperactive child VI: Prenatal and paranatal factors associated with hyperactivity. *Dev Med Child Neurol, 10*:355-363, 1968.

O'Leary, K. D., and Becker, W. C.: Behavior modification of an adjustment class: A token reinforcement program. *Except Child, 33*: 637-642, 1967.

O'Leary, K. D., Becker, W. C., Evans, M. B., and Saudergas, R. A.: A token reinforcement program in a public school: A replication and systematic analysis. *Journal of Applied Behavior Analysis,* 2:3-13, 1969.

Riddle, I.: *Aspects of de-institutionalization.* Paper presented at the meeting of the Great Lakes Region of the American Association on Mental Deficiency, Champaign, Illinois, October, 1973.

Sprague, R. L.: Minimal brain dysfunction from a behavioral viewpoint. *Ann NY Acad Sci, 205*:349-361, 1973.

Sprague, R. L., Barnes, K. R., and Werry, J. S.: Methylphenidate and thioridazine: Learning, reaction time, activity, and classroom behavior in emotionally disturbed children. *Am J Orthopsychiatry, 40*:615-628, 1970.

Sprague, R. L., and Toppe, L. K.: Relationship between activity level and delay of reinforcement. *J Exp Child Psychol, 3*:390-397, 1966.

Sprague, R. L., and Werry, J. S.: Methodology of psychopharmacological studies with the retarded. In Ellis, N. R. (Ed.): *International Re-*

*view of Research in Mental Retardation.* New York, Academic Press, Vol. 5, p. 147-219.

Sprague, R. L., and Werry, J. S.: Psychotropic drugs and handicapped children. *The Second Review of Special Education.* Philadelphia, JSE Press, 1974, p. 1-50.

Strauss, A. A., and Kephart, N. C.: *Psychopathology and Education of the Brain Injured Child. Vol. II Progress in Theory and Clinic.* New York, Grune and Stratton, 1955.

Strauss, A. A., and Lehtinen, L. E.: *Psychopathology and Education of the Brain Injured Child.* New York, Grune and Stratton, 1947.

Werry, J. S.: Studies of the hyperactive child IV: An empirical analysis of the minimal brain dysfunction syndrome. *Arch Gen Psychiatry, 19*:9-16, 1968.

Werry, J. S.: Organic factors in childhood psychopathology. In Quay, H. C., and Werry, J. S. (Eds.): *Psychological Disorders of Childhood.* New York, Wiley, 1973, p. 83-121.

Werry, J. S., and Quay, H. C.: Observing the classroom behavior of elementary school children. *Except Child, 35*:461-472, 1969.

Werry, J. S., and Sprague, R. L.: Hyperactivity. In Costello, C. G. (Ed.): *Symptoms of Psychopathology.* New York, Wiley, 1970, p. 397-417.

## Chapter V

# PSYCHIATRIC RESPONSE TO THE MINIMAL BRAIN DYSFUNCTION CHILD

PAUL C. LAYBOURNE, JR.

TRADITIONALLY, CHILD PSYCHIATRY has focused on the disturbed child in the context of his family and society in general. An understanding of the nature of his problems usually entails long and difficult work with the child, his parents and the school. Often the nature of the therapeutic effort is unclear and the precise relationship between what we do and the observed improvement is *sometimes* puzzling. Perhaps it is because we have been forced to work in such a difficult and frequently unrewarding field, that *child* therapists in general have approached the whole syndrome of minimal brain dysfunction (MBD) in an entirely different manner. The MBD syndrome has gradually evolved over the years to include children with (1) a hyperkinetic syndrome who manifests a short attention span, over-activity, distractibility, impulsiveness and excitability. The other part of the syndrome (2) related to the specific learning disabilities which impair one or more of the basic psychological processes involved in understanding and/or using spoken or written language. These may be disorders of listening, thinking, talking, reading, writing, spelling, or arithmetic. They include conditions which have been referred to as perceptual handicaps, brain injury, minimal brain dysfunction, dyslexia, developmental aphasia, etc. (The National Advisory,

1967). A staggering amount of literature, both in the professional and lay press has appeared in recent years. Child psychiatric facilities have been inundated by parents who want treatment for their children after their home-bound diagnosis of hyperkinesis. A surprisingly high percentage of children referred by physicians to psychiatric clinics have already taken either methylphenidate or amphetamines as treatment of their "hyperkinesis." Periodically, articles have appeared in the papers reporting that a child has been transformed from a demon into a wonderful child by the use of stimulant medications. Switchboards then become jammed by parents wanting their child transformed by similar magic. Let us investigate how this state of affairs evolved and see if a more rational approach to treatment can be developed.

In 1937, Dr. Charles Bradley reported the effects of Benzedrine® on overactive children. Much to his surprise the Benzedrine seemed to have a "paradoxical effect" and overactive children were quieted (Stewart and Olds, 1973). This report received little attention until the late 1950's to early 1960's when publicity through the lay press, professional journals, and drug advertising created unwarranted optimism regarding the drug therapy of hyperactive children. In recent years books have been published advising parents how to control their hyperactive children. In all cases the disorder is viewed as existing in the child (Wender, 1973). The possibility that the parents may have contributed to the difficulty within the child is viewed as a secondary importance. In other words, the notion is discounted that a hyperactive child may create emotional problems in the parents which may subsequently result in emotional problems in the child. Psychotherapeutic intervention has been played down or dismissed as ineffective. I hasten to point out that the psychotherapy referred to in these books has been defined in a very narrow frame of reference including only psychoanalytically oriented technicians and excluding all behavior modification techniques and environmental manipulation. A very narrow definition of psychotherapy indeed!

There is no intent in this paper to rehash the standard techniques of treating the child with MBD, but rather to point out misconceptions, misdiagnoses, and anti-therapeutic efforts of some professionals in the field.

## WHAT IS MINIMAL BRAIN DYSFUNCTION

Since a therapist does those things which he thinks will bring about a favorable change in a disorder, it is appropriate to attempt to define the nature of the disorder before considering the kinds of therapeutic interventions which might be helpful. Since Wender (1973) has viewed the disorder as caused by an inborn temperamental difference in the child, he has seen treatment as often relatively simple. It almost always requires the services of a physician. He has seen medication as of the greatest importance in most instances; therefore, non-medical specialists such as psychologists, educators, and social workers cannot assume primary responsibility for treatment.

Stewart (1973), on the other hand, has listed a number of possible etiologies for the disorder and has emphasized a number of possible treatment modalities before even mentioning the use of drugs. However, he excluded emotional disturbance within the home as a cause of hyperactivity. He stated the following:

> If the child has been brought up in a very unstructured environment without a reliable pattern to depend upon in a chaotic atmosphere, he will tend to exhibit some of the traits of hyperactivity—high level, a general lack of self-control, and a tendency to flit from one activity to another, tune out on verbal instructions, act impulsively without considering the consequences, and become easily bored. This is not true of hyperactivity as we have been discussing it, and yet children whose apparent hyperactive behavior stems from lack of proper teaching can benefit from many of the techniques of management discussed in this book, such as emphasis on structures and routine, program or verbal training, and impulse control and rewards for good behavior.

This statement by Stewart is interesting since the therapeutic response to stimulants has been utilized by various investigators to prove the existence of minimal brain dysfunction.

Reitan and Boll (1973) have used the response of hyperactive dogs to amphetamines to suggest that they are the canine equivalent to the behavior problem child. If parental neglect and lack of structure can produce a child with the symptomatology described above by Stewart, then how does one actually differentiate these children from the so-called hyperkinetic or MBD child, and how can one be sure that these children will not respond to stimulant drugs with improved behavior? Or on the other hand, if they failed to respond to stimulant drugs, will the tendency to see them as organically damaged keep the therapist from investigating the real reason for the disturbance; that is, the disturbance in the parent-child relationship?

Anthony (1973) spoke to this point as follows:

> Experience has shown that organic patients, once so diagnosed are frequently separated from the content and process of their minds. Even sympathetic dynamic observers are inclined to approach them exclusively from the outside as if the internal sphere was empty or solidified into predictable and stereotyped, concrete slabs of expression. If it requires patience to communicate in a rewarding way with emotionally disturbed individuals, in the case of MBD children with their built-in disconnections between thought, feeling, and action, the persistence that is demanded is well beyond the average. If the extra effort is made, however, a view of the interior opens up that may be quite surprising to anyone expecting little other than concreteness and rigidity.

Viewing all of the overactive, aggressive, and disobedient children as hyperkinetic, which is frequently done by teachers, parents, pediatricians, and some child psychiatrists, probably is a disservice to these children.

The prevalence of MBD is almost impossible to establish since the nature of this confusing syndrome and the accuracy with which it can be diagnosed is really not known. For example, studies of learning disabilities indicate an incidence ranging all the way from 5 percent to 41 percent, but it is obvious from reading the descriptions of the children included in these handicapped groups that definitions of MBD vary greatly from study to study (Minskoff, 1973). Even the results of drug studies have been of little help in making a diagnosis. It is startling to note that uncontrolled studies by Knobel (1962) report 90 percent improved, and Lytton and Knobel (1958) reported 75 percent improved. On the other hand, a carefully controlled study by Millichap and colleagues (1973) of thirty MBD children yielded the following results. "A significantly improved performance during treatment with methylphenidate was observed in six of the seven neuropsychological tests. The effect of the drug was specific and greater than that of the placebo in the Draw-A-Man and Frostig Figure Ground Tests. In the parents' subjective evaluation of conduct and immaturity, improvements in scores during treatment of methylphenidate were not different from evaluations based on placebo response." Similar results are not unusual in carefully controlled drug studies. Differences between placebo and experimental groups are usually small and limited to certain specific tests. It should be noted that parents do not bring their children in for treatment to increase their ability on the Draw-A-Man and Frostig Figure Ground Tests, or even to demonstrate improvement on neuropsychological tests. They bring them in because of gross symptomatology which causes the parents considerable distress.

## THE PSYCHIATRIC ASPECTS OF HYPERKINESIS

It has been our experience that those children who do not respond to drug therapy and structured schooling experiences have severe emotional disturbances in the family which must be dealt with in a traditional psychotherapeutic manner. If correction of this conflictual situation is neglected, therapeutic results are unsatisfactory. The following case is an example of a child who was diagnosed as having MBD, treated with drugs, not only ineffectively but with a worsening of the condition, and successfully treated only after dealing with the family pathology.

George, a six year old boy, was admitted to the University of Kansas Medical Center with a chief complaint of wild, violent episodes of throwing himself around, breaking objects, and hurting other children. Approximately three weeks before his admission, George began displaying bizarre behavior. He became violent, banging his head, cutting himself, and was apparently impervious to pain. He hallucinated bugs at this time and expressed considerable fear of them. He was taking 5mg of Ritalin® three times a day. When this was discontinued the hallucinations ceased. George then regressed into a more infantile-like state, cursing, wetting his bed, going in trance-like conditions, apparently unaware of his environment and unable to be awakened.

When he was four and one-half years old, George was seen by a neurologist who recorded the chief complaint by the mother,

"He just seems to throw himself around and does not mind if he gets hurt. He seems sort of turned off and I can't get his attention. The other day in the restaurant I slapped him when he was misbehaving and he didn't seem to know. A few minutes later when he had settled down and I mentioned that he had finger marks on his face, he asked how that happened." The mother noted that during the afternoon nap he usually slept with his eyes open although he was completely limp.

Neurological examination at that time indicated that George appeared to be an essentially normal youngster, somewhat restless, with distinctly reduced muscle tone. His reflexes were within normal limits. Alterating movements were made with fair speed, more quickly with the right hand. He was somewhat restless and perhaps hyperactive, but could be controlled by verbal suggestions. His electroencephalogram showed multiple spike wave activity compatible with a seizure disturbance. Photic stimulation produced paroxysmal polyspike activity. He was given 10 mg of Ritalin in the morning to see if this would reduce his undesirable behavior.

Five months later he was seen by another physician. His mother complained he had bizarre seizure episodes, characterized by twenty minutes of wild fits during which he threw himself about, yelled, used filthy language, was incoherent and unaware of his surroundings. His mother also complained that George had staring episodes which would last from sixty to 120 minutes during which she could not get through to him. But he could recall all of the activities which occurred during that time. The physician diagnosed the condition as organicity, convulsive disorder with mild cerebral palsy. The dosage of Ritalin was increased and Thorazine® was added in an attempt to improve his behavior.

Approximately nineteen months later George was admitted to the University of Kansas Medical Center with the previously mentioned symptoms of violent episodes, throwing himself about, breaking objects, hallucinations, and dreamlike states. For the first time the family was evaluated psychiatrically. In the hospital the patient was oriented as to time, place and person. He said that he was in the hospital to straighten out. He admitted that he had broken furniture, cursed and held up his nasty finger. His affect was inappropriate. He constantly grinned while relating his problems and stated he wasn't sorry that he did them. The patient was generally well behaved in the hospital. His misbehavior seemed to be confined to the evenings, specifically when his mother was visiting. He interacted well with the other patients and took part in occupational and recreational therapy activity. He responded reasonably well to structure and behavior modification techniques.

An evaluation of the mother indicated that he had an extremely unhappy childhood in which she was constantly scapegoated by her mother and made to feel that any misfortune that befell the family was her fault. The father was severely obsessive-compulsive and bad tempered toward the children and his wife. The marital situation was very poor.

According to the father, the patient got along reasonably well until about three months before admission to the hospital when they adopted a retarded girl. At that time he became jealous of the new child and quite aggressive toward her. It was also discovered from interviewing the father that the mother considered herself an amateur psychologist and manipulated the patient's dose of Ritalin according to what she thought he needed.

During the child's hospitalization, the mother began to talk about the sexual relationship between George and herself. At about one year of age he began coming in at night to sleep with his parents. As soon as he became too large for the three to sleep in one bed he would bring his pillow into the parent's bedroom and sleep next to the bed on his mother's side. As soon as the father got out of bed in the morning, George would get into bed with his mother. The mother-son relationship progressed from closeness to active fondling of his mother's breasts and body. Shortly before hospitalization, George had been getting erections during these sessions and had apparently been enjoying this. The mother always reacted to this behavior by in her term, ignoring it. Sometimes she would remove his hand, but for the most part she simply ignored it. There had been several incidents during the day at home and in public when George fondled his mother. The mother contended that by ignoring it the situation would go away. However, she did admit that it had not gone away, but was getting worse.

After fifteen days of hospitalization George was transferred to out-patient treatment. Therapeutic work with the child was directed toward getting him to control his behavior. At home he became more manageable but he developed several rituals such as being obsessed with the idea of saying "goodbye" over and over again. He also started hoarding paper. However, this activity was discouraged and he soon gave it up. In play therapy George wanted to hoard paper drinking cups but was required by his therapist to give them up. This provoked anger on his part but soon he responded to firmly enforced limits. He related that his mother and father fought all the time because all his father cared about was work.

In four months he had given up hoarding, and eight months after his admission to the hospital he was able to enter public school in the second grade and make an adequate social and academic adjustment to school. As a matter of fact, he was elected student of the week by the class which, of course, made him and his parents very happy. Psychotherapeutic efforts with the parents were directed toward helping them to set more realistic limits with the child, to stop the sexual stimulation and seduction of the boy, and to improve the marital relationship. Nine months after hospitalization this had been partially successful and the relationship between the parents had improved markedly. A battery of psychological tests done while George was in the hospital indicated that he was in the bright normal range of intellectual ability, he possessed generally average academic skills and factual knowledge, he demonstrated a keen sensitivity to social situations which probably accounted for his facility at manipulating others. His perceptual motor development was age-appropriate and there was no indication of organic dysfunction.

This case then has illustrated how important it is to study all aspects of hyperkinetic behavior. This child was unsuccessfully treated with medication and amateur attempts on the part of the mother to cope with his behavior. Once a thorough psychiatric study was made, it became obvious how all members of the family played into his hyperkinetic, uncontrolled behavior and when attention was directed to remedying the pathological situation in the family, the behavior of the child improved markedly. The case has also illustrated the important fact that drugs do not always have a salutary effect on hyperkinesis but sometimes complicate matters by producing psychotic episodes in the child. We cannot be sure that the mother had not over-medicated the child in her attempts at adjusting his dosages according to his needs, but there is little doubt in our minds that the hallucinatory episodes were a reaction to methylphenidate.

Hyperkinesis is not the only disorder which can result from emotional disturbance. A specific learning disability certainly can be simulated by emotional disturbance to the point that extensive testing will fail to determine the exact nature of the disorder, as the following case will demonstrate.

Mark, a six year old boy, was referred as an out-patient to the University of Kansas Medical Center, Division of Child Psychiatry, by the home-school coordinator. The chief complaint was that he had begun kindergarten in September at the age of five years, but acted like a two year old. He was hard to test, cried a great deal, and was uncontrollable. A pediatrician had told the family he would outgrow it. The public school recommended withdrawal for a year; subsequently, he was placed in a preschool program. The following year the parents entered in the first grade; however, after a period of time he was put back in kindergarten. According to reports, his total verbal output was profanity. The schoolteacher reported that he could read some words.

Mark's history revealed that his parents were not yet through high school when the mother became pregnant. Shortly after birth, he was taken to an apartment where there was a gas leak. He was four months old before the leak was repaired. Shortly after that he became ill with bronchial pneumonia and was hospitalized with a high fever. According to his parents, Mark appeared quite nervous and tense from birth; he was easily startled by lights and noises, and he was described by his mother as hyperactive from the beginning. It was reported that he crawled all over the bed when he was four and one-half days old. Also, according to the mother, he was toilet trained at four months of age.

At the time he first entered kindergarten, Mark was one of the youngest children in the district. He was immediately recognized as more immature than the other children and twelve complaints were registered against him by teachers: (1) he tired easily, (2) he couldn't adjust to changes from the regular routine, (3) he couldn't remember simple directions, (4) he had a very short attention span, (5) he had poor coordination, (6) he had repeated tantrums, (7) he repeated phrases over and over (8) he continued to ask where his mother and daddy were (9) he started laughing when nothing was funny, (10) be became overly excited when around other children, (11) he cried daily, and (12) there was an unusual and persistent use of profanity. His mother told the home-school coordinator that he was an only child and had never played with other children. He didn't mind her, he sassed her back, and picked up the curse words from his grandfather. At that time his Stanford Binet IQ was 60. His visual motor ability was a 3.6 year level; his verbal fluency was at the 3.0 year level; his memory, concentration and general comprehension were at the 2.6 year level. On the Kindergarten Screening Test he was below 99 percent of the children entering kindergarten. Because of these findings he was placed in nursery school.

The following year when Mark was barely six years old, he was enrolled in the first grade. He immediately distinguished himself by being below 96 percent of the children entering the first grade on the tasks that he was able to master. He absolutely refused to do a human figure drawing, and never willingly entered into any kind of test situation with the counselor. Because of these findings, he was placed in kindergarten at age six. He never entered into group activities, and according to reports, never watched one film all year. When a film was running in the classroom he kept his head turned away from the screen. He also had frequent sprees of cursing. Eight months after entering school, Mark was given a WISC and achieved a Verbal IQ of 85, a Performance IQ of 118, and a Full Scale IQ of 101. Although he did very poorly on formal tests, he would give occasional indications that he was brighter than he appeared. For example, he noted that the calendar was set on the wrong month. He was given a Criterion Reading Levels Test in the spring of his kindergarten year. He had pronounced difficulty with eye tracking, he couldn't throw a beanbag, he couldn't balance on one foot, he held his scissors incorrectly, couldn't follow a line, couldn't copy shapes, couldn't find different words in a group of four. When asked to draw himself, the child began to scribble. The tutor took the paper, gave it to Mark and told him to do it right. He then drew an age-appropriate human figure, all the time saying, "Shit ass, shit ass, shit ass."

He was seen by the Division of Child Psychiatry in the summer of the same year in which he had failed all the tests in the spring. In the playroom he quickly read the labeling on a number of trays of toys which were labeled "cowboys and Indians," "trains," "trucks and cars," with no difficulty. However, he did this at his own initiation. When asked to read a book he refused to look at it and denied that he could recognize any word in the book. Even when the therapist took his finger and pointed to such things as kittens he acted as though he couldn't even identify the picture. It seemed evident that the youngster probably could do any age-appropriate task if he wanted to. He was then brought from the playroom back into the office and was tested on some of the things he had failed in school only a few months before. He could balance on one foot, he could identify his right and left side, he could throw and catch a beanbag fine, he even looked out the window and said, "I see downstairs," although he had failed concepts of above and below only a few months before in school. He also showed great dexterity with scissors, volunteering to cut a circle and demonstrating that he could indeed cut in a straight line. Apparently his failures were based on extreme negativism rather than any intrinsic lack of ability to perform at that level.

At the time of the evaluation his parents had expressed the idea that their child performed his tasks adequately at home and only pretended not to be able to do them in school. They felt that if the school would not put up with the foolishness and would exert firm control and supervision, Mark would perform adequately in school. We supported them in this belief, telling them that he was indeed of normal intelligence and coordination, and that he should be expected to behave as a normal child and not as a mentally retarded handicapped child. We also had a conference with the school personnel and shared our findings with them. They agreed to put Mark in a small learning disability class, not on the basis that he had a learning disability, but simply that he needed structure and a specially trained teacher. He re-entered school in the fall and did very well academically. He utilized the isolation screens, referring to them as his office. When he became upset he would often go to his office until he had regained his composure. The class was structured on a behavior modification system and there was an "ugly box" that the children sat in when they behaved in an "ugly manner." He sat in the "ugly box" twice, but after that decided that behaving properly was considerably more fun than sitting in the box. On one occasion he did lapse back into profanity but the school called his parents and his parents told him they would not put up with his profanity. This brought an end to the problem.

Here again we have an example of an evaluation of the child within the context of his family. This demonstrates the importance of utilizing the strengths of the family to support limits set at school as well as at home, and the necessity of understanding clearly the nature of the problem when dealing with the child. Once this was done, what appeared on the surface to be a very organic type of disability disappeared. This is not to say that the child did not have some kind of a learning disability substrate, but that focusing on the child as a handicapped child rather than clearly identifying what he could and couldn't do prepetuated the myth that he was inadequate and perhaps even severely mentally retarded. It is certain that the school would have had a more difficult time in bringing about the salutary changes in this child without the cooperation and understanding of the parents which was a direct result of the psychotherapeutic efforts of the Division of Child Psychiatry.

## DISCUSSION

The classical techniques of treating children with hyperkinesis and learning disorder are not to be discarded. The use of medication when indicated can be of great help and of great value in helping the child to cope more adequately with his environment. Structured situations and special learning techniques are also valuable and it is not the intent of this paper to in any way impune their value. The intent of this paper is, however, to call attention to those working in the field that a hyperkinetic or learning disabled child is still a child and subject to all of the emotional disabilities that any other child can demonstrate. It should be remembered that all children bring into the world a constitution, and that within the limits of that constitution they cope with their environment as best they can. If we neglect the whole concept of understanding the kinds of conflicts that exist in children who are already predisposed to having difficulty in coping, we are doing the child and ourselves a disservice.

## REFERENCES

Anthony, E. J.: A psychodynamic model of minimal brain dysfunction. In de la Cruz, F. F., Fox, B. H., and Roberts, R. H. (Ed.): *Minimal Brain Dysfunction. Ann NY Acad Sci., 205*:52-60, 1973.

Greenberg, L. M., Deem, M. A., and McMahon, S.: Effects of dextroamphetamine, chloropromazine, and hydroxyzine on behavior and performance in hyperactive children. *Am J Psychiatry, 129*:532-539, 1972.

Millichap, J. Gordon: Drugs in management of minimal brain dysfunction. In de la Cruz, F. F., Fox, B. H., and Roberts, R. H. (Ed.): *Minimal Brain Dysfunction. Ann NY Acad Sci, 205*:321-334.

Minskoff, J. G.: Differential approaches to prevalence estimates of learning disabilities. In de la Cruz, F. F., Fox, B. H., and Roberts, R. H. (Ed.): *Minimal Brain Dysfunction. Ann NY Acad Sci, 205*:139-145, 1973.

Reitan, R. M., and Boll, T. J.: Neuropsychological correlates of Minimal Brain Dysfunction, In de la Cruz, F. F., Fox, B. H., and Roberts, R. H. (Ed.): *Minimal Brain Dysfunction. Ann NY Acad Sci, 205*:65-88, 1973.

Stewart, M., and Olds, S.W.: *Raising A Hyperactive Child.* New York, Harper & Row, 1973, p. 237.

The National Advisory Committee on Handicapped Children, U. S. Office of Education, Washington, D.C., 1967.

Wender, P. H.: *The Hyperactive Child.* New York, Crown, 1973, p. 31.

---Chapter VI---

# EFFECTS OF MEDICATION ON LEARNING EFFICIENCY RESEARCH FINDINGS REVIEW AND SYNTHESIS

VIRGINIA I. DOUGLAS

I TRUST THAT YOU WILL not feel that I am abusing your excellent Texas hospitality if I begin by saying that I hope the time will soon come when we stop holding symposia with titles like "learning disabilities" and "minimal brain dysfunction." Certainly, the discussions that we heard this morning made it clear that diagnosing a child as having a "learning disability" contributes little or nothing to an understanding of his problems and provides few clues about how we should go about trying to help him.

Indeed, it may well be that vague, global labels of this sort have actually stood in the way of progress toward arriving at specific treatment plans for individual children and have encouraged, instead, the development of faddish approaches toward treatment. Witness, for example, the popularity of the perceptual motor training approach which is still being used indiscriminately in some settings with children demonstrating a wide range of learning problems. Potentially more serious has been the recent fad toward prescribing stimulant drugs for the "learning disability" group. I would argue that there are no short cuts to helping a child with a learning problem. We can help only if we are willing to engage in intensive detective work to diagnose exactly which aspects of learning are difficult for him. Then and only then will we be in a position to design a programme to help correct his difficulties.

I am equally disenchanted with the notion of "minimal brain dysfunction." What do we accomplish when we give a child this label? At best we have communicated the idea that we do not think his problems are psychogenic in origin; at worst we have set the stage for indiscriminate reliance on drug treatment for him.

At our clinic we have been working with another label, that of "hyperactivity." I must confess that I am not completely happy with this term, either, for reasons which I shall try to make clear shortly. Nevertheless, the term "hyperactivity" does at least point to specific symptoms which can be observed and, to some extent, objectively defined. It has the advantage, as well, of not making unwarranted assumptions about the cause of a particular child's symptoms. When we take into account the paucity of properly controlled studies to establish reliable evidence of brain damage in children diagnosed within the "minimal brain dysfunction" category, this advantage assumes considerable importance.

Before I leave this issue of minimal brain dysfunction it is important to let you know that in our samples of hyperactive children we have found little neurological evidence of brain damage. This may be because we deliberately chose "hyperactivity" as the main symptom by which our samples were defined and also because we deliberately exclude from our studies children who showed clear evidence of brain damage. Nevertheless, I am sure that a large proportion of our children would be placed in the "minimal brain dysfunction" category by many clinicians and we were rather surprised that our rather diligent efforts to find evidence of neurological dysfunction failed. As a cautionary note I would add that if we had not run control groups, we would have had little difficulty convincing ourselves that we had found the "evidence" we sought. It is an embarrassing fact that, when "blind" controls are used, a disturbing number of apparently normal children demonstrate neurological "signs" that are usually associated with brain dysfunction.

Since you will be hearing several speakers today who have worked with rather different samples of children, let me say a little more about how we have gone about selecting subjects for our studies. In the early days we relied heavily on reports of parents and teachers. In our interviews with them we looked for descriptions of hyperactive behavior and chose children for whom this seemed to be the *major* presenting symptom. The children were included only if the hyperactivity was creating serious problems at home and at school and had been a problem over several years. Excluded from our samples were children with IQ's below eighty, those who showed evidence of neurosis or psychosis and also, as I have mentioned, children who demonstrated clear evidence of neurological damage.

As you will see from the data I will discuss, our studies of these children have convinced us that hyperactive behavior is usually accompanied by other symptoms that we have come to consider even more important. These include the inability to sustain attention, to keep impulsive responses under control, to engage in organized, planful behavior and to cope realistically with frustration. For this reason, we now are relying far more heavily on these symptoms in defining our samples of children.

This emphasis on attention and impulsivity in our diagnostic battery is also reflected in our therapeutic approach to these children. I am willing to admit that hyperactive behavior can interfere seriously with learning and can create serious interpersonal problems but I have come to believe that it would be a mistake to focus too heavily on hyperactivity per se. Although it would be helpful to find a therapeutic approach that would reduce hyperactivity, I believe that it is even more important to prove that our therapeutic interventions can help the child deal with what I have come to think of as an inability to "stop, look and listen."

Let me summarize the basic argument I want to make today. I believe that our studies of hyperactive children and matched controls have revealed that the hyperactives demonstrate a serious defect in the ability to "stop, look and listen." I am willing to wager that similar studies with children diagnosed in the minimal brain dysfunction category would yield several children with similar problems and I suspect that this syndrome also plays a major role in many children in the learning disability group.

If I am correct, then it would follow that our best strategy would involve putting together a diagnostic battery to tap the "attention—impulsivity" syndrome. For those children who fall into this category, we could concentrate on therapeutic techniques specifically designed to improve functioning on the abilities that define the syndrome and we would be able to evaluate the effectiveness of our therapeutic interventions by measuring changes in the child's performance on measures of these same abilities.

This is the goal that we are currently pursuing. Now that I have told you where we are heading, let me review for you the evidence that convinced us of the importance of the "stop, look and listen" syndrome in our hyperactive group. In this way I can also acquaint you with the measures we have used thus far to define the syndrome and I will report, as well, on drug studies in which we have investigated the effects of methylphenidate treatment on some of these attention-impulsivity measures.

In our early investigations we concentrated on learning about our children's performance at school, on scholastic achievement tests and on a large battery of tests commonly used by clinical and school psychologists. We found ample evidence that the children were doing badly in school; their problems were not limited to particular school subjects but covered pretty much the entire curriculum. They were also significantly behind their classmates on the group achievement tests administered in the schools. When we administered individual achievement tests, on the other hand, they did not do as badly. Observations in the classroom showed that they were spending a good deal of their time in activities not directly related to the ongoing classroom activity.

We found that our hyperactives performed rather well on several of our test measures. We could find no particular pattern of difficulties on the Wechsler Intelligence Scale for Children except that they showed significantly more variability from subtest to subtest than the normal controls. There were no significant hyperactive-normal differences on the tests of short term memory or auditory discrimination and there was no evidence of language problems as measured by the Illinois Test of Psycholinguistic Abilities. Interpretation of results from tests of abstract reasoning and concept formation is somewhat less clear. The hyperactive children can solve these problems under some conditions but there

# Effects of Medication on Learning Efficiency

are other conditions that seem to "waylay" them and we are investigating this issue further.

Their performance on tests tapping perceptual motor functioning is also somewhat puzzling. They do badly on the Bender-Visual-Motor Gestalt Test, on the Lincoln-Oseretsky Schedule of Motor Development and on the Goodenough Draw-A-Person Test. They had some difficulty with the Frostig Developmental Test of Visual Perception but the hyperactive-normal comparisons were significant on only one subtest. We were somewhat surprised to discover recently that they perform very well on the Pursuit Rotor Test. This is a test in which the subject must attempt to keep a stylus on a small disc which is moving rather quickly in a circular motion.

These findings give no clear indication of the nature of the hyperactive children's problem. They did suggest, however, that their difficulties become more evident when they are required to work alone and when they are asked to attend carefully to tasks that others have set for them. The apparent perceptual motor disability may be a separate problem or it may be part of this more general difficulty. It was at this point that we decided to move to more specific measures that might tell us more about the nature of the children's disability. Several of the studies I shall report were done by doctoral students working with me at McGill University.

Sykes (1969) studied the performance of hyperactives and controls on several different measures of attention. The one on which the hyperactives did most badly was the continuous performance task. This is a vigilance task on which the child is required to push a button only when particular letters appear. The hyperactive children missed more of the target letters than the controls and they also pushed more frequently for wrong letters. Thus, their errors seemed to be due to both lapses of attention and an inability to hold back impulsive responding to the wrong letters. When the children were required to stay at this task over time, errors of both kinds increased more for the hyperactives than for the controls (Sykes, Douglas and Morgenstern, 1972; Weiss and Minde, 1971; Sykes, Douglas and Morgenstern, 1973).

Three doctoral students, Cohen (1970), Parry (1973) and Firestone (1974) have examined the performance of hyperactives and normal controls on several versions of the delayed reaction time task. On this task the child hears a warning signal which is meant to alert him. This is followed by a reaction signal and his task is to respond as quickly as possible, usually by pressing a key. Once again, our hyperactive subjects have had difficulty with this task in two different ways. First, their reaction times are slow and erratic. Secondly, they seem unable to hold back impulsive responses to the warning signal and they also anticipate the reaction signal and push the key before the signal arrives. Once again, their performance deteriorates badly over time (Cohen, Douglas and Morgenstern, 1971).

Campbell (1969) investigated the performance of hyperactives on the Matching Familiar Figures Test of Reflection-Impulsivity (Kagan, 1965). This is a task in which the child is shown a picture of a familiar object and is asked to find an identical picture among six possible choices. Since each of the choices is very similar to the target picture, success on the task depends on the child's ability to hold back responding until he has made a careful search of the alternatives. This hyperactive children cannot do; they are inclined to choose too quickly and, as a result, make significantly more errors than a control group. In a follow-up study with a group of adolescent hyperactives, Cohen, Weiss and Minde (in press) found that similar difficulties were still occuring in the adolescent group.

Parry (1973) looked at the performance of hyperactives on the Porteus Mazes. This is a paper and pencil task in which the child must find his way without going into blind alleys or crossing lines. Thus, the test probably measures several abilities including planfulness, impulse control and perceptual motor coordination. Here again, the performance of the hyperactives was significantly worse than that of the controls.

Another test that has turned up hyperactive-normal differences is the story completion test. I have been using various versions of this test over the past several years to study the reaction of children to frustrating and disappointing events. The stories used by Parry portray child heroes faced with various kinds of frustration and the subject is asked to choose from among several possible endings for the stories. The scores for the hyperactive children on this measure revealed relatively immature responses to frustration;

they tended to deny frustrating events and also reacted to them with open aggression.

This is a rather quick overview of our findings from the hyperactive-control comparisons that have been made thus far. I believe, however, that they do provide considerable evidence to suggest that the difficulties of our hyperactive subjects become most evident when they are required to sustain attention, keep impulsive responses under control, engage in planful behavior and cope with frustration.

Let me turn now to a brief review of our drug studies with these same hyperactive subjects. These studies have convinced us that short term treatment with methylphenidate produces positive changes on several of these same measures. On the continuous performance task the hyperactive subjects responded to more correct letters and fewer incorrect letters when they were receiving methylphenidate. On the delayed reaction time task, subjects on methylphenidate showed faster and less erratic response times and they also made fewer impulsive responses both to the warning signal and also before the appearance of the reaction signal. Thus, in both of these studies the drug seemed to increase attention and reduce impulsivity.

On the Matching Familiar Figures Test of Reflection-Impulsivity, reaction times slowed when the hyperactives were receiving the drug and the children also made fewer errors. Although we have not used the Porteus Mazes in our own drug studies, several investigators have reported improved performance in hyperactive children on this test when they are receiving treatment with stimulant drugs.

There is also considerable evidence that the stimulants produce positive changes on the hyperactivity scale developed by Conners (Conners, 1971; Sprague and Werry, 1974). The items on this scale include the following descriptions of behavior: "restless," "impulsive," "disturbs other children," "short attention span," "constantly fidgeting," "inattentive," "easily frustrated," "cries often and easily," "mood changes quickly and drastically" and "temper outbursts." I think that you will agree that these descriptions match rather closely the ones that I have drawn from our investigations of the performance of these children on our objective test measures.

Thus, Conners' work with parents' and teachers' ratings has suggested a symptom complex very similar to the one we have found with our objective tests. Also, his teacher's rating scale has proved to be a very sensitive measure of the effects of stimulant drug treatment, a finding which parallels the positive changes we have seen on our measures.

These findings strongly suggest that the Conners' Rating Scales, in conjunction with a judicious selection from the tests I have described, would provide a promising battery of instruments for both diagnosing this syndrome and for evaluating the effectiveness of therapeutic intervention.

I would like to end, however, on two cautionary notes. Before such a battery is ready for clinical use, a good deal of work must be done to develop adequate norms for some of the tests. I would also like to see modifications in the scoring systems for a few of the more commonly used instruments that would make it possible to separate errors due to the attention-impulsivity factor from ones caused by other kinds of disabilities. Even more important, we must add to our battery measures that come closer to evaluating the demands made on the child in his everyday world. These might include, for example, objective ratings of school progress such as samples of academic work and classroom observations. Sroufe (in press) has quite rightly pointed out that drug studies with these children have failed thus far to establish solid evidence that the stimulants produce changes on these more meaningful measures.

This leads to my second cautionary note. Although our own data and those from several other laboratories have yielded encouraging results in short-term studies with the stimulants, evidence is accumulating to suggest that these drugs may have serious shortcomings. It is difficult to design a well-controlled study on the long-term effects of the stimulants, but I am forced to conclude from our own efforts and those of others that the long-term results thus far are not promising (Sroufe, in press). Data are also beginning to accumulate to suggest that long-term use of these drugs may produce negative effects on heart rate (Sprague, 1973) and may interfere with normal gains in weight and height (Safer, Allen and Barr, 1972). The debate about the danger of addiction is still being waged but certainly this potential danger should inspire great caution. For these reasons, we have decided to shift our efforts, at least for the next year or two, toward an attempt to help these children through a training approach.

In recent years, good progress has been made toward the development of training techniques for dealing with behavorial problems in children and some of these (Meichenbaum and Goodman, 1971; Palkes, Stewart, and Kahana, 1968; Santostefano and Paley, 1964) emphasize the teaching of strategies to combat poor attention and impulsivity. Thus, they seem particularly relevant to the constellation of problem behaviors which have been defined in our research.

We have also derived some of our techniques from the behavior modification literature. It is important to mention, however, that we have data to suggest that hyperactive children may have rather unique reactions to some aspects of reinforcement contingencies and so special care must be taken in developing behavior modification programs for them.

It will be some time before we know how the results of our training approach compare with those achieved in the drug studies. It is my hope that we can show longer-lasting changes on the test instruments I have described and on the "real life" samples of academic performance which I mentioned earlier. It must be admitted that this approach will involve considerably more "man hours" than the typical drug treatment regime. I am hopeful, however, that our results will prove that the investment is justified.

## REFERENCES

Campbell, S.: *Cognitive styles in normal and hyperactive children*, McGill University, Unpublished doctoral dissertation, 1969.

Cohen, H. J., Douglas, V. I., and Morgenstern, G.: The effect of methylphenidate on attentive behavior and autonomic activity in hyperactive children. *Psychopharmacologia*, 22:282-294, 1971.

Cohen, H. J., Weiss, G., and Minde, K.: Cognitive styles in adolescents previously diagnosed as hyperactive. *J Child Psychol Psychiatry*, in press, 1974.

Conners, C. K.: Drugs in the management of children with learning disabilities. In Tarnopol: *Learning Disorders in Children: Diagnosis, Medication, Education*. Boston, Little, 1971a.

Conners, C. K., and Rothschild, G.: Drugs and learning in children.

In *Learning Disorders.* Seattle, Special Child Publications, 1968, vol. 3.

Firestone, P.: *The effects of reinforcement contingencies on the performance of hyperactive children,* Unpublished paper, 1974.

Kagan, J.: Impulsive and reflective children; Significance of conceptual tempo. In Krumboltz, J. D. (Ed.): *Learning and the Educational Process.* Chicago, Rand McNally, 1965.

Meichenbaum, D. H., and Goodman, J.: Training impulsive children to talk to themselves: A means of developing self-control. *J Abnorm Psychol,* 77:115-126, 1971.

Palkes, H., Stewart, W., and Kahana, B.: Porteus maze performance of hyperactive boys after training in self-directed verbal commands. *Child Dev, 39*:817-826, 1968.

Parry, P.: *The effect of reward on the performance of hyperactive children,* Unpublished doctoral dissertation, McGill University, 1973.

Santostefano, S., and Stayton, S.: Training the preschool retarded child in focusing attention: A program for parents. *Am J Orthopsychiatry, 37*:732-743, 1967.

Safer, D., Allen, R., and Barr, E.: Depression of growth in hyperactive children on stimulant drugs. *N Engl J Med, 289*:217-220, 1972.

Sprague, R., and Boileau, R.: Are Drugs Safe? In Sprague R. L. (Chm.): *Psychopharmacology of Children with Learning Disabilities.* Symposium presented at the American Psychological Association, Montreal, Canada, August, 1973.

Sprague, R., and Werry, J.: Psychotropic drugs and handicapped children. *The Second Review of Special Education.* Philadelphia, JSE Press, 1974, p 1-50.

Sroufe, L. A.: Drug treatment of children with behavior problems. *Review of Child Development Research,* in press, 1973.

Sykes, D. H.: *Sustained attention in hyperactive children,* Unpublished doctoral dissertation, McGill University, 1969.

Sykes, D. H., Douglas, V. I., and Morgenstern, G.: The effect of methylphenidate (Ritalin) on sustained attention in hyperactive children. *Psychopharmacologia, 25*:262-274, 1973.

Sykes, D. H., Douglas, V. I., Weiss, G., and Minde, K.: Attention in hyperactive children and the effect of methylphenidate (Ritalin). *J Child Psychol Psychiatry, 12*:129-139, 1971.

Sykes, D. H., Douglas, V. I., and Morgenstern, G.: Sustained attention in hyperactive children. *J Child Psychol Psychiatry, 14*:213-220, 1973.

## Chapter VII

# VISUAL EFFICIENCY AND LEARNING DISABILITIES

### Max Kaplan

MANY CHILDREN WITH learning disabilities are brought to the family practice physician, opthalmologists or optometrist, for assistance in the identification of factors causing or contributing to classroom difficulties. Because reading involves seeing, the child who is not learning to read, or who is learning at a slower rate than expected, is frequently suspected of having a visual deficit. A short attention span, or a lack of interest in classroom activity, may cause the teacher to suspect that the child's poor performance is due to a problem in "seeing." Also, if a child presents a typical picture of biologic perpetual motion, constantly fidgeting and squirming, questions frequently arise as to the medical basis for such behavior.

Both parents and teachers justifiably expect the physician to help them classify and identify the basic causes of learning disabilities, whether visual, auditory, developmental, emotional or environmental. Such identification and sorting out may be difficult because one or more of these factors are frequently found to be contributing to a given educational or learning problem. The sound and valid medical perspective of this large problem must include a consideration of all of the areas of importance to the physician in the management of children with learning disabilities —including both the diagnostic and therapeutic implications.

The specific assignment which I have been given in the area of medical perspective is to discuss visual efficiency and learning disabilities. In this discussion, I shall accept a definition for learning disabilities that is, perhaps, somewhat loose, but nevertheless practical and clinical. I recognize that it may not be a totally and definitely accurate definition that would be acceptable to authorities in all of the disciplines concerned with learning disabilities. This practical, clinical definiton adopted from Schain (1972) is that a learning disability refers to a condition wherein a child's learning performance on academic subjects in school is not commensurate with his intellectual abilities. In an amplification of this definition, Schain (1972) stated:

> A convenient objective method for assessing learning performance is the measurement of reading skills utilizing some standard test of reading ability. This approach . . . will not recognize children who are failing to enter the learning process during the first years of classroom instruction but it does provide a means of identifying the existence, and estimating the prevalence of this disorder. A reading score two or more grades below expected grade level is generally regarded as evidence that a child manifests a significant degree of reading retardation.

It is evident that this approach does not recognize children with learning disabilities prior to their entrance into school. Schain noted that most good definitions of learning disability tend to imply the presence of some type of selective central nervous system dysfunction that is responsible for the suboptimal learning processes, whatever the causes of this selective dysfunction may be. He points out that, ". . . the definitions do not require positive evidence of the presence of cerebral dysfunction; rather it is deduced from the absence of known causes of learning disorders, i.e. recognizable emotional disturbance, environmental disadvantage, sensory deficits or frank neurological disorders," and may not provide total explanations for the dysfunction in all individuals.

In a monograph entitled *Congenital Word Blindness* an ophthalmic surgeon in Glasgow, Scotland, James Hinshelwood (1917), was one of the early workers to study in some depth the nature of specific learning disabilities. He stated that the reading difficulties in his cases were not of ocular origin; moreover, he concluded that minor refractive errors and muscle imbalance were not significant or causative in his patients with reading and writing problems. In the half-century or more since that time, not all workers in the field have agreed with the conclusions of Hinshelwood. Many theories have been propounded relating ocular and ocular-motor problems to reading and learning difficulties. These theories have held that definitive and causative relationships exist between reading disabilities and many peripheral sensory and nervous system abnormalities, such as defects in visual acuity, binocular coordination, extraocular muscle balance, mixed and cross dominance, preferential use of the hand, foot and eye, and others. The belief is also held widely, especially among optometrists, that orthoptics and various types of visual-motor exercises are successful in the treatment of reading and learning disorders.

It is more generally accepted that poor visual acuity is rarely a deterrent to learning to read, even if the acuity is less than 20/200. When the acuity is poor, the print may have to be held closer to the eyes and reading may be slow, but it will be accurate. To interfere significantly with reading, poor vision, due to high degrees of astigmatism or other causes, must be bilateral and very poor indeed. Impaired visual acuity can contribute to slow reading, to frustration, and to fatigue. Thus, occasionally a poor or slow reader may become a better reader after acquiring glasses which improve vision and visual comfort. Glasses should be prescribed, therefore, to correct significant refractive errors in children with reading disabilities. However, as Campion (1965) pointed out, the threshold of what a significant refractive error is may be different for some practitioners than it is for others. The prescription of glasses for refractive errors should be given only when the lenses offer definite prospects for improving visual acuity or visual comfort. Providing glasses to a patient always carries with it the optimistic hope that such treatment will promptly correct the child's reading and learning difficulties. Since this is only rarely the case, disappointment and discouragement, plus loss of confidence in the physician, will often ensue.

Many authors have pointed out that muscle imbalance and problems in convergence are possible causes of reading difficulties. However, Critchley (1964) and others have shown in many studies that true reading disabilities are independent not only of errors of refraction, but also of muscle imbalance and binocular fusion. For example, Rutter, *et al.* (1970) compared three groups of children; one group was defined as reading disabled, one group as mentally retarded, and the control group consisted of normal children. Contrary to popular expectation, the children with reading disabilities did not have a higher incidence of strabismus or visual defect than the control group.

Campion (1965) has emphasized that oculo-motor problems do not interfere with the recognition of symbols and states that, "This is also true of strabismus or squint." Most ophthalmologists will probably agree with his revealing observation that it is very difficult to convince the parents of a cross-eyed child that the eyes are not the cause of the reading disability; there will sometimes be a token nod of agreement, but in their hearts they know that the doctor is wrong. Parenthetically it should be noted that teachers are also difficult to convince. Most ophthalmologists can cite examples of children with strabismus, even when accompanied by one amblyopic eye, who were excellent high-achieving readers.

It is interesting to note that certain congenital disorders of eye movement, such as congenital nystagmus, may result in some slowness of reading. This is related to the net efficiency of vision affected by the constant oscillatory motion and the unsteady fixation of the eyes. However, congenital nystagmus rarely produces a true reading disability. It is true that the presence of other congenital central nervous system disorders, which may accompany the nystagmus, frequently have significant effects upon the child's learning disabilities, depending upon the type, focus and severity of the nervous system pathology. Dr. Albert E. Sloane (1968) has asked editorially a telling question. "Why does a child with marked nystagmus and high refractive error, associated with refractive amblyopia and who is legally blind, show no difficulty in learning to read, and yet another boy with 20/15 vision and no muscle imbalance confuses the simplest words?"

Just as significant refractive errors should be corrected with glasses, so should significant muscle imbalances be treated. Treatment of muscle imbalances is particularly important where there is inconstant and variable binocular coordination and fusion, and when convergence difficulties or convergence insufficiencies exist.

The ophthalmologist may need the orthoptic technician's help in the treatment of some patients with inconstant binocular coordination and patients with convergence insufficiency. Nevertheless, it should be emphasized that such oculo-motor difficulties are probably not the primary causes of the reading disability. Successful achievement of the orthoptic treatment goals may have some, but probably not great or dramatic beneficial effects on the child's reading problems. Psychological factors, and increased concentration, may be the primary ingredients in the achievement of any reading improvement that results from such treatment. In addition, the increased personal attention received by the child may be most important in increasing motivation and achievement.

If the eye is functioning perfectly in receiving light rays, focusing the rays accurately on the retina, sending the electrochemical impulses into and along the optic nerve and thence through the optic pathways to the brain, the process of seeing is still not complete until that which is "seen" is interpreted by the observer. This phenomena is called visual perception, defined as the interpretation of sensory stimuli into the organization that leads finally to understanding, or conception. Visual perception is the ability to recognize stimuli and to correlate them with previous experiences. This process of recognition and integration of stimuli occurs in the brain, not in the peripheral receiving organ, the eye. Thus, vision takes place in the occipital lobe and from there the impulses pass onto the angular gyrus and thence to the frontal lobes.

The significance of visual experiences in animal physiologic functioning at the neuronal level has been the subject of some basic and fascinating experiments by Wiesels and Hubel (1963). Kittens deprived of vision from birth do not have normal pattern responses in nerve cell recordings if tested visually after a few months. However, if they were deprived of vision after an initial period of being able to see normally, responses were the normal expected responses. These experiments indicate that normal function may be critically important at certain stages of development for the normal physiological maturation of cortical visual responses. Experience may, therefore, play more than a purely psychologic role.

Maximum visual perceptual development normally occurs between the ages of three and a half and seven and a half years. The causes of disability in visual perception may be pathological, as in minimal brain dysfunction. On the other hand, the disability may also result from emotional disturbances, or from a "nonspecific" mechanism, such as a lag in perceptual development. Not with standing background factors, it is accepted that there is a definite correlation between visual-perceptual ability and reading achievement (and the two often run somewhat parallel in the course of development).

All of the disciplines involved in diagnosis and treatment of children with learning disabilities should be aware of the visual-perceptual aspects of these problems. This applies to medical practitioners who function individually as consultants, as well as those who are members of a multidisciplined team. Not only the ophthalmologist, but also the pediatrician, family physician, the otolaryngologist and neurologist as well as psychiatrist—each must maintain a high level of awareness of the importance of perception as it relates to learning.

An example of what can happen, indeed what has happened, when the concept of perception is lost or ignored, is the use of the ophthalmograph or the electronystagmograph to photograph eye movements during reading. The machines are quite adequate to photographically record ocular movements during the process of reading, but the analysis and interpretation of the graphs may often be incorrect and invalid. Such incorrect interpretations may result in recommendations for treatment by orthoptics or muscle exercises in an effort to train ocular movements in the belief that this would be helpful in improving reading. Abnormalities in the tracings may be interpreted as evidence of the cause of the reading disorder. Stated differently, the interpretation states that the abnormal eye movements cause the difficulty. In fact, the abnormal tracing may be only the evidence of the motor signs of the disability, that is, the absence of a smooth rapid and accurate binocular activity of the eyes moving across the line of print.

Goldberg and Schiffman (1972) investigated this subject by recording with the electronystagmograph the eye movements of fifty dyslexic children and an adequate number of controls. First, each child was asked to read material below his frustration level and a graph was obtained of eye movement. Second, he was asked to read material above his frustration level. The second graph of eye movements demonstrated abnormalities which varied with the difficulty of the word or sentences. There were changes in the graph which were synchronous with difficulties in the reading material. In another experimental condition, the frustration words were taught to the child in advance of the reading material. Under this condition the graph of eye movements showed definite improvement over the previous untutored graph recordings. Goldberg concluded, "... in actuality it is not the eyes that read, but it is the brain that reads" (1972). He points out that ocular motility does not determine the degree of comprehension, but rather the ability to perceive determines the fluidity of reading. Thus, ocular motility simply denotes the degree of fluidity. At least from the standpoint of this experimental evidence, improper eye movements seem to be the result rather than the cause of poor comprehension.

Somewhat more cautiously Schain (1972) has stated, "Treatment programs based upon improving reading skills through training of ocular motor abilities seem to be based upon highly debatable theories, and lack of support of a scientific data base indicating the value of such treatments." A number of research studies on the effectiveness of visual training on reading have been carried out, many of them by optometrists. Most of the results were favorable, but the studies can be justifiably critized because they lack control groups and/or accurate data analysis. One well controlled study was that of Olson, Mitchell and Westberg (1953) who attempted to determine the effects of visual training upon the reading ability of college students. Although comprehension scores improved under visual training, the gains were not found to be statistically significant, indicating that in a college population the reading rate may be the skill most amenable to improvement. Other groups have shown significantly greater gains in visual perceptual skills at the end of the training period, but have not shown correspondingly significantly gains in reading achievement tests. Cohen (1966) for one, concluded that, "The significant gains in visual perception ... were not reflected in gains in reading."

Rubino and Minden (1971) followed up on the earlier work of Eames. Eames (1935) worked on the hypothesis that educational disability cases present smaller visual fields than normal in unselected cases and that the differences in the visual fields were greater in the left eye. The early Eames work was based on the assumption that visual field limitation would require more fixations per line and therefore slower, more mechanical reading. Rubino and Minden (1971) went on to demonstrate in a group of twenty-three children with learning disabilities that the visual fields, both central and peripheral, were in essence within normal limits. They suggested that further investigation be carried out in this field including in the study a matched sample of children without reading problems.

The human species was originally ambidextrous. The emergence of laterality in mankind, with dominance of one side of the body, usually the right eye, the right hand and foot under the control of the left cerebral hemisphere, has been explored by many workers through the years. The precise age at which this handedness is settled is subject to great individual variation. By the age of two in most children the passive hand has become more subordinate. Generally hand differentiation begins in the child at about nine months and is virtually complete by two years of age.

The role of cerebral dominance in the development of speech and reading abilities and the relationship of cerebral dominance to eye, hand and foot dominance has also been the subject of many investigations. Our interest at this time is whether eye dominance is related to the development of reading skills. If it is related, then the prospects for a more accurate diagnosis, leading to more effective treatment procedures, should be explored.

Goldberg (1972) has cited the figures that 7 percent of people are left handed, while left eyedness occurs in about 30 percent of the population. Ninety percent of the individuals are right handed, but only 66 percent of them are right eyed. About 33 percent of the population has mixed dominance. He stated:

> The master eye is usually the one with preferential visual acuity; in some person's the optically weaker eye may be preferred for sighting. In determining cerebral dominance, eyedness is a more significant finding because the person is not aware of his preferred eye and environmentally is not encouraged to change this dominance.

There is no absolute and universal separation of left and right, and many grades of ambidexterity exist. The laterality of the brain is genetically determined, and generally it is a recessive trait.

I shall not attempt to cite the clinical reports detailing various aspects of the proof of cerebral dominance as related to the location of the center of the brain as well as the dominance of the hand and eye. However, it may be stated that many of the reports lead to the conclusion that the dominant brain hemisphere for language is most often the left one. This is usually true even in individuals who are left hand dominant by ordinary standards. Exception to this lies in the fact that an injury to the dominant hemisphere incurred in childhood can be compensated for by a shift in dominance to the opposite hemisphere; thus, the right hemisphere can assume the capabilities of language function if the task is forced upon it.

There is evidence that dyslexia can occur from a dysfunction in either the major or minor hemisphere. For example, Goldberg (1972) has stated:

> In a study of 100 achieving students, there would be no statistically significant difference between the dominance of those who are achieving poorly and those who are successful. The theory that individuals with severe reading disability have poorly lateralized dominance may be because 30 percent of these children may have some form of brain dysfunction, which may lead to poor lateralization and poor learning. In these cases, the poor lateralization might be the result of brain dysfunction; the poor learning is associated with the dysfunction and not with crossed dominance.

Brain (1972) has stated, "It is probable that in such cases the failure to establish a dominant hemisphere is the result, and not the cause, of congenital abnormalities of brain function, which also express themselves in disabilities of speech, reading, and writing." Goldberg and Schiffman (1972) argue the converse, namely that, the great majority of poorly lateralized children do not have reading disability. An impairment of visual efficiency or visual perceptual ability, due to poor lateralization or crossed dominance, has not been established, and many surveys have failed to support crossed dominance as a consistent link with reading problems.

Goldberg, et al. (1972) stated that, "It is not the loss or absence of laterality that produces the disorder of language, but if there is a delay in the acquisition of language, most often it is accompanied by other signs of cerebral immaturity, including delayed or incomplete establishment of laterality." He goes on to argue against forcing the child to use one hand or patching one eye in an effort to establish dominance of one hemisphere.

Benton, et al. (1965) studied 250 children referred with reading problems and found 93 with crossed dominance, 53 with mixed dominance and 104 with incomplete dominance. They concluded that eye and hand dominance were significant factors in the causation of the reading problems. They went on to report very good results in treating these children by encouraging and reinforcing the dominance of one hand and by treating the crossed dominance of the eyes with strong retinal rivalry by occlusion or by medically blurring the non-controlling eye. However, in 1969, after further follow up on their patients and examination of their data, Benton and McCann (1969) again reported on the same group, reversing their position and stating that they now felt that eye dominance was not an important measurement in evaluation or treatment in most cases of dyslexia. They argued that the poor performance of over half of all the dyslexic patients in visual motor testing was possibly due to immature functioning of higher correlative activities of the brain.

Ocular dominance cannot be explained by eye anatomy, just as hand dominance cannot be explained by known anatomical findings in the brain. There is no anatomical arrangement in the eyes themselves, or in their known brain connections, that could account for the dominance of, say, the right eye. Shifting the controlling eye therefore can be expected to have little effect upon hand and/or brain dominance.

One can conclude that, when dominance of the eye, hand or foot are inconsistent, and when there might be existing learning difficulties, the presence of the peripheral lack of consistent dominance does not indicate the cause of a learning disability, but merely a corollary associated with a central dysfunction. Just as there are no known anatomical facts about the brain, eye or hand that account for cerebral dominance, neither do we know of any right-to-left anatomic reversals in the eye, or up and down anatomical reversals, that account for the reversals of letters and words manifested by some children in their reading and writing.

What then is the currently acceptable status for the relationship of visual efficiency to reading and learning disabilities?

Ocular fatigue, and visual handicaps such as high degrees of far sightedness (hyperopia), astigmatism, muscle imbalances, and intermittent control of binocular coordination may result in slowing of the individual's reading rate and make reading more difficult. These factors are not important because they interfere with the child's understanding of symbols or his perception of reading material. The same may be said about other causes of reduced visual acuity such as congenital ocular anomalies, and other abnormalities of control of eye movements, such as nystagmus and oculo-motor apraxia. All such peripheral visual handicaps, in addition to their direct effects upon visual comfort and reading speed, may have some frustrating effects upon the learning child that result in shortening of his attention span and reducing the useful time available for the reading-learning act.

Unfortunately, a child who needs glasses may also be living in a cultural environment that contributes to his learning difficulties. The learning disability team must constantly be alert to combinations of causes that may be contributing to the child's learning difficulties.

The obscure role of homolateral v. mixed dominance and the importance placed by some in the interpretation of binocular movements, patterns of fixation, hesitation, or regression, while attempting to read, have not contributed any solid additions to our diagnostic success or our therapeutic armamentarium in the management of these children. The child who has difficulty in learning to read will inevitably hesitate, refix and regress as he tries to interpret uncertain or incompletely learned symbols.

> Keeney (1969) has summed up the case against eye exercises: It must be recognized . . . that neither ocular exercises relating to the eyeball and their muscles, nor gross motor coordination pro-

grams, have any direct relation to the symbol-interpretive function of the brain. Nearly blind children who have only one eye and are forced to read with materials held an inch or two from the remaining eye may be rapid and bright learners, just as may the child with gross deformities of polio-myelitis or leg injuries. Until more specific understanding of the neuro-physiology, neuropathology and neuropharmacology of the learning process is achieved, it is necessary to utilize every route of therapy and sensory augmentation that can logically be directed to the child's program.

The complexities of this entire field need no emphasis before a group such as this. What does merit emphasis is the importance of recognizing these very complexities in evaluating the practical, clinical approaches to diagnosis and treatment of these children. One is certainly justified in questioning the validity of a total plan of treatment that is based entirely upon the diagnosis of one clinical discipline—whether ophthalmology, optometry, neurology, psychiatry, or psychology. Unless specialists from each of these disciplines has had the opportunity to study the child from his/her unique prespective and the plan for treatment is developed out of the totality of input, then the child is not being given the best of what present-day science and education have to offer. Beware of the practitioner, in whatever area of practice, who launches a learning disabled child on a solo treatment regimen based on a solo treatment diagnosis.

Casual, isolated clinical observations may add a few bits of rewarding and helpful knowledge, but only research that is critical, scientific, well designed, and well-controlled offers real promise for progress and greater success in helping these children.

## REFERENCES

Benton, Jr., C. O., McCann, Jr., V. W., and Larsen, N.: Dyslexia and dominance. *Journal of Pediatric Opthalmology*, 2:53-57, 1965.

Benton, Jr., C. O., and McCann, Jr., J. W.: Dyslexia and dominance: some second thoughts. *Journal of Pediatric Opthalmology*, 4:220-222, 1969.

Brain, W. R.: Speech and handedness. *Lancet*, 2:837, 1945.

Campion, George S.: Visual problems and reading disorders. In Flower, R., Gofman, H., and Lawson, L. (Ed.): *Reading Disorders: A Multidisciplinary Symposium*. Philadelphia, Davis, 1965, pp. 41-44.

Cohen, R. I.: Remedial training of first grade children with visual perceptual retardation. *Educational Horizons, 45*:60-63, 1957.
Critchley, MacDonald: *Developmental Dyslexia.* London, Heinemann, 1964.
Eames, J. H.: A frequency study of physical handicaps in reading disability and unselected groups. *Journal of Educational Research, 29*:1-5, 1935.
Goldberg, H. K., and Schiffman, G. B.: *Dyslexia: Problems of Reading Disabilities.* New York, Grune and Stratton, 1972.
Hinshelwood, J.: *Congenital Word-blindness.* London, Lewis, 1917.
Keeney, A. H.: Medical diagnostics and counseling of dyslexia. *Med Clin North Am, 5*:1123-1129, 1969.
Olson, H. C., Mitchell, C. C., and Westberg, W. C.: The relationship between visual training and reading and academic improvement. *Am J Optom, 30*:3-13, 1953.
Rubino, C. A., and Minden, H. A.: Visual-field restrictions in cases of reading disability. *Percept Mot Skills, 33*:1215-1217, 1971.
Rutter, M., Tizard, J., and Whitmore, K. (Ed.): *Education, Health, and Behavior.* London, Longman, 1970.
Schain, Richard J.: *Neurology of Childhood Learning Disorders.* Baltimore, Williams and Wilkins, 1972.
Sloane, A. E.: Reading disability and the opthalmologist. *Journal of Pediatric Ophthalmology, 5*:4, 1968.
Wiesel, T. N., and Hubel, D. H.: The effects of visual deprivation on morphology and physiology of cells in the cat's lateral geniculate body. *J Neurophysiol, 26*:978-993, 1963.

# Chapter VIII

# THE EFFECTS OF PERCEPTUAL MOTOR TRAINING ON READING ACHIEVEMENT

Steven M. Hirsch and Robert P. Anderson

The purpose of this paper is to evaluate the experimental literature concerning the effects of perceptual motor training on academic achievement and, in particular, reading achievement. It has been argued by proponents of perceptual motor training that the exercises should have a direct effect upon some aspect of an LD child's academic achievement. Furthermore, it is suggested that if the learning disabled child has no perceptual motor training, he will not gain as much in his academic achievement as one who has had such training. Cratty (1971) has taken a skeptical view of the transfer phenomena; he stated "there should be sufficient proof that the unusual remedial techniques employed will truly transfer in a direct way . . . ." The authors share Cratty's skepticism. We have an admitted bias; that is, perceptual motor training in all its various forms as delineated by Kephart, Getman, Frostig, Delacato, and others, does not significantly effect academic achievement, particularly in the area of reading by altering the cognitive structure which underlies the learning of reading, spelling and writing skills. We believe that the effects of this training must be shown in some positive way to affect the cognitive development of the child before we can accept the transfer hypothesis.

The authors acknowledge that youngsters defined as having

minimal brain dysfunction, learning disabilities, or reading deficits are different from normal children in terms of their levels of coordination and perceptual motor development. These differences have been substantiated by research. It is apparent that special attention and special programs may have some positive effects upon youngsters with learning problems. As a result of participation in special programs the children feel more self-confident, and in a better frame of mind to attack academic subjects. Moreover, we have observed clinically, that training children in a specific series of exercises may result in an improvement of their ability to perform the exercise for which they are being specifically trained. For example, if children are trained to walk on a balance beam they will become better at walking on a balance beam, and if they are trained in the Frostig exercises they will do better on a repeat of the Frostig test. However, to argue that these training exercises have some direct causal effect on reading achievement is another matter.

A recent review by Keogh (1974) examined the literature related to optometric visual training for learning disabled children. The review was intended as an objective analysis, ". . . shunning the position of both advocate and adversary." Keogh concluded, ". . . that confounding of sampling program procedures, and research methodology make existing evidence too limited for a decision on the program effects." In short, she appeared to adopt a cautious stance and while some positive effects were attributed to developmental vision training programs, the basis for the success, as well as failure, could not be determined from the reported research.

In order to evaluate the experimental literature on the effects of perceptual motor training, the authors have adopted the criteria provided by Campbell and Stanley (1969) in assessing educational research. Campbell and Stanley looked at two broad factors in evaluating any research project. The first was internal validity; that is, "did in fact the experimental treatments make a difference in the specific experimental instance?" Some of the extraneous variables associated with internal validity are as follows: *history* (specific events affecting the experimental subjects between the first and second measurement in addition to the experimental variable), *maturation* (biological and physiological processes within the subjects operating as a function of the passage of time; e.g. growing older, better coordinated, etc.), *testing* (the effects of taking a test upon the scores of a second testing), *statistical regression* (the inevitable tendency of persons whose scores are extreme to be less extreme on a repeat of a test), *selection* (all biases which conspire to make the experimental and control groups unequal at the beginning of an experiment), *mortality* (the differential loss or dropping out of subjects from the comparison groups). The second factor relates to external validity; that is, "to what population, settings, treatment variables, and measurement variables can this effect be generalized?" The interested reader is referred directly to Campbell's article for a technical description of these factors.

Campbell and Stanley classified education research into two broad groups. First, there were the pre-experimental designs including the one shot case study and the one group pretest-posttest design. Second, there were the true experimental designs which included the pretest-posttest control group design. The studies reported in the literature related to perceptual motor training can be classified in terms of these three designs. The organization of the paper followed Campbell and Stanley's classification schema. A total of fifty-one studies were reviewed. Studies using subjects defined as mentally retarded were excluded from the review. This review overlaps to some extent with the previously cited article by Keogh (1974); some of the articles were reviewed in common with Keogh.

### PRE-EXPERIMENTAL DESIGNS

At least four studies classified as one shot case studies have been reported (Painter, 1966; Early and Sharpe, 1970; Early and Kephart, 1969; Emrich, 1971). Each of these investigators reported careful studies of a single subject; their general conclusions were based upon an expectation of what the data would have been had training not occurred. The studies all involved male subjects between the ages of six and nine years of age. All of the studies reported improvement in achievement based on descriptive statistics and behavioral observations. The inferential conclusion drawn from these case studies was that remedial programs lead to an increase in academic skills and perceptual motor training does enhance reading skills. However, if one applies Campbell and Stanley's criteria these conclusions cannot be justified because some of the major factors affecting internal validity include history, maturation, selection, testing and mortality. In other words, the positive gains in achievement could be attributed to other significant events occurring in the history of the boys, such as increased attention. In addition, there is a gain in achievement associated with age, and the subjects in these studies may have improved simply because they grew older. The selection of the subjects was not carried out on a random basis and one could ask why a particular subject was selected as opposed to another. The more critically minded investigator could also question why others who may have dropped out of the program were not selected for evaluation. In short, there are numerous reasons why these gains could have occurred aside from the experimental treatment itself. It must be concluded that the studies do not demonstrate the positive effects of perceptual motor training, nor can any of the effects reported be generalized beyond single subjects.

A second type of pre-experimental design is the one group pretest-posttest design. No control group is utilized in this design either. Lewis (1968) studied the effects of Frostig training on reading achievement and interpreted the results as supportive of this type of visual perceptual training for youngsters exhibiting reading difficulties. The positive gains in achievement attributed to the Frostig training cannot be supported by his data. Some of the defects in the study include a lack of control for history, maturation, and testing effects, statistical regression and a biased, small (N=5) sample. In addition, the author used inappropriate statistics; e.g. treating percentiles as scores which could be added and subtracted.

Frieden, Van Handel, and Kovalinsky (1971) studied the effects of perceptual training on eleven children ranging in age from seven to eleven years. No significant gain in reading was found after eight months of treatment but the authors did report significant gains in reading after twenty months. In addition to the problems associated with the lack of a control group, the authors confounded perceptual motor training and regular academic training, which made it impossible to attribute effects or gains to the special training. Moreover, the positive results in reading were based on a twenty month period; with this long period of time the effects of maturation on the outcome should have been considered. The authors' claim of positive effects for their training program goes beyond the data and design limitation of the study.

Frostig and Maslow (1969) reported a study in which they attempted to investigate the effects of the Frostig program on WISC scores of sixty-one children between the ages of six and nine. Although the great majority of subtests showed gains in a positive direction, the gains and losses for the sample were all within the standard error of measurement. Any positive claims by the authors can be accounted for in terms of the natural and expected fluctuations of the Wechsler scales as the test is repeated. In addition, there are alternative explanations, such as history or maturation, which could account for changes in scale scores. Thus, this study cannot be considered an example of possible benefit attributable to the Frostig program.

Four pre-experimental studies were found which are in support of Delacato's theory of neurological organization. In Delacato's study (1959) on the effectiveness of eight weeks of Doman-Delacato therapy, at least three sources of gain other than the positive effects of therapy can be identified. First, the regression effect would be expected to produce gains from pretest to posttest. A second influence is the practice effect from having taken the same test eight weeks before. The third factor is that the children advanced in age and a gain could be expected of 0.2 years from normal reading instruction. Piper (1963) conducted an experiment in which she attempted to measure the effect of Delacato's therapy by administering four forms of the Gates Basic Reading Test over a seven month period. At least four explanations of why posttest scores exceeded pretest scores can be identified. They include: 1) the inevitable phenomenon of regression toward the mean, 2) the practice effect of the testing, 3) the lack of equivalence of the alternate forms of the test, and 4) maturation or normal growth of the subjects.

McGrath (1966) examined the results of six weeks of neurological testing. He reported positive results, but made no attempt to control for the effect of maturation, testing, and regression. In addition, he appeared to have confounded the treatment. That is, students received neurological training plus reading therapy, and one cannot be sure what may have helped these youngsters. Noonan's study (1966) is open to the same influences which invalidated the McGrath study. It is difficult to logically relate the significant improvement in reading skills to the specific therapy of neurological organization used in these studies.

## TRUE EXPERIMENTAL DESIGNS

Campbell and Stanley classified the true experimental design as one following the paradigm of a pretest, posttest, control group design. Many of the objectives of the pre-experimental designs can be overcome by careful utilization of a control group. A major difficulty existed in evaluating this research area because there was no consistent definition of what was meant by perceptual motor or visual perceptual training. Thus, it was difficult to generalize from one study to the next, with the exception of those studies dealing with the Frostig training procedures, and the Doman-Delacato patterning program. The experimental data related to Kephart's training procedures was limited; this seemed surprising in view of the apparent wide spread use of his particular techniques.

The "true experimental" studies are divided into three groups: 1) studies measuring visual perceptual training in general, without reference to a particular school of training, 2) studies which examine the Frostig procedures, and 3) studies which assess the Doman-Delacato method.

Falik (1969) examined the efficacy of providing perceptual motor training as part of a general kindergarten curriculum. He addressed himself to the problem of determining whether or not a program designed after the work of Kephart would show a differential effect on reading readiness after one academic year of training. The results were negative in that no between group differences could be demonstrated. Falik stated, "We need to reevaluate our thinking on the role of perceptual motor training as part of the curriculum for the average child." In another experiment, Keim (1970) studied a kindergarten population in terms of the effect of perceptual motor training on reading readiness. Keim reported negative results, in that the Winterhaven program "did not result in significant gains in readiness-for-learning scores and measured intelligence." Cornish (1970) investigated effects of neurological training on the psychomotor abilities of a group of thirty kindergarten children. He gave his experimental group a program of cross-patterning experiences for three minutes a day over a three month period. It was concluded that the neurological training program did not significantly improve the psychomotor functioning of the children. Cornish is quite restrained in his conclusion and is aware of the limitation of his study. He recognized that his experimental group had a brief exposure to preceptual motor training each day, and stated "the present study due to its inherent weakness does not offer evidence for either position. Carefully controlled research is necessary."

Anderson (1965) evaluated the effects of cross-pattern creeping and walking exercises in the reading achievement of intermediate level students. The experimental group did the cross-pattern exercises for thirty minutes per day for a ten week period. He found no evidence that the training had any appreciable effect upon reading. In a second experiment he evaluated the effects of perceptual motor training in kindergarten classes. Again, the results were negative, demonstrating no significant gains in readiness.

McLees (1970) examined seventh grade students in a remedial reading class of one school. The experimental group received forty-five minutes of a motor pattern type program for ninety-two school days. She concluded that for the pupils studied, "addition of perceptual motor training . . . serves no useful purpose." McLees goes on to say in support of the author's bias, "the fact that simple motor patterns can be improved by practice is of no practical consequence unless the improvement can be related to more complex functions."

Manley (1969) reported a study in which he gave evidence that perceptual motor therapy enhances the learning ability of children. The subjects of his study were forty-six children diagnosed as having learning disabilities. The perceptual training program was for a period of forty-five minutes each day for six months. Since subjects in the experimental and control groups were not randomly assigned, one could not be confident that the two groups being compared are equivalent. The author made some attempt to match the subjects on intelligence and socioeconomic variables, although the exact criteria used were not mentioned. It appeared that history and selection factors may have biased the positive results reported by the author. Interestingly, the same teacher taught both of the experimental classes in the same building while different teachers taught classes for the control group on two other elementary campuses. One could certainly question whether this study measured the effectiveness of a perceptual motor training program or the effectiveness of one particular teacher.

No statistical analysis of the data was presented. The results of the testing program are reported in terms of the total average gain per student. Since it is not known how the experimental and control group compared initially, it is difficult to conclude that either training method is superior. The results can be accounted for further on the basis that the experimental program, "Operation Moon Shot," made school more fun for those students. The numerous probable sources of bias and invalidity in this experiment render the reported positive results of the study suspect. At best, the results of Manley's experiment should be regarded cautiously until additional data are published.

Faustman (1966) investigated the effects of perceptual training in kindergarten on first grade success in reading. Although the author reported significant mean growth scores on the Gates Word Survey Test in favor of the experimental group, a number of sources of possible error render the results dubious. No information is given on how the original thirty-two kindergarten classes were selected and some questions might be raised concerning the equivalence of the experimental and control groups. The experimental group received training in perception over and above regular classroom instruction and other factors accompanying the perceptual training (individualization of instructions, diagnosis of learning needs, and better opportunities for teachers to gain knowledge of child growth and development) might have favored the experimental group aside from the actual training itself.

Dawson (1966) studied the effects of visual and auditory perceptual training as a supplement to the regular reading program on the reading scores of low achieving second graders. No significant differences existed between the experimental and control groups on the Sight Vocabulary, Word Discrimination, and Total Reading subtests, but a significant difference did exist, favoring the experimental group on the Reading Comprehension subtest. Aside from the relatively small sample size (N=15) of the experimental group, the method of selecting the groups did not appear to be random. In addition, the effects of special attention were not adequately controlled and the inclusion of auditory training makes it difficult to attribute any possible gains directly to the visual motor training.

Cohen (1969) studied the effects of visual perceptual training on the reading achievement of disadvantaged children. He found no significant changes in reading achievement as a result of perceptual motor training. Cohen argued strongly against the concept of transfer when he stated, "in the reading field the surest way to get urban ghetto kids to read is to teach some letters and words and do it thoroughly." Jensen and King (1970) also reported negative results in their study which evaluated the effectiveness of visual motor discrimination training on learning to read a word list. The kindergarten children studied showed no significant differences on reading task as a result of different training methods. Gorelich (1965) examined the effectiveness of visual perceptual discrimination training in a prereading program. Again, the results were essentially negative and Gorelich reported no significant increase in word recognition skill as a result of the visual discrimination training.

McCormick, Schnobrich, Footlik and Poetker (1968) studied forty-two underachieving children matched on IQ, age, sex and reading grade level. The children were randomly divided into three groups; one group received perceptual motor training, the second group received a regular physical education (PE) program, and the third group received no PE or special attention. From a design standpoint the study looked good, in spite of the small number of subjects in each group (N=14). However, some statistical manipulations were used to find positive results in favor of the perceptual motor group. An analysis of variance was appropriately used to test the significance of differences between groups and the results were negative showing no significant intergroup differences. The authors then rejected these findings and proceeded to test if the group gains differed significantly from zero. They ended up making three tests of significance instead of one. Their procedures were not consistent with acceptable statistical methodology.

Elkind and Deblinger (1969) investigated the effects of a nonverbal perceptual training program on a sample of fifty-four disadvantaged children. They found that the experimental group did significantly better than the control group (using Bank Street Readers) on two of the six achievement measures. The authors pointed out the possibility of experimenter bias influencing the results since the investigators worked with both groups. Furthermore, the selection of subjects was not done randomly and a differential dropping out of subjects for discipline reasons from the experimental group may have biased the results.

Halliwell and Solan (1972) studied the effects of a supplemental perceptual training program on reading achievement for first grade children. The sample of 105 students were divided into three groups of thirty-five children each; experimental I which received supplementary perceptual training in addition to the regular reading program, experimental II, which received traditional supplementary reading instruction in addition to the regular reading program and the control group, which received no supplementary instruction. The analysis of the data indicated that, of all the groups, only the experimental I total group and the experimental I boys read significantly better than the respective control groups. None of the comparisons between the two experimental groups was significant, indicating that the supplemental perceptual motor training was no more effective than the supplemental traditional reading instruction, toward increasing reading achievement. It must be concluded that this study does not provide adequate evidence for the superiority of perceptual motor training over more traditional approaches to the teaching of reading skills.

Painter (1966) examined the effects of a rhythmic and sensory motor activity program on perceptual motor spatial abilities of kindergarten children. Twenty youngsters representing the lowest 50 percent of a group in terms of "intelligence" were selected for the study. The youngsters were divided into experimental and control groups. The former received a modified Barsch-Kephart type of training program while the latter received no special help. Painter recognized that she did not control for attention effects. Positive gains were reported for several of the dependent variables (ability to draw a human figure, distortion of body image) however, the study was not directed toward examining the effects on reading, or reading achievement. The best one can conclude is that perceptual motor training may affect some specific skills in a positive direction but one can only inferentially conclude that these skills are related to the intellectual processes associated with reading, writing, spelling and language production.

Silver, Hagin, and Hersch (1967) studied eighty boys with reading achievement problems. The boys were divided into experimental and control groups. A crossover type of design was used. The statistical analysis of the results had not been completed when the authors published their study. Only descriptive statements about selected subjects from each group were given. Since the statistical results comparing the two groups were not available, the effect of the perceptual motor training could not be adequately studied. Halgren (1961) also reported positive benefit from a perceptual motor program administered to a group of thirty-one high school boys. While a control group was used, the author did not report sufficient information to effectively evaluate the study. The method of selecting the groups did not appear to be random. Furthermore special attention effects were not adequately controlled and the dependent variable measures were not specified. Finally the results were not reported in terms of any accepted statistical procedures. These sources of invalidity cast serious doubts on the results of the experiment.

McCormick, Schnobrich, and Footlik (1969) conducted a second study of young children at the first grade level. The children were divided into an experimental and a control group with the experimental group receiving perceptual motor training in addition to the regular school program. Two subgroups of twelve in each group were formed who were of average intelligence but reading below grade level. The authors stated that differences in reading gain were not significant for the group as a whole but positively significant for the poor reading group. It was argued that perceptual motor training does not have a positive effect on reading achievement for a group of poor readers. The authors recognized that special attention effects were not controlled. They utilized a nonparametric statistic and concluded there was a significant difference between the experimental and control group at the .01 level. We utilized a simple $t$ test to analyze the significance of difference between the experimental and control subgroups. The results showed the $t$ to be significant at the 5 percent level but not at the 1 percent level. Thus, the gains were still evident but not to the degree to which the authors suggested. This appears to be one of the few studies we found where significant differences may exist. Unfortunately, the design of the experiment does not allow one to rule out an alternative hypothesis, that the gains are due to the special attention received by the experimental group.

Ismail and Gruber (1967) examined the effect of a physical education (PE) program on IQ and academic achievement in normal elementary school children. The authors divided a matched sample of 142 subjects into an experimental group which received an organized program of physical education and a control group which spent a similar amount of time in a "free play" situation. The results of the experiment indicated that the PE program had no effect on IQ but did have a significant effect on academic achievement scores. Although the subjects were pre-tested on reading achievement, no data were presented to indicate initial comparability of the two groups. In addition, the authors made no attempt to control for the possibility of a Hawthorne or special attention effect. While this study represents one of the better controlled experiments reviewed, the above mentioned sources of invalidity render the reported results questionable. Furthermore, the subjects in the study only included normal healthy children, carefully screened to eliminate handicaps in vision, hearing and speech. It would be difficult to meaningfully generalize the results of this study to a population of handicapped children.

## THE FROSTIG PROGRAM

Ten true experimental studies using the Frostig training program were found, and eight of these studies reported negative results. Cohen (1966) evaluated 155 first graders who received training with the Frostig program for ten weeks. No significant relationship was found between the visual perceptual training and gains in reading achievement. Rosen (1966) also studied the effects of the Frostig program on 305 first graders. He found that improvement in abilities did not reflect itself in comparable improvement in scores of reading ability. Indeed, in two of the analyses the control group excelled the experimental group with the implication that added reading instruction produced more desirable results than perceptual training.

Buckland (1969) studied the effect of an eight week Frostig program on perceptual, readiness, and word recognition skills of low readiness first grade children. No significant differences on any measures were found between the Frostig training group and a control group which listened to taped stories. Similarly, Bennett (1968) compared two second grade classes which had received sixteen weeks of instruction with the Frostig training program with two control classes. He found no significant differences in reading achievement between the two groups.

Jacobs (1968) investigated kindergarten children and concluded from his data that subjects who received nine months of Frostig training performed no better on a reading readiness test than a control group. In a follow-up evaluation of the Frostig Visual Perceptual training program, Jacobs, Wirthlin, and Miller (1968), reported that "pupils who take the Frostig program seem to have no particular advantage as far as future reading achievement is concerned as compared to pupils who do not take the Frostig program." Thus, the authors finished by stating that "if the goal is to increase reading achievement beyond normally expected, the evidence obtained from this study would not tend to support the notion that this will occur."

In an investigation of the effectiveness of the Frostig program, Brown (1969) reported that eighteen weeks of perceptual training produced no significant gains on either the Frostig Test or on the Gilmore Reading Test. Brown concluded that the utilization of the Frostig Program had a negative value "because it occupied time which could be better spent with reading instruction." Cox (1969) also evaluated the effects of the Frostig program and obtained negative results between the experimental and control groups after ten weeks of training. The mean differences in reading achievment were no greater than expected by chance when one group had been given the Frostig and the other group had been given additional reading for a similar period of time.

Alley, Snider, Spencer and Angell (1968), reported on a posttest only, control group type of experimental design in which they examined the effect of eight months of a Frostig training program on reading readiness. The subjects for the experiment were 108 culturally deprived kindergarten children of unselected mental ability. The authors make no mention of the number of the subjects in either the experimental or control groups. In addition, no clear indication of how subjects were designated experimental and control was given. Since this design can only be used with "true randomization" of subjects, one can question the initial comparability of the two groups with respect to reading readiness and the potential to acquire reading readiness by means other than Frostig training during the eight month experimental period.

The results revealed that five out of eight variable mean scores on the Metropolitan Reading Readiness Test significantly differentiated the two groups under investigation. Of the thirteen Frostig test variable means only one achieved significance at the 5 percent level and when the mean raw scores were used no significant difference between the group mean scores was found. In addition to those factors which may have been at work to make the experimental and the control groups unequal at the outset of the experiment, the study failed to control for differences in presentation, personality, interests, and classroom management of the two kindergarten teachers. These are serious sources of experimental invalidity and it must be concluded that the study does not offer credible evidence for the effectiveness of the Frostig training program.

Linn (1968) studied thirty kindergarten children equally divided into experimental and control groups. The experimental group was given the Frostig program over a period of time. The author reported that the experimental group improved on a posttest of the Frostig Test. These results are to be expected since the children in the experimental group were essentially taught to perform better on a repeat of the Frostig test. The author then went on to follow the children for another year. She maintained that at the end of the first grade the children who had received the Frostig training the previous year gained more in reading than the control group. Since there were no statistics for the differences between the means of the two groups, the author's conclusion of gains cannot be justified by the data.

Taken as a group, the ten studies reviewed show little, if any, relationship between the Frostig Visual Perceptual Training Program and reading achievement. In fact, the data seems to indicate that additional reading instruction may be more beneficial than visual perceptual training.

## THE DOMAN-DELACATO PROGRAM

There were a series of studies (Alcuin, 1966; Delacato, 1966; Edwin, 1966; Glaeser, 1966; Kabot, 1966; Masterman, 1966; Miracle, 1966; Vivial, 1966) in support of Delacato's theories which utilized some version of the pretest-posttest, control group design. Each study can be criticized on several points. Experimental mortality was not controlled in a number of the studies. This results in a mortality rate which ran as high as 33 percent in the Masterman study. In at least four studies (Edwin, Glaeser, Alcuin, Miracle) the selection of students for the experimental and control groups was biased. Furthermore, in the experiment by Delacato and Masterman inappropriate assignment of subjects introduced the regression phenomena as an alternative and plausible explanation of positive results. None of the studies used a sufficient number of intact groups so that random assignment of classrooms into experimental and control conditions could have been implemented. Thus, factors such as time of day and studying under different teachers were never adequately controlled.

Another source of possible bias related to the novelty, interest, and motivational effects generated by the enthusiasm of the experimeter. For example, Vivian described a program of neurological organization which also included spinning yo-yos, bouncing balls, and playing games. This confounding makes it difficult to specifically attribute possible gains to the therapy. Several of the studies contained omission of data. Some subjects who were included in the pretest data disappeared during the posttest analysis. In addition, several authors (Masterman, Kabot, Alcuin, and Edwin) failed to include sufficient information for the reader to determine how subjects were matched and how the experimental and control groups compared at the outset of the experiment.

The lack of adequate experimental procedures made it difficult to arrive at conclusions similar to Delacato. The results of each of the studies can be accounted for in terms of alternative hypotheses based on a scrutiny of the errors in the execution of the experiments as well as in the analysis and reporting of the data.

Delacato's theories have also been tested by Robbins (1966) and and O'Donnell and Eisenson (1969) and Forester (1965). The Robbins study is one of the few reported in the literature which attempted to utilize a research design that could control the various sources of invalidity. He divided his population into experimental, control, and nonspecific groups. The results of the experiment were negative and he concluded that "the data did not support the postulated relationship between neurological organization and reading achievement." O'Donnell and Eisenson investigated the usefulness of the Delacato program as an adjunct to the curriculum of disabled readers. The experimenters gave careful attention to the selection and assignment of subjects into experimental and control groups. The results showed no change in reading as a result of the modified Delacato program of neurological organization. Forester studied the effects of Delacato mobility training on reading achievement and intelligence test scores of fourth and fifth grade boys having mixed dominance. Three groups matched in reading achievement and intelligence test scores were formed. One group of twenty-six subjects received a Delacato type program for thirty minutes a day. The second group with twenty-eight subjects received training considered to be opposite that recommended by Delacato's theory. The third group with twenty-seven subjects, received the regular school program and served as a control group. The study was conducted over a five month period; training was carried out at the same time of day in each school for thirty minutes during the regularly scheduled physical education period. Forester found no significant differences among the groups at the conclusion of the program in posttest scores on reading achievement or intelligence.

## CONCLUSION

The experimental literature on the effects of perceptual motor training was reviewed with respect to adequacy of experimental design. Numerous sources of error and invalidity were identified which made the reported results questionable. Alternative and plausible hypotheses can be used to account for the ostensibly positive gains which have been attributed to perceptual motor training. The authors must conclude that these studies do not provide sufficient evidence that perceptual motor therapy, in any of its forms, has a significant effect on academic achievement. More specifically, it has not been demonstrated that perceptual motor training can cause positive changes in reading achievement because it effects changes in cognitive abilities. More adequate designs than those which have been employed thus far are needed to reach a conclusion concerning the merits of perceptual motor training.

## REFERENCES

Alucin, S., Sister: The effect of neurological training on disabled readers. In Delacato, C. (Ed.): *Neurological Organization and Reading.* Springfield, Thomas, 1966.

Alley, G., Snider, W., Spencer, J., and Angell, R.: Reading readiness and the Frostig training program. *Except Child*, 35:68-69, 1968.

Anderson, R. W.: *Effects of neuropsychological techniques on reading achievement,* Unpublished doctoral dissertation, Colorado State College, 1965.

Bennett, R. M.: *A study of the effects of a visual perception training program upon school achievement, I.Q., and visual perception,* Unpublished doctoral dissertation, University of Tennessee, 1968.

Brown, J. L.: *The Frostig program for the development of visual perception in relation to visual perception ability and reading ability,* Unpublished doctoral dissertation, University of Southern California, 1969.

Buckland, P. A.: *The effect of visual perception training on reading achievement in low readiness first grade pupils,* Unpublished doctoral dissertation, University of Minnesota, 1969.

Campbell, D. T., and Stanley, J. C.: *Experimental and Quasi-experimental Designs for Research.* Chicago, Rand-McNally, 1969.

Cohen, R. I.: Remedial training of first grade children with visual perceptual retardation. *Educational Horizons*, 45:60-63, 1966.
Cohen, S. A.: Studies in visual perception and reading in disadvantaged children. *Journal of Learning Disabilities*, 2:498-503, 1969.
Cornish, R. D.: Effects of neurological training on psychomotor abilities of kindergarten children. *Journal of Experimental Education*, 39:15-19, 1970.
Cox, C. A.: *Remediating visual perceptual skills in lower socio-economic children*, Unpublished doctoral dissertation, Arizona State University, 1969.
Cratty, B. J.: *Active Learning: Games to Enhance Academic Abilities.* Englewood Cliffs, Prentice Hall, 1971.
Dawson, D. K.: *An instructional program for children with perceptually related learning disabilities*, Unpublished doctoral dissertation, Ohio State University, 1966.
Delacato, C. H.: *The Treatment and Prevention of Reading Problems.* Springfield, Thomas, 1959.
Delacato, C. H.: *The Diagnosis and Treatment of Speech and Reading Problems.* Springfield, Thomas, 1963.
Delacato, C. H.: *Neurological Organization and Reading.* Springfield, Thomas, 1966.
Early, G. H., and Kephart, N. C.: Perceptual-motor training and academic achievement. *Academic Therapy Quarterly*, 4:201-206, 1969.
Early, G. H., and Sharpe, T. M.: Perceptual-motor training and basic abilities. *Academic Therapy Quarterly*, 5:235-240, 1970.
Edwin, M., Sister: Neurological training as a Pre-reading readiness measure. In Delacato, C. (Ed.): *Neurological Organization and Reading.* Springfield, Thomas, 1966.
Elkind, D., and Deblinger, J.: Perceptual training and reading achievement in the disadvantaged child. *Child Devel*, 40:11-19, 1969.
Emrick, C. D.: Treatment of conceptual and perceptual deficits. *Academic Therapy Quarterly*, 6:293-303, 1971.
Falik, L. H.: The effects of special perceptual-motor training in kindergarten on reading readiness and on second reading grade performance. *Journal of Learning Disabilities*, 2:395-402, 1969.
Faustman, M. N.: *Some effects of perceptual training in kindergarten on first grade success in reading*, Unpublished doctoral dissertation, University of California, Berkeley, 1966.
Ferinden, W. E., Jr., Van Handel, D., and Kovalinsky, T.: A supplemental instructional program for children with learning disabilities. *Journal of Learning Disabilities*, 4:194-203, 1971.
Forester, J. M.: *Effects of mobility training upon reading achievement and intelligence*, Unpublished doctoral dissertation, University of California, Los Angeles, 1965.

Frostig, M., and Maslow, P.: Treatment methods and their evaluation in educational therapy. In Hellmuth, J. (Ed.): *Educational Therapy*. Seattle, Special Child Publications, 1969, Vol. 2, 413-432.

Glaeser, G., Dewaide, S., and Levi, R.: Reading improvement program at Miguel High School reading clinic. In Delacato, C. (Ed.): *Neurological Organization and Reading*. Springfield, Thomas, 1966.

Gorelich, M. C.: The effectiveness of visual form training in a pre-reading program. *The Journal of Educational Research, 81*:315-318, 1965.

Halgren, M. R.: Opus in see sharp. *Education, 81*:369-371, 1961.

Halliwell, J. W., and Solan, H. A.: The effects of a supplemental perceptual training program on reading achievement. *Except Child, 38*:613-621, 1972.

Ismail, A. H., and Gruber, J. J.: *Motor Aptitude and Intellectual Performance*. Columbus, Merrill, 1967.

Jacobs, J. N.: An evaluation of the Frostig Visual Perception Training Program. *Education Leadership Research Supplement, 25*:332-340, 1968.

Jacobs, J. N., Wirthlin, L. D., and Miller, C. B.: A follow-up evaluation of the Frostig Visual Perception training program. *Educational Leadership Research Supplement, 26*:169-175, 1968.

Jenson, N. J., and King, E. M.: Effects of different kinds of visual motor discrimination training on learning to read words. *J Educ Psychol, 61*:90-96, 1970.

Kabot, R. R.: A study of improvement in reading through improvement of neurological organization. In Delacato, C. (Ed.): *Neurological Organization and Reading*. Springfield, Thomas, 1966.

Keim, R. P.: Visual-motor training, readiness and intelligence of kindergarten children. *Journal of Learning Disabilities, 3*:256-259, 1970.

Keogh, B.: Optometric vision training programs for children with learning disabilities: review of issues and research. *Journal of Learning Disabilities, 4*:219-232, 1974.

Lewis, J. N.: The improvement of reading ability through a developmental program in visual perception. *Journal of Learning Disabilities, 1*:652-653, 1968.

Linn, S. H.: Achievement report of first-grade students after visual perceptual training in kindergarten. *Academic Therapy Quarterly, 3*:179-180, 1968.

Manley, M.: Potential through perceptual training in a public school classroom. *Ideas for Action*, Houston, 1969, 36-40.

Masterman, J.: The effect of neurological training on reading retardation. In Delacato, C. (Ed.): *Neurological Organization and Reading*. Springfield, Thomas, 1966.

McCormick, C. C., Schnobrich, J. N., and Footlik, S. W.: The effect of perceptual motor training on reading achievement. *Academic Therapy Quarterly,* 4:171-176, 1969.

McCormick, C., Schnobrich, J., Footlik, S., and Poetker, B.: Improvement in reading achievement through perceptual-motor training. *The Research Quarterly,* 39:627-633, 1968.

McGrath, F., Father: The St. Philip summer remedial reading course. In Delacato, C. (Ed.): *Neurological Organization and Reading.* Springfield, Thomas, 1966.

McLees, M. P.: *The effectiveness of activities designed to improve basic perceptual-motor patterns for increasing achievement among seventh grade remedial reading pupils,* Unpublished doctoral dissertation, University of South Carolina, 1970.

Miracle, F. B.: The linguistic effect of neuropsychological techniques in treating a selected group of retarded readers. In Delacato, C. (Ed.): *Neurological Organization and Reading.* Springfield, Thomas 1966.

Noonan, J. D., Jr.: A one-year study of the effects of neurological organization as a factor in reading retardation. In Delacato, C. (Ed.): *Neurological Organization and Reading.* Springfield, Thomas, 1966.

O'Donnell, P., and Eisenson, J.: Delacato training of reading achievement and visual-motor integration. *Journal of Learning Disabilities,* 2:441-446, 1969.

Painter, G.: The effect of a rhythmic and sensory motor activity program on perceptual motor spatial abilities of kindergarten children. *Except Child,* 67:113-116, 1966.

Painter, G.: Remediation of maladaptive behavior and psycholinguistic deficits in a group sensory-motor activity program. *Academic Therapy Quarterly,* 3:233-243, 1968.

Piper, G. L.: Results of a twelve-week therapy program in neurological organization and dominant laterality. In Delacato, C. (Ed.): *The Diagnosis and Treatment of Speech and Reading Problems.* Springfield, Thomas, 1963.

Robbins, M. P.: A study of the validity of Delacato's theory of the neurological organization. *Except Child,* 32:517-523, 1966.

Rosen, C. L.: An experimental study of visual perceptual training and reading achievement in first grade. *Percept Mot Skills,* 22:979-986, 1966.

Silver, A., Hagin, R., and Hersch, M.: Reading disability: teaching through stimulation of deficit perceptual areas. *Am J Orthopsychiatry,* 37:744-752, 1967.

Vivian, Sister M.: An experiment with the concept of neurological organization. In Delacato, C. (Ed.): *Neurological Organization and Reading.* Springfield, Thomas, 1966.

Chapter IX

# A REVIEW OF THE RESEARCH ON CONCEPT FORMATION AND THE CHILD WITH LEARNING DISABILITIES

MARY R. PARUCKA

## INTRODUCTION

CONCEPT FORMATION IS considered to be one of the most important aspects of learning (Bourne, 1966) and one of the most frequently noted deficit areas for children with learning disabilities (Johnson & Myklebust, 1967). A critical review of the literature would appear to indicate that traditional approaches to the investigation of concept formation emphasizing either task variables or subject variables alone are not sufficient for an understanding of this process in children with learning disabilities (Parucka, 1972; 1973). First, the studies on concept formation in children with learning disabilities are reviewed. Second, the implications of these studies for clinical practice are discussed followed by suggestions for alternative approaches.

## REVIEW OF STUDIES

Early investigations of conceptual difficulties in the children with learning disabilities generally centered around abstract concepts and implied such deficits from poor academic performance attributing them to (1) global cognitive and/or intellectual impairments (Rosenfelt & Bradley, 1948), (2) inefficient brain processing and patterning (Burks, 1960), and (3) malfunction in the capacity to selectively scan and screen incoming stimuli (Clements & Peters, 1962). More recently studies have emphasized evaluation of both cognitive-intellectual and motivational-attentional variables in the subject. Additionally, emphasis has been placed on an examination of task requirements. Freibergs and Douglas (1969) compared both normal and learning disabled, male and female subjects of different intellectual levels, between six and twelve years of age, in an untimed concept formation task which involved two types of concepts — a naturalistic one and a numerical one. The children were tested under three experimental conditions: continuous reinforcement, partial reinforcement and delayed reinforcement. In the continuous reinforcement condition the subjects received 100 percent token reinforcement for correct responses with a four second intertrial interval. The partial group received 50 percent reinforcement on a fixed ratio two schedule with a four second intertrial interval. The delayed reinforcement group received 100 percent reinforcement for correct responses with an eight second intertrial interval. The trials themselves were self-paced. The primary results of the study indicated that learning disabled children were just as cognitively efficient as normals for both types of concept formation when untimed. They experienced no greater difficulty with numerical concepts than did the normal subjects. A secondary but important finding noted that under partial reinforcement schedule learning disabled children showed significant performance decrements. This unexpected result, explained in terms of Amsel's theory of frustration (1962), was corroborated by test records indicating many of the subjects abandoned attempts at rational solutions and began employing defense mechanisms like denial insisting there was no way to solve the problem.

In a similar but timed experiment Parucka (1972; 1973) examined concept formation in seven to nine year old male learning disabled subjects of two different intelligence levels. Two types of concepts were utilized, concrete and abstract (numerical). There were three experimental conditions, continuous reinforcement, partial reinforcement, and no reinforcement for the control group. A behavorial rating scale for learning disabled children developed by McCullom (1971) was completed by classroom teachers on all subjects.

Subjects under the continuous reinforcement condition received 100 percent reinforcement for correct responses while subjects under the partial reinforcement condition received 50 percent reinforcement on a fixed ratio two schedule. The controls received no reinforcement. The stimuli were presented for fifteen second trials with a one second intertrial interval. Both trials to criterion and median reaction time were evaluated. The results indicated a significant interaction between type of reinforcement and type of concept. The learning disabled children trained under partial reinforcement showed significant decrements in retaining the abstract (numerical) concept. Somewhat similar to the findings of Friebergs and Douglas (1969), Parucka (1972; 1973) also noted on the raw test records a giving up or frustration-type response on the part of some subjects under the partial reinforcement condition. Examiners' notes indicated these youngsters appeared frustrated, sat back passively, removed their hands from the response levers, and refused to continue responding.

The results of the median reaction time data indicated that recognition of the abstract (numerical) concept took an average of 3.75 seconds longer for the learning disabled group. This finding appeared to corroborate the results of Dykman, *et al.* (1970) that learning disabled children takes longer to process information. It is also substantiated by the speculations of Freibergs and Douglas (1969) that if their stimuli had been presented for a fixed interval at a predetermined rate, the children with learning disabilities would have performed more poorly than the normals.

A final result of Parucka's (1972; 1973) study was that only one factor, social assertiveness, on McCullom's (1971) behavorial rating scale for children with learning disabilities differentiated the learning disabled children whose performance improved at retest from those whose performance was unimproved. The factor generally describes learning disabled children who are considered to be more hyperactive, dominant, demanding and disruptive in the classroom.

## CLINICAL IMPLICATIONS

Thus far an examination of the work on concept formation with learning disabled children appeared to have some potent implications for clinical practice. One of the most striking implications is that the full scale intelligence level as measured by traditional instruments does not differentiate between ability and inability to form and retain concepts for the learning disabled group. The question then arises from a methodological as well as a remedial standpoint as to what instrument or set of procedures could function as an accurate predictor of concept formation ability in the learning disabled group.

A second implication for clinical practice and a most difficult finding to deal with from a viewpoint of experimental psychology is (1) that learning disabled children under partial reinforcement show significant decrements in performance (Friebergs and Douglas, 1969; Parucka, 1972, 1973) and (2) more importantly that this type reinforcement appears to produce highly undesirable personality traits and/or behavorial response styles in the learning disabled group. For remedial purposes this finding would appear to suggest that continuous reinforcement, possibly administered by a computer system, would be ideal for learning disabled children in the classroom. From a research/theoretical viewpoint, it leads to a two-sided question: First, exactly what is the function of continuous reinforcement in a concept learning task with learning disabled children? Second, why does partial reinforcement produce such inappropriate behavior? To answer the first part of the question, it appears that although the experimenters believed the function of continuous reinforcement was to reinforce correct choices, that for the learning disabled groups in these studies, continuous reinforcement may have functioned at the onset of the task to reinforce attending to stimuli, listening to instructions, etc., and during the task served to refocus subjects on the task. If this explanation of the function of continuous reinforcement is accepted, it would appear that under partial reinforcement learning disabled children in the studies reviewed earlier were reinforced less often for orienting to, attending to, and refocusing on the task and thus afforded less opportunity to receive and process information necessary for completion of the task. It is quite understandable then that the performance of these learning disabled youngsters under partial reinforcement would show decrements. The second part of the question as to why partial reinforcement produces inappropriate behavior is more difficult. Amsel's (1962) contention that the nonreinforced trials during partial reinforcement produce a frustrating effect which interferes with rational solutions as the task seems to afford a reasonable explanation. In both Freibergs and Douglas (1969) and Parucka's (1972, 1973) studies some learning disabled children under partial reinforcement were noted in the experimenter's raw test records to use defense mechanisms like denial or to sit passively refusing to press response levers thus withdrawing from the task.

A third and final implication for clinical practice involves the finding that learning disabled children rated as more socially assertive and disruptive also showed more improved performance (Parucka, 1972, 1973). It appears that within the learning disabled group there are activity-behavorial-personality differences (Dykman, *et al.* 1970; McCullom, 1971), and that these differences interact with reinforcement conditions definitely in concept formation task and most probably in other learning situations as well.

## ALTERNATIVE APPROACHES

In summary it can be said that the territory of concept formation in learning disabled children needs a great deal of further exploration. Two major areas stand out. The first task involves breaking down the concept formation task itself into component parts such as orienting to stimuli, abstracting bits of information, encoding, decoding and categorizing bits of information, the role of memory, etc. Herein the recent work of Anderson, *et al.* (1973) utilizing the vigilance task to measure attentional deficits in learning disabled children appears to be a useful first step.

A second outstanding area in need of further work stems from the assertion by an increasing number of experimenters

(Dykman, et al, 1970; Luria, 1961; McCullom, 1971, Parucka, 1972, 1973) that learning disabled subjects appear to be a more heterogenous than a homogenous group. Whether these differences are more a question of activity level (Dykman, et al, 1970; Luria, 1961) or personality-behavioral variables (McCullom, 1971) presents an interesting challenge in addition to assessing their interaction in learning tasks.

## REFERENCES

Amsel, A.: Frustrative nonreward in partial reinforcement and discrimination learning. Some recent history of a theoretical extension. *Psychol Rev, 69*:306-328, 1962.

Anderson, R. P., Halcomb, C., and Doyle, R.: The measurement of attentional deficits. *Except Child, 39*:535-541, 1973.

Bourne, L. E.: *Human Conceptual Behavior.* Boston, Allyn and Bacon, 1966.

Burks, H. R.: The hyperkinetic child. *Except Child, 27*:18-26, 1960.

Clements, S. D., and Peters, J. E.: Minimal brain dysfunction in the school-aged child. *Arch Gen Psychiatry, 6*:185-197, 1962.

Dykman, R. A., et al.: Children with learning disabilities: Conditioning, differentiation and the effect of distraction. *Am J Orthopsychiatry, 40*:766-782, 1970.

Freibergs, V., and Douglas, V. I.: Concept learning in hyperactive and normal children. *J Abnorm Psychol, 74*:388-395, 1969.

Johnson, D. J., and Myklebust, H. R.: *Learning Disabilities: Educational Principles and Practices.* New York, Grune and Stratton, 1967.

Luria, A.: *The Role of Speech in Regulation of Normal and Abnormal Behavior.* New York, Liveright, 1961.

McCullom, P. S.: *Group counseling as an adjunctive remediation technique for learning disabilities,* Unpublished doctoral dissertation, Texas Tech University, 1971.

Parucka, M. R.: *An Investigation of Concept Formation in Children with Learning Disabilities,* Unpublished doctoral dissertation, Texas Tech University, 1972.

Parucka, M. R.: *Concept formation in children with learning disabilities,* Paper presented at Southwestern Psychological Association, Dallas, 1972.

Rosenfield, C. B., and Bradley, C.: Childhood behavior sequelae of asphyxia in infancy with special reference to pertussis and asphyxia neonatorum. *Pediatrics, 2*:74-84, 1948.

## Chapter X

# THE VIGILANCE TASK AND THE MEASUREMENT OF ATTENTIONAL DEFICITS

ROBERT B. DOYLE

ONE OF THE FACTORS most clearly differentiating between children who are considered to be academically adequate and children who are diagnosed as having some specific learning disability is the presence of an attention deficit. An attentional deficit syndrome was suggested by Dykman, Walls, Suzuki, Ackerman, and Peters (1970) as the most common denominator of the learning disabilities syndrome. They also found it necessary to investigate the dimension of activity level when considering the attentional deficit syndrome. They divided their learning disability population into subgroups representing three activity levels: hyperactive, hypoactive, and normoactive. The children with learning disabilities (CLDs) were classified hyperactive when they were rated by teachers and parents as exhibiting restless or fidgety behaviors. CLD's who demonstrated extremely slow execution of purposive movements such as talking, walking, buttoning clothes, etc., were classified as hypoactive. If the CLD's did not fit either the hyperactive or hypoactive classification they were considered to be normoactive.

The results of Dykman, *et al.* supported similar research by Luria (1960, 1961) who discussed the "cerebro-asthenic" syndrome (the Russian diagnostic term most similar to the term learning disabilities in current vogue among American investigators). Luria also divided cerebro-asthenic children into activity subgroups. One subgroup described as those whose inhibitory processes were weak or deranged with a consequent increase in distractibility and impulsiveness was descriptively similar to Dykman's hyperactive children. A second type described by Luria was similar to Dykman's hypoactive children. They were characterized as distractible and impulsive, with behaviors/behaviorial inhibition predominating over excitation. Regardless of activity classification both investigators found that all of the children demonstrated deficits in attention which contributed to their failure to keep pace academically with their classmates.

## THE VIGILANCE TASK

Jerison (1967) and other investigators (J. Mackworth, 1970; Bakan, 1966) have contended that certain critical questions about the nature of attention could best be studied by utilizing a vigilance paradigm. Jane Mackworth (1970) summarized the literature in which the vigilance task allowed investigation of the physiological-psychological parameters of human attention. Excellent examples of this approach to the study of attention are provided by her work which related vigilance to habituation and levels of arousal, and by the work of Kaider, Spong, and Lindsley (1964) which related vigilance performance to evoked cortical potentials.

Norman Mackworth (1950) foresaw the discovery of a relationship between attention and vigilance when he observed the similarity between monitoring failure and failures of alertness in patients with brain damage. The term "vigilance" was adopted to describe his research primarily because it was the term in current vogue among British neurologists at that time to characterize the dimension of behavior involving arousal and activation. Mackworth applied the term "vigilance" to that dimension of behavior critical to the missing of signals by radar observers. A result of his work was the development of the Mackworth Clock Test (Mackworth, 1950), a vigilance task which simulated the attention-demanding features of the radar system monitored by the observer.

In current vigilance research, the typical vigilance experiment is structurally indistinguishable from many detection or discrimination experiments, except in terms of the experimental parameters (e.g. stimulus duration, frequency, and strength). An observer in a vigilance task is presented with stimuli, some of which are signals which are to be reported, and others which are nonsignals which require no action on the part of the subject. The critical features of the vigilance experiments are the parameters which are utilized. First, the vigil or watch is maintained without interruption for a period of at least a half-hour. A watch may last longer. Second, signals are presented infrequently and without forewarning. Third, the signals are considered strong in a psychophysical sense (superliminal and nearly always correctly reported by the alert observer with few if any false alarms in a two-alternative forced-choice setting), but they would be described as weak by many observers because they are not "attention demanding." These conditions require the observer to be continuously alert in order to detect and report all signals. Therefore, detection failures can be identified with failure of attention.

From the viewpoint of the observer the signals during a vigilance task can appear at any point in time. Stimuli are normally presented at a regular interval, with the stimulus presentation rate determining the timeframe for the observer. The average frequency (probability) of signals in a vigilance task is thus relative to the stimulus frequency or rate.

The major vigilance effect is the decrement function which is a reliable drop in the average number of correct detections as the vigil progresses. In a well-designed experiment the average rate of correct detections will drop significantly to a lower steady-state level. N. H. Mackworth (1950) reported that the detection decrement occurred after the first half-hour of a vigil. A finer grain analysis was performed by Jerison (1963) which indicated a continuous decrement within the first half-hour of observation; which was complete after approximately fifteen minutes and which was followed by the plateau.

Another important aspect of the vigilance task is that it is seen to provide an accurate simulator of attention-demanding situations in real life. The observer as an experimental subject is required to make the same kind of responses as he does when he is required to respond to the less measured and controlled environment of everyday life. This brings certain problems of attention within the reach of analysis which would not be available in other more highly controlled laboratory settings.

In most highly controlled experiments using children as subjects, it is almost inevitable that the child will adopt the set and role of the experimental subject and attempt to conform to the demand characteristics of the task. This set will interact in unpredictable ways with his performance during the experimental session. This same uncertainty principle also extends to the procedures and methods used by the experimenter and results in an unknown reaction to the experimental setting. The vigilance task was found by Jerison (1963) to be less susceptible to the reactive consequences of this uncertainty principle than other experimental paradigms utilized to investigate attention. In using a vigilance task to study the parameters of attention, Jerison found: (1) stimuli and signals were much less esoteric, much more the sort of thing one normally sees in the everyday world; and (2) the relative isolation and the long uninterrupted vigil was conducive to the eventual nonlaboratory oriented response sets, even if the observer started by seeing himself as a guinea pig. While it is true that the situation presented by a vigilance task can hardly be considered normal in the sense of representing typical activities of children, Jerison has pointed out that the situation is acceptable as one which will produce typical observing patterns distributed over time, in which the actual observing responses of the subjects are similar in kind to those made in response to more everyday requirements.

Not only does the vigilance task present the experimenter with a simulation of normalcy for investigating attention, a vigilance task can also be simple enough to keep the analytic problems manageable. To maintain manageability in studying the parameters of attention, simplicity must be utilized in the vigilance task selected, especially when the problem is to decide whether or not a specific stimulus is a signal. For example, by requiring a search and scanning operation to take place during performance of a vigilance task the experiment is complicated by adding complex sensory analyses (i.e. higher order information processing and memory). Therefore, in studying attention deficits of children with learning disabilities and using a vigilance task, the task should not be one in which cognitive processes of a higher order than simple temporal certainty or uncertainty are present. Even then, when the location of the stimulus is known, there is the problem of whether or not it will be observed, and, if observed, how adequate an observation will be made in light of the presence of any irrelevant stimuli.

## ATTENTION DEFICITS AMONG CHILDREN WITH LEARNING DISABILITIES

Dykman, *et al.,* (1970) hypothesized that the critical variable determining the inattentiveness of children with learning disabilities required to perform a simple signal detection task was their inability to process information at the same rate as normal children. They concluded that children with learning difficulties were "... lacking in those specific arousal or emotive supports necessary for sustained attention and learning." At the same time, Dykman and his associates stressed that the organic conclusion which they reached could explain only in part slower reaction times, slower learning, slower assimilation of information, shorter attention spans, and the increased physiological activity of children with learning disabilities. Their conclusion was in agreement with Anderson (1970) who postulated that learning disabilities appeared to be the result of interaction between complex neurogenic and psychogenic factors.

## THE VIGILANCE TASK AND ATTENTIONAL DEFICIT RESEARCH

A series of studies using a vigilance task to quantify attention deficits among children with learning disabilities was initiated through the Psychology Department of Texas Tech University in 1972. The initial study (Anderson, Halcomb, & Doyle, 1973) demonstrated that the vigilance task was a simple yet technically sophisticated means of obtaining an experimental analysis of attention deficits. It was possible for the authors to conclude that the methodology of the vigilance task provided a most hopeful means of examining the complex parameters of attention deficits expressed by CLD's. The results of this study also supported Dykman, *et al.* (1970) and Luria (1960, 1961) in the classification of

CLD's into activity level groups of hyperactive, normoactive and hypoactive.

A simple vigilance task was used by the Texas Tech group to systematically examine attention deficits. The subjects were required to sit before a console in a 4 x 4 foot booth. The booth was carpeted, air conditioned, and had indirect incandescent lighting. It provided a pleasant environment that had none of the characteristics associated with laboratory experimentation. The entry was a pleasant, carpeted waiting room with chairs, lamps, etc. The subject's parents could sit and wait in the area while the experiment was in progress.

The subjects were instructed to observe a pair of flashing lights which appeared in front of them. The lights flashed in red-red, green-green, or red-green, green-red combination at a rate of one flash each two seconds. When the red-green combination appeared, subjects were told to press a button mounted in a bicycle handle bar grip. The handle bar grip was connected to the console by a two foot wire so subjects could hold the grip in their hands and move about the booth. The subjects could hold the handle bar grip in either hand and were not required to maintain a certain position in order to make a response.

When the subjects responded to the red-green combination by pressing the button, they were credited with a correct detection. Pressing the button to the red-red or green-green combination was considered a false alarm. The program continued for thirty minutes with a total of sixty red-green combinations appearing during this period. These combinations occurred randomly with the restriction that ten signals occur during each five minute interval. There were a total of nine hundred red-red, green-green, red-green combinations during the thirty minute vigil. Thus, the subjects were required to attend to the display in order to make the correct detections. The sequence of flashing lights and the recording of data were programmed and controlled through a Digital Equipment Corporation PDP-8/e computer housed in the Engineering Psychology Laboratory at Texas Tech University. The entire experimental task was under absolute computer control assuring uniform presentation of the stimuli from subject to subject and accurate recording of data. Instructions were presented to the subjects by means of a tape recorded message and supplemented with individualized instruction when required.

The initial study utilized thirty CLD's and thirty academically adequate children. All of the subjects were considered to be average to above average intellectually, but the CLD's were all experiencing difficulty keeping pace scholastically. A completely randomized analysis of variance yielded significant differences between the two populations on both the correct detection and false alarm variables. On correct detections the $F$ ratio of 9.339 (df=1/62) was significant beyond the .01 level and on false alarms the $F$ ratio of 4.326 (df=1/62) was significant beyond the .05 level. The $F$ ratios from the analyses of variances between the three activity level groups of CLD's (N for each group = 10) were as follows:
1. On correct detections:
    a. Between hyperative and normoactive, $F=17.9$, $p<.01$.
    b. Between hyperactive and hypoactive, $F=10.6$, $p<.01$.
    c. Between normoactive and hypoactive, $F=4.9$, $p<.05$.
2. On false alarms:
    a. Between hyperactive and normoactive, $F=8.1$, $p<.05$.
    b. Between hyperactive and hypoactive, $F=3.8$, $p<.10$.
    c. Between normoactive and hypoactive, $F=1.1$, NS

In essence, this first study showed that the hyperactive CLD's made fewer correct detections than the hypoactive and normoactive youngsters. Also, the hyperactive children made more false alarms than either of the other two groups. The activity dimension appeared to be on a continuum on which the hyperactive children were categorized as being more subject to attentional deficits and the hypoactive children demonstrated some deficit but quantitatively less of a decrement than the hyperactive children. The normoactive children manifested almost correct performance.

## Effects of Medication

During the initial study it was noted that there appeared to be differences between the performances of hyperactive children who were taking a medication such as Ritalin and those who were not taking medication to control their hyperkinesis. Therefore, another study was initiated (Anderson, Halcomb, Ozolins and Gordon, 1974) to study the effects of medication on vigilance performance using each subject as his own control by requiring him to perform the task on medication and then after being taken off medication. The results of this investigation did not yield significant differences between the on and off medication performance of the entire population of hyperactive CLD's. However, when the subjects were divided into age groups (older—10 to 12 years, younger—7 to 9 years) significant differences were found between the on medication and off medication performance on the correct detection task for the younger subjects while no such differences were found for the older group of subjects. A cautious conclusion was drawn from this investigation to the effect that medications such as Ritalin appeared to increase the attention span for younger hyperactive CLD's, but not for older hyperactives. The possibility of an age x task difficulty interaction is offered as a tentative explanation of these findings.

## Effects of Visual Distraction

Another progression in the investigation of attention deficits was the effect of distraction, both visual and auditory. In order to avoid contamination, a visual distraction study was conducted separately from an auditory distraction study. The visual distraction investigation (Doyle, Anderson, & Halcomb, 1973) utilized a total of thirty-five CLD males between the ages of eight and twelve. This group of CLD children was subsequently divided according to their activity level yielding groups of ten normoactive and hypoactive children and a group of fifteen hyperactive children. These children were matched with a group of thirty-five children considered academically adequate on age, sex, and intellectual ability.

The analysis of variance yielded significant differences between the CLD population and the academically adequate population, not only on the variables of correct detections and false alarms, but also in the frequency and duration of eye contact with the visual distractor. The visual distractor consisted of fifteen sequences of numerical and color-number signals presented every twenty seconds throughout the thirty minute task period. They were presented on a seven-frame display located ten inches to the lower left of the task display. Each frame (1x1 inch) had the capability of displaying three numerical figures, and the color red. All fifteen sequences followed the same time pattern with a signal occurring every second for seven seconds followed by a three second pause. In other words, the visual distraction was assumed to be far more attractive, more meaningful, and occurred more rapidly than did the stimulus events. Each subject was instructed not to attend to the distraction as it had nothing to do with the task that they were to perform. The eye contact which the subjects made with the distraction task was recorded by stationing two observers standing behind a one-way mirror. Their observations were recorded by means of an event recorder, thus allowing a record not only of the frequency of eye contacts with the distractor, but also of the duration of the eye contact. The vigilance task, the visual distractor, and the recording of task results were controlled completely by means of the PDP-8/e computer.

A series of randomized block analyses of variance between the CLD and control subjects yielded the following results:
1. Correct detections, $F=8.16$, $p<.01$.
2. False alarms, $F=7.57$, $p<.01$.
3. Frequency of eye contact, $F=5.81$, $p<.05$.
4. Duration of eye contact, $F=7.67$, $p<.01$.

Randomized block analyses of variance between the three CLD activity level groups yielded the following results:
1. Correct detections, $F=.66$, NS
2. False alarms, $F=4.90$, $p<.05$.
3. Frequency of eye contact, $F=4.26$, $p<.05$.
4. Duration of eye contact, $F=3.09$, $p<.10$.

Within group analyses of variance for the CLD's yielded the following results:
1. Hyperactive vs hypoactive
    a. Correct detections, $F=3.085$, $p<.05$.
    b. False alarms, $F=7.980$, $p<.01$
    c. Frequency of eye contact, $F=5.993$, $p<.01$.
    d. Duration of eye contact, $F=3.866$, $p<.05$.
2. Hyperactive vs normotactive
    a. Correct detections, $F=2.504$, $p<.05$.
    b. False alarms, $F=5.608$, $p<.05$.
    c. Frequency of eye contact, $F=2.783$, NS
    d. Duration of eye contact, $F=3.462$, $p<.05$.

3. Normoactive vs hypoactive
   a. Correct detections, $F=2.010$, NS
   b. False Alarms, $F=.174$, NS
   c. Frequency of eye contact, $F=2.372$, NS

The vigilance task in this study again demonstrated that CLD's and academically adequate children could be differentiated by means of their correct detection and false alarm performances on the vigilance task, and also that CLD's as a whole tended to perform even more poorly when faced with visual distraction than did the non-CLD children. When the CLD's were subdivided into the three activity groups, it was evident that the hyperactive CLD'S were the most affected by the distraction stimulus, the hypoactives the least affected, with the normoactive being quite similar to the control subjects in terms of their ability to inhibit responses to the distraction.

A more detailed analysis of their task performance was achieved by looking at the task performance during each five minute interval of the vigil. From interval analyses it was possible to conclude that hyperactive CLD'S expressed extremely poor stimulus selection processing, poor focusing (inhibitory weakness), and had erratic sustained attention throughout the task period. Hypoactive CLD's expressed attention postures similar to hyperactives in their poor detection performances but in the case of the hyperactives the major attention deficit appeared to be centered around weak arousal processes. For the hypoactive a sustained process of attention appeared to be functioning throughout the task, but the process broke down in stimulus selection where inhibitory processes predominated over arousal. The attention deficits across time intervals for the normoactive CLD's were quite dissimilar from either the hyperactive or hypoactive CLD's. Normoactives did not manifest any attention differences from the normal control subjects during the initial intervals of the task. The performance data revealed that after a period of time on task the sustained attention processing of the normoactives began to collapse. There were no indications that the drop in performance was due to either failure of arousal or stimulus selection processes, but rather there was evidence that it was the result of additional stimulus-seeking exploratory behavior. The normoactive CLD's stimulus-seeking exploratory behavior resulted in a deterioration of task performance and an increase in responding to irrelevent stimuli as the task progressed. The performance of normoactives across time intervals of the task had the appearance of individuals who began quite strongly with a great deal of effort, but who after only a few minutes, stopped performing the task at their initial attending level and began seeking out other external sources of stimulation. These results indicated that for normoactive CLD's the attention deficits might be more related to psychogenic factors of attention than to neurogenic factors.

### Effects of Auditory Distraction and Response Latency

A fourth study (Anderson, Holcomb, Ozolins & Hopson, 1974) was conducted to determine the effects of auditory distraction upon the performance of CLD's during a vigil. Two types of auditory noise were used in this study (with each subject serving as his own control). The two types of noise were wide range random noise and classroom noise. In addition to the usual measures of correct detection and false alarms an additional variable, response latencies, was used to measure the effects of the auditory distraction upon vigilance performance. Response latency was measured by obtaining the time interval between the onset of the light stimulus and the occurrence of the subject's response. In this study twenty-two CLD's and twenty-two control subjects were utilized. Using a four way analysis of variance significant differences were found between the CLD's and the controls only on the correct detection measure. The differences in the number of correct detections was not significant for conditions of wide range random noise, but was markedly different under the conditions of classroom noise ($F$-4.564, $p$ .05.) No differences were found between the CLD's and normals for the false alarm variable using either type of auditory distraction. The false alarm data for the CLD's contained some extreme scores necessitating an examination of the differences between the median false alarm scores for these two groups. Significance might have been achieved by eliminating the extreme scores at the cost of losing statistical power. It would seem from the results of this study that CLD's have more difficulty tuning out extraneous auditory distraction than do normals; and that they are likely to show their distractibility by a lack of accuracy in any task which requires them to carefully attend to detail.

The results of this study are consonate with the results of the visual distraction study (Doyle, et al., 1973) CLD's have a difficult time tuning out visual distraction; with the hyperactive CLD being particularly susceptible. Both studies of distraction (visual and auditory) indicate, that under controlled conditions, CLD's do indeed have problems with attention which influence their efficiency of performance.

By examining the response latencies, it was possible to test an often untested assumption that CLD's tend to respond "faster" because of the incidence of hyperactivity. Hyperkinesis has at times been related to a fast response latency; but Dykman, et al. (1970) demonstrated that this was not necessarily the case. Analyses of the present study demonstrated that there were no significant differences between the response latencies of the CLD's and control subjects. However, both groups did take significantly longer to respond under conditions of classroom noise than they did under the condition of wide range random noise. There was also a change in latency observed over the time intervals of the task. All children responded slower toward the end of the task than they did during the first five minute segment.

## Effects of Knowledge of Results

The effect of knowledge of results on vigilance performance was of particular interest to the Texas Tech investigators. Several previous studies have addressed the problem of shaping attention behavior utilizing the vigilance task and reinforcement through knowledge of results (Perryman, 1972). Perryman demonstrated that the mentally retarded subject with a presumed profound attention deficit could be conditioned by means of positive reinforcement to perform adequately on a vigilance task. Chinn and Alluisi (1964), using a watch-keeping task, presented three kinds of knowledge results (KOR); missed signals, correctly detected signals, and false responses. Their results indicated that knowledge of results regarding missed signals produced a significant decrease in the proportion of missed signals. Hardesty, Trumbo and Bevan (1963) utilized six groups in which all groups were retested without KOR one and seven days after the initial test with KOR. They found that subjects receiving verbal KOR from the experimenter showed a smaller decrement and significantly higher overall performance.

Similar studies with different approaches, such as Hartlage (1965), McCormack (1959), Sipowicz, Ware and Baker (1962), Weidenfeller, Baker and Ware (1962), Weiner (1962), and Weiner (1963), discovered basically the same thing. When subjects were presented with KOR while performing a vigilance task, the overall effect was an increase in correct detections and a decrease in false alarms, thus indicating a higher state of attention for the organism. Baker (1961) states that KOR was more powerful in task performance than the decrements due to division of attention (distraction) resulting from introduction of the feedback.

A fifth study was conducted at Texas Tech (Ozolins, Anderson & Halcomb, 1974) in which twenty hyperactive and twenty hypoactive CLD's performed the vigilance task under conditions of wide range random noise, positive KOR, and negative KOR. This study also considered the latency of response variable.

The analyses of variance for both correct detections and false alarms indicated that differences (significant at the .01 level) could be attributed to the treatment effect (positive and negative KOR and wide range random noise) and that the interaction between treatment and activity level (hyperactive and hypoactive), was also significant at the .01 level. In other words, hyperactive CLD's and hypoactive CLD's did respond differently to feedback.

In terms of correct detections, hypoactive CLD's performed less well than did hyperactive CLD's when they received negative KOR. Although both groups achieved about the same number of correct detections under positive KOR, the hyperactive CLD's were also committing a significantly greater number of false alarms. It appeared, therefore, that in terms of remediation of the attention deficit, hyperactive CLD's should be exposed to conditions of negative KOR (told when they are wrong); while hyperactive CLD's should be taught under conditions in which they receive positive KOR (told when they are right).

## SUMMARY

One major difference between academically adequate children and children with learning disabilities is that the latter group seems to have an attention deficit of some sort. Using the vigilance task to study this attention deficit has indicated that CLD's are consistently and significantly inferior in performance when compared with non-CLD's and that this difference may be directly attributed to defective arousal, stimulus selection, focusing and/or sustained attentional processes on the part of the CLD's. These differences have been demonstrated in studies utilizing a simple vigilance task, a vigilance task with visual distraction, a vigilance task with auditory distraction and a vigilance task in which knowledge of results is provided to the subjects.

As a result of these investigations it becomes apparent that the heterogeneous CLD's cannot be considered a homogenous group in regards to the expression of attention deficits. The activity level classification of hyperactive, hypoactive, and normoactive may provide one differentiation for studies utilizing the vigilance task. The use of medication provides yet another. The three groups of CLD's were found to differ significantly in the performance of the vigilance task under visual distraction and in their responses to both positive and negative knowledge of results. Auditory distraction appeared to affect the performance of all CLD's when classroom noise was the auditory distractor. Medication appeared to alter the sustained attention performance of only the younger children. Latency of response did not differentiate any of the CLD's from their control counterparts. Both groups demonstrated the decrement of response latencies throughout the experimental session which one would predict from the past vigilance literature.

In studying attention deficits of CLD's the vigilance paradigm provided the advantage of: (1) experimental conditions which were controlled rigidly without the necessity of creating a cold, austere, laboratory-type environment; (2) a task that was easy and was "learned" within a few minutes; (3) stimulus events that were programmed and completely computer controlled, thus assuring uniformity of presentation; (4) response characteristics that were measured with extreme accuracy on more than one dimension;

(5) an objective measure of attention which could be obtained on the basis of performance independent of the judgments of potentially biased observers; and (6) with the basic tool of a vigilance task it was possible to increase the stimulus complexity by introducing visual and auditory distraction and the effects of medication on the attention process.

## REFERENCES

Anderson, R. P.: *The Child with Learning Disabilities and Guidance.* Boston, Houghton Mifflin, 1970.

Anderson, R. P., Halcomb, C. G., and Doyle, R. B.: The measurement of attentional deficits. *Except Child, 39*:534-539, 1973.

Anderson, R. P., Halcomb, C. G., Ozolins, D., and Hopson, J.: *The effects of auditory distraction on vigilance task performance in learning disabled children,* Paper presented Southwestern Psychological Association, El Paso, 1974.

Anderson, R. P., Halcomb, C., Gordon, W. J., and Ozolins, D.: Measurement of attention distractibility in LD children. *Academic Therapy, 9*:261-266, 1974.

Bakan, P. (Ed.): *Attention: An Enduring Problem in Psychology,* Princeton, Van Nostrand, 1966.

Baker, C. H.: Maintaining the level of vigilance by means of knowledge of results about a secondary vigilance task. *Ergonomics, 4*:311-316, 1961.

Chinn, R. McC., and Alluisi, E. A.: Effect of three kinds of knowledge-of-results information on three measures of vigilance performance. *Percept Mot Skills, 18*:901-912, 1964.

Doyle, R. B., Anderson, R. P., and Halcomb, C. G.: *Attention deficits and the effects of visual distraction,* Paper presented Southwestern Psychological Association, Dallas, 1973.

Dykman, R., Walls, R., Suzuki, R., Ackerman, P., and Peters, J.: Children with learning disabilities: Conditioning, differentiation, and the effect of distraction. *Am J Orthopsychiatry, 40*:766-781, 1970.

Haider, M., Spong, R., and Lindsley, D. B.: Attention, vigilance and cortical evoked-potentials in humans. *Science, 145*:180-182, 1964.

Hardesty, D., Trumbo, D., and Bevan, W.: The influence of knowledge of results on performance in a monitoring task. *Percept Mot Skills, 16*:629-634, 1963.

Hartlage, L. C.: Knowledge of results and cautiousness in signal detection. *Psychonomic Science, 2*:347-348, 1965.

Jerison, H. J.: On the decrement function in human vigilance. In Buckner, D. N., and McGrath, J.: *A Symposium.* New York, McGraw-Hill, 1963.

Jerison, H. J.: Signal detection theory in the analysis of human vigilance. *Human Factors, 9*:285-288, 1967.
Luria, A.: *The role of speech in the regulation of normal and abnormal behavior,* U. S. Department of Health, Education and Welfare, NIH, Russian Scientific Translation Program, Bethesda, Maryland, 1960.
Luria, A.: *The Role of Speech in the Regulation of Normal and Abnormal Behavior.* In Tizard, J. (Ed.). New York, Liverright, 1961.
Mackworth, J. F.: *Vigilance and Attention.* Harmondsworth, Penquin, 1970.
Mackworth, J. F.: Vigilance, arousal and habituation. *Psychol Rev, 75*:308-322, 1968.
Mackworth, N. H.: *Rsearches on the Measurement of Human Performance.* Medical Research Council Special Report, No. 268, London: H. M. Stationery Office, 1950.
McCormack, P. D.: Performance in a vigilance task with and without knowledge of results. *Can J Psychol, 13*:68-71, 1959.
Ozolins, D., Anderson, R., Halcomb, C., and Gordon, W.: The effects of medication on performance on a vigilance task by hyperactive children with learning disabilities. 1973. Unpublished.
Perryman, R.: *Operant conditioning of the mental retardate-visual monitoring behavior,* unpublished doctoral dissertation, Texas Tech University, May, 1972.
Sipowicz, R. R., Ware, J. R., and Baker, R. A.: The effects of reward and knowledge of results on the performance of a simple vigilance task. *J Exp Psychol, 64*:58-61, 1962.
Weidenfeller, E. W., Baker, R. A., and Ware, J. R.: Effects of knowledge of results (true and false) on vigilance performance. *Percept Mot Skills, 14*:211-215, 1962.
Weiner, B., and Feldman, R.: Information processing related to stimulus novelty and complexity in a signal detection paradigm. *Br J Psychol, 58*:69-75, 1967.
Wiener, E. L.: Knowledge of results and signal rate in monitoring: A transfer of training approach. *J Appl Psychol, 47*:214-222, 1963.

## Chapter XI

# RESEARCH WITH THE SMART READING PROGRAM

BONNIE W. CAMP

### INTRODUCTION

FOR SEVERAL YEARS, several investigators at the University of Colorado Medical School, have been interested in studying reading progress in upper elementary and junior high school children with severe reading retardation. The extent of reading retardation in these children was generally disproportionate to their intelligence. Recognizing that many of the perceptual problems thought to interfere with learning in early grades should no longer interfere with learning at this level, the investigators started by examining the response of these children to a tutorial program called SMART (Camp, 1970; Camp & van Doorninck, 1971). SMART (Staats Motivation Activation Reading Therapy) is basically a behavioral-therapy approach to tutoring in reading. It was first described by Staats and Butterfield (1965) as a procedure for teaching reading to a nonreading adolescent delinquent boy. The procedures were later expanded and used successfully with both junior-high (Staats, Minke, Goodwin, & Butt, 1970) and elementary-school children (Camp, 1971; Camp & van Doorninck, 1971; Ryback and Staats, 1970) tutored by high-school and adult volunteers (Camp, 1971; Camp and van Doorninck, 1971; Staats, *et al.*, 1967) and parents working with their own children (Ryback & Staats, 1970).

The unique features of SMART included the following: (1) it utilized a general drill and practice procedure which could easily be adapted to a variety of materials, (2) it utilized incentives for eliciting good work and attention from reluctant readers, (3) it recognized the importance of consequences of behavior in improving retention of materials learned, and (4) it could be learned by nonprofessionals in a short period of time.

## DESCRIPTION OF SMART

Our basic program was a simplified version (Camp, 1971) of the procedure introduced by Staats and Butterfield (1965). In this version, graded rewards were used as incentives in a drill-and-practice-type reading lesson which used a "look-say" method to teach new vocabulary as it was encountered. Tokens ranging in value from one to five points were used as rewards, with money as the back-up reinforcer.

Each lesson was designed to cover four phases: new vocabulary, paragraph reading, silent reading, and comprehension. In the first phase (new vocabulary), new vocabulary words were presented to the child one at a time. He was asked to pronounce each one first without help. If correct on the first trial, he received a five point token, and the word was eliminated from the list. If he was incorrect, the correct answer was given, and he was asked to rehearse this aloud and keep it in the list for another trial. After all the new words had been tried once, the child went through the words remaining in the list a second time. If he pronounced a word correctly the second time, he received a two point token, and the word was eliminated from the list. If incorrect, the word was rehearsed again and retained in the list for another trial. This procedure continued until the child finally got each word without prompting, at which time he received a one point token whether it took three or more trials.

Once each new vocabulary word had been pronounced without prompting, the child proceeded to the paragraph-reading phase. Each paragraph was read aloud with the goal of reading each word in the paragraph correctly. If this occurred on the first trial, the child received a five point token, and the paragraph was eliminated. If an error occurred on any word in the paragraph, the word was rehearsed and the paragraph retained for another time. After all paragraphs had been read once, the child went through the remaining paragraphs again. On the second time, he received a two point token for each correct paragraph. Paragraphs in which errors occurred were again retained and re-presented until all words had been read correctly. A one point token was given for each paragraph requiring more than two times.

Once each paragraph had been read correctly, the child read the entire story silently or aloud. No corrections were made. A five point token was presented for reading through the story irrespective of errors. Then a series of comprehension questions were presented. During this phase, he could use the story material in any way he desired. For each correct answer, the child received a five point token. Each incorrect answer was corrected for a two point token.

The child and tutor then counted tokens and converted these to points. The child was permitted to accumulate points or trade for money immediately. The rate of exchange could be decided arbitrarily; however, we traded ten or twenty points per penny, depending on the child. Usually a child was started at ten points per penny and changed to twenty points per penny after the program had been going for a while. For children who earned less than 100 points in a lesson, a bonus was given to ensure that they earned at least ten cents per lesson

Records were kept of all errors in each lesson. Children were started at a level of difficulty one-half to one full grade level below their tested achievement level. Lessons were one-half hour in length and occurred three to five days per week. Lessons were held at school during school hours or outside school depending on the situation. At the end of each block of fifteen to twenty lessons at the same level of difficulty, the child had a review lesson covering all vocabulary words missed during the block of lessons. During this lesson, words were presented only once, and each correct word earned a five point token. If errors on review totaled more than 20 percent of the total new vocabulary for the set of lessons, the child was asked to repeat the block of lessons.

An emphasis in the program was placed on the business like nature of the session. The general attitude was that the child had a problem for which help was being provided. The tutor was expected to be generous but to reward for success and not effort alone. Haggling over points was discouraged. If any question arose concerning delivery of a token, the policy was to decide in favor of the child. The child was encouraged to insist upon his "payment" if a tutor forgot to deliver a token. A mistake on the tutor's part in delivering a token not earned was handled by allowing the child to keep the token. Children were also encouraged to count their own tokens, to understand and to check the tutor's calculations; thus, a general level of fairness was attempted at all times.

In our experience, money was the easiest back-up reinforcement to teach, distribute, and handle when the program was being carried out in many different schools by many different tutors. There was no reason, however, why other types of back-up reinforcements which have been used in other programs could not be used in a program such as the one described here.

The SMART program has received the support of the Denver Public Schools and was offered in any school which could provide individual tutors at least three days per week. Any child was eligible for a trial in the program if he or she was at least nine years old, had an IQ above 75, was reading at or below grade 3.0. Tutors were volunteers, paid aides or anyone who was literate, kindly in attitude toward children, dependable and able to follow instructions. A standard training program (Camp, in press) was developed with manuals (Camp & Staats, 1970), proficiency checks and regular monitoring so that we could reasonably claim that all children received similar instruction.

The average child in the program was ten years old, in fifth grade and had an IQ of 87. Each year we followed 100 to 120 children in ten to fifteen schools. Over a calendar year we usually trained seventy to eighty tutors who gave approximately 7000 to 7500 lessons.

## RESEARCH RESULTS

Our initial studies demonstrated that improvement in general attitude, behavior and school performance often accompanied enrollment in the tutorial program irrespective of whether the reading improved (Camp, 1971). We have also shown that a gain in reading was clearly related to the number of lessons completed irrespective of how long it took. Thus, it took approximately five months to complete 100 lessons, if a child received one lesson a day during the school week. As originally set up, the average child in our program made approximately three months of grade level progress in reading for each 100 lessons completed. Further, children in the tutoring program made significantly greater gains as compared to controls (Camp and van Doorninck, 1971).

The program also provided an opportunity to look at factors which affect learning. To do this some method for characterizing learning had to be developed. After examining several possible ways of describing learning, it was decided to look at the rate of error production in relationship to the number of correct respon-

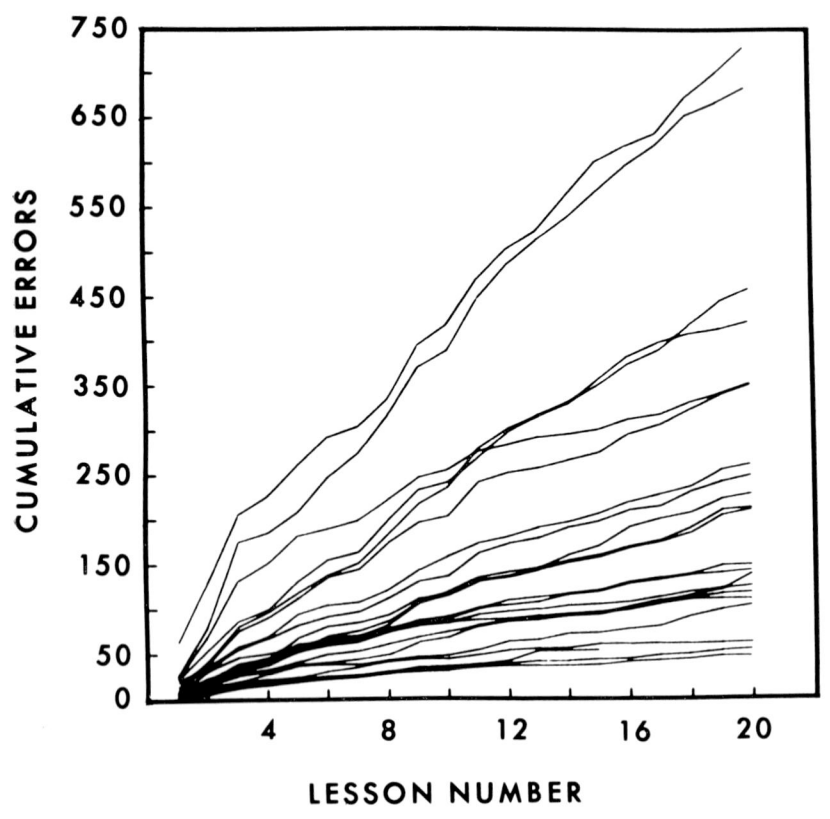

Figure XI-1. Learning Curves: SMART program.

ses. To do this all of the words in each lesson were counted and then curves were plotted showing the cumulative number of errors versus the cumulative number of words read correctly.

Initially it was expected that children with heterogenous learning problems would show diverse patterns in these curves. However, to our surprise the majority of children, despite their severe reading problems, showed learning curves characterized by an initial acceleration followed by a gradual deceleration. This is the same type of curve which has been observed in other learning tasks with normal children (Stake, 1961). Figure XI-1 displays a group of such curves for the least difficult lessons. These curves were chosen for display because there was more variation at this level than at any subsequent level.

Because of the regularity with which this characteristic curve appeared, we were encouraged to find a way of comparing slopes of curves obtained by children working at different levels of difficulty. Since learning curves have been known to vary with difficulty we needed to know whether learning rate would change as difficulty changed. A technique described by Rao (1958) for comparing growth curves was found to be applicable in this situation. Essentially this technique converts each curve to a straight line so that curves can be compared by an analysis of covariance of origin and slopes. Figure XI-2 shows a plot or origin and slopes of five different difficulty levels after transformation by the Roa technique. As expected from visual inspection, only the line for the sixty-one to eighty group differed significantly from the others. Inspection of the raw data indicated that the six children in this group were started on much easier material for their skill level than children in the other groups. Consequently we concluded that the curves did not differ from one level of difficulty to another if the relative difference between entering skill and difficulty was similar.

Based on these findings we grouped children together who actually worked with different lesson material for purposes of determining whether our measure of learning rate was related to any traditional variables. First it was shown that the learning rate was highly correlated with measures of retention and ability to progress to higher levels of difficulty (Camp, 1973a). Since some

*Learning Disability/MBD Syndrome*

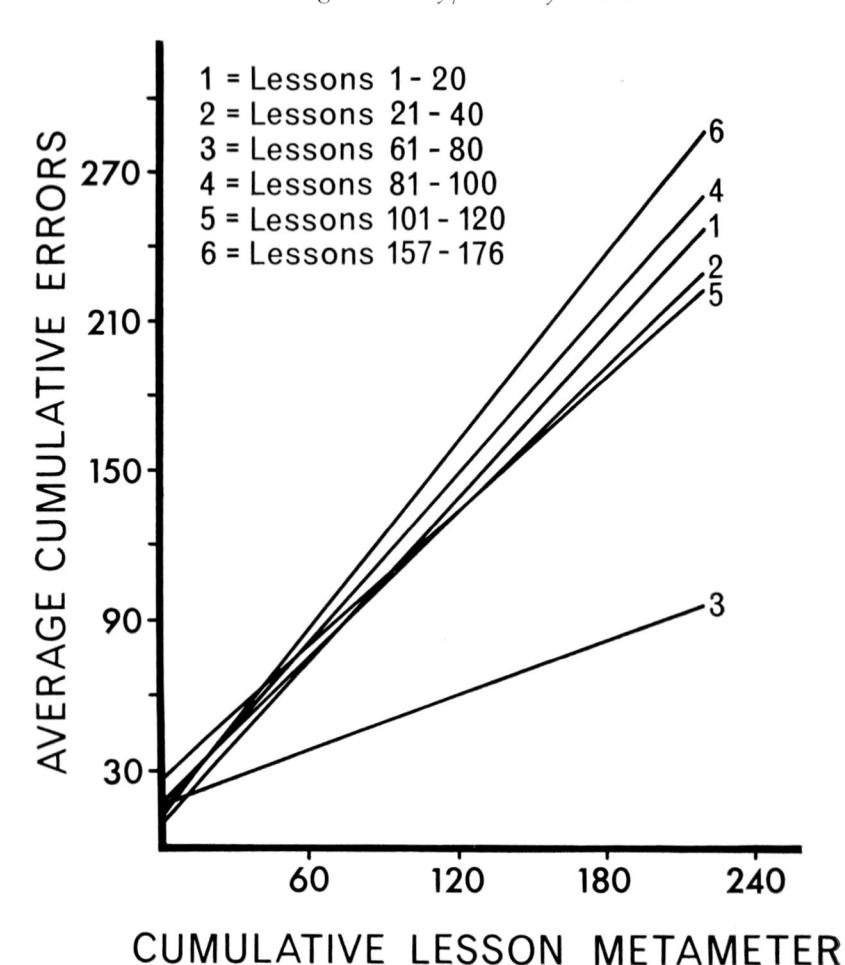

```
1 = Lessons   1 - 20
2 = Lessons  21 - 40
3 = Lessons  61 - 80
4 = Lessons  81 - 100
5 = Lessons 101 - 120
6 = Lessons 157 - 176
```

Figure XI-2. SMART program: Rao transformation learning curves.

children obviously did better than others, both in rate of learning and degree of retention, we next considered the question of whether psychometric tests used to make diagnostic statements about children would help to distinguish, ahead of time, between those who would and those who would not progress in the program. Selected tests were introduced prior to tutoring and then learning rate in the initial period was related to tests results (Camp, 1973b).

Tests were selected largely because of previous claims made either in terms of differentiating between good and poor readers or because of clinical experience with interpretation of these tests. The Bender-Gestalt for example was selected, despite literature negating its usefulness, because clinicians so often rely upon this test to make interpretations of visual-perceptual problems. We felt that if subjects in the present study were demonstrated to have equally or more severe problems with the Bender-Gestalt than normal children, this would at least support the contention that they were indeed representative of disabled children. The test of auditory-visual integration, on the other hand, was selected because differences had been demonstrated between good and poor readers at upper grade levels (Kahn & Birch, 1968; Sterritt & Rudnick, 1966; Zigmond, 1969) and by implication, could be causally related to persistence of the reading problem at that level. Sterritt and Rudnick's (1966) visual-spatial test of perception was used primarily to demonstrate that subjects in the present study did not have significant problems with input of visual materials. The Raven Progressive Matrices was selected as a potentially useful measure of intelligence and brain damage (Aftanas & Royce, 1969).

Tests were given prior to tutoring and every four to six months as long as children remained in the program. In addition, IQ scores, either from the Kuhlman-Anderson given by the schools, the WISC Verbal Scale, or the Stanford-Binet were available. From these scores, and an initial reading level obtained from the Wide

TABLE XI-I
DESCRIPTIVE STATISTICS OF TEST SCORES

| Variable | N | Mean | S.D. | Age Equiv. |
| --- | --- | --- | --- | --- |
| Age (in years) | 69 | 10.8 | 1.3 | 10.8 |
| School Grade | 69 | 5.1 | 1.2 | 10.5 |
| K-B[1] | 68 | 10.5 | 3.2 | 7.5 |
| Bender[1] | 66 | 5.7 | 2.7 | 7.5 |
| Raven[1] | 69 | 22.0 | 5.5 | 9.0 |
| S-R[1] | 68 | 19.9 | 2.5 | — |
| WRAT[1] | 69 | 2.3 | 1.1 | 7.5 |
| IQ | 44 | 87.7 | 10.1 | 9.5 |
| LQ | 37 | 83.0 | 10.0 | — |
| Learning Rate | 43 | .87 | .54 | — |

[1]Initial test administration
Adapted from B.W. Camp, "Psychometric Tests and Learning in Severely Disabled Readers," *Journal of Learning Disability*, 6:512 (1973).

Range Achievement Test (WRAT), a learning quotient (LQ) was calculated using Myklebust's (1968) formula.

Table XI-1 shows the initial scores and approximate age equivalent for the variables under consideration.

It is quite clear from the above table that children in this reading program showed the expected deficiency on the tests selected. Inter-correlation among the psychometric tests, LQ, IQ, and learning rate were then obtained. Significant correlations were found among all of the psychometric tests. However, neither LQ, IQ, nor performance on any of the reference tests were significantly related to learning rate.

A multiple regression analysis of variables influencing the follow-up WRAT score indicated that 84 percent of the variance could be accounted for by an equation combining $WRAT_1$, LQ, number of lessons between tests and time between tests. Using this equation to predict WRAT, we grouped children according to whether their actual WRAT was above or below expectancy. Table XI-II shows the test scores of the groups so constituted. The two groups do not differ significantly on reference tests but do show significant differences in learning rate and achievement.

TABLE XI-II

DESCRIPTIVE STATISTICS OF ALL MEASURES FOR GROUPS ACHIEVING ABOVE AND BELOW EXPECTANCY

|  | Below Expectancy | | | Above Expectancy | | |
| --- | --- | --- | --- | --- | --- | --- |
| Variable | N | Mean | S.D. | N | Mean | S.D. |
| K. B. | 17 | 10.7 | 3.0 | 15 | 10.3 | 3.5 |
| Bender | 16 | 5.2 | 2.9 | 14 | 5.9 | 2.2 |
| Raven | 17 | 21.8 | 6.0 | 15 | 23.3 | 3.9 |
| S-R | 17 | 20.5 | 2.3 | 15 | 20.1 | 2.3 |
| WRAT1 | 17 | 2.2 | .3 | 14 | 2.3 | .4 |
| WRAT2* | 17 | 2.3 | .4 | 17 | 2.8 | .6 |
| IQ | 17 | 88.6 | 5.3 | 15 | 91.2 | 12.0 |
| LQ | 17 | 83.0 | 8.4 | 15 | 85.0 | 10.2 |
| Initial Errors | 14 | 18.6 | 14.5 | 13 | 11.1 | 8.6 |
| Learning Rate** | 14 | 1.12 | .5 | 12 | .63 | .3 |

*Mann-Whitney U between groups = 75.5, p .02
**Mann-Whitney U between groups = 48.5, p .05
Reprinted from B.W. Camp, "Psychometric Tests and Learning in Severely Disabled Readers," Journal of Learning Disability, 6:512 (1973).

## SUMMARY AND CONCLUSIONS

We have demonstrated a significant relationship between our measures of learning rate and two types of achievement in the tutoring program but no relationship between psychometric tests and either our measure of learning rate or gain in the program. Though this may surprise clinicians, it is no surprise to those who have studied individual differences in learning among normals (Glaser, 1967; Jensen, 1967).

Since the measure of learning rate seemed robust, we decided to abandon the diagnostic testing and approach the problem from a different direction. First, we stated the problem as an attempt to define which variables determine whether a child will or will not make progress in this tutorial program. We also developed a working distinction between "no" progress and "slow" progress. Slow progress was present when the error rate showed a "normal" shaped curve with initial acceleration followed by a gradual deceleration and improvement occurred with repetition; "no progress" was defined as an instance in which either a high and linear error curve was noted or continuous acceleration occured over a set of lessons. Further, we centered attention on the development of decoding skill in the most severely disabled.

To explain differential rates of progress in decoding, we conceptualized the learning process in a manner resembling Miller's (1956) "leaky bucket" theory of memory. Thus, we reasoned that each exposure to a word placed it in a short-term memory store. Each lesson consisted of either placing words in the response pool for the first time (new vocabulary), or replacing lost words. A minimum requirement for learning to occur would be for the rate of placement (or replacement) to be greater than the rate of loss. A child making one error for every two correct responses would have a slope of .5. As the slope increases to 1.0, responses would be increasingly lost as fast as they were being placed or replaced in the memory store. At a slope of 1.0, the rate of loss would be proportional to the rate of placement. At this point, the error rate might be expected to remain the same, irrespective of changes in difficulty, etc., varying only with the number of words presented. Learning would not be occurring, however, because nothing would be accumulating. Between a slope of .5 and 1.0, the rate of loss would be so close to the rate of placement that for all practical purposes learning would be too slow to measure. On the other hand, the one situation in which learning must be occurring is the one in which there is evidence of a decreasing error rate even as difficulty increases. To demonstrate learning unequivocally, then, the goal of altering instructional procedures could be to produce a decreasing error rate. Our next step was to begin a series of procedural alterations to do precisely that. As we worked over a few obvious procedural changes aimed at increasing mastery at each stage before proceeding to more difficult material, shifts to harder material were easier and the average gain in reading increased from three months to five months after five to six months of lessons.

In one sense none of these observations are likely to be startling to educators. However, when one is dealing with a group of children carrying the stigmata of learning disability, it seems useful to point out that the *learning process* appeared to be intact in most of these children. The *rate* of learning did indeed vary from none to fast depending on the difficulty of the material facing the child and his or her level of mastery over prerequisite material. Thus, our findings support Hull's (Estes, 1970) view that individual differences in learning result from different values being attached to the set of variables related to growth of habit strength and not to differences in the learning process.

It is, of course, still possible that pathological pattern(s) of learning will yet be demonstrated. Indeed we continue to study very closely the children who remain in the "no progress" group after each procedural alteration has been made. Although it is tempting to neurologize about this non-learning group, we believe it will ultimately be more profitable to continue pursuing the question of how to modify learning rates through altering instructional procedures.

## REFERENCES

Aftanas, M. S., and Royce, J. R.: A factor analysis of brain damage tests administered to normal subjects with factor score comparisons across ages. *Multivariate Behavioral Research,* 4:459, 1969.

Camp, B. W.: Remedial reading in a pediatric clinic. *Clin Pediatr,* 10:36, 1971.

Camp, B. W.: Learning rate and retention in retarded readers. *Journal of Learning Disability,* 6:65, 1973 (a).

Camp, B. W.: Psychometric tests and learning in severely disabled readers. *Journal of Learning Disabilities, 6*:512, 1973 (b).
Camp, B. W.: Training tutors for a behavior-therapy reading program. In Bernal, M. E. (Ed.), *Training Social Agents in Behavior Modification.* Brooks-Cole, (In press).
Camp, B. W., and Staats, A. W.: *Staats Motivation Activation Reading Technique. A Guide to the Technique with Accompanying Lesson Materials,* unpublished manuscript, University of Colorado Medical School, 1970.
Camp, B. W., and van Doorninck, W. J.: Assessment of "motivated" reading in elementary school children. *Behavior Therapy, 2*:214, 1971.
Estes, W. K.: *Learning Theory and Mental Development.* New York, Academic Press, 1970, p. 101.
Glaser, R.: Some implications of previous work on learning and individual differences. In Gagne, R. M. (Ed.): *Learning and Individual Differences.* Columbus, Merrill, 1967.
Jensen, A. R.: Varieties of individual differences in learning. In Gagne, R. M. (Ed.): *Learning and Individual Differences.* Columbus, Merrill, 1967.
Kahn, C., and Birch, H. G.: Development of auditory-visual integration and reaching achievement. *Percept Mot Skills, 27*:259, 1968.
Miller, G. A.: Human memory and the storage of information. *IRE Trans Inform Theory, IT-2*:129-137, 1956.
Myklebust, H. R.: Learning disabilities: Definition and overview. In Myklebust, H. R. (Ed.): *Progress in Learning Disabilities.* New York, Grune and Stratton, 1968, vol. 1.
Rao, C. R.: Some statistical methods for comparison of growth curves. *Biometrics, 14*:1, 1958.
Ryback, D., and Staats, A. W.: Parents as behavior therapy-technicians in treating reading deficits (dyslexia). *Behavior Therapy and Experimental Psychiatry, 1*:109, 1970.
Staats, A. W., and Butterfield, W. H.: Treatment of nonreading in a culturally deprived juvenile delinquent; an application of reinforcement principles. *Child Dev 36*:925, 1965.
Staats, A. W., Minke, K. A., Goodwin, W., and Landeen, J.: Cognitive behavior modification; "motivated learning" reading treatment with sub-professional therapy-technicians. *Behav Res Ther, 5*:283, 1967.
Staats, A. W., Minke, K. A., and Butts, P.: A token-reinforcement remedial reading program administered by black therapy-technicians to backward black children. *Behav Ther, 1*:331, 1970.
Stake, R.: Learning parameters, aptitudes and achievements. *Psychometric Monographs,* No. 9, 1961.

Sterritt, G. M., and Rudnick, M.: Reply to Birch and Belmont. *Percept Mot Skills, 23*:662, 1966.

Zigmond, N. K.: Auditory processes in children with learning disabilities. In Tarnapol, L. A. (Ed.): *Learning Disabilities: Introduction to Educational and Medical Management.* Springfield, Thomas, 1969.

---Chapter XII---

# TWO BLINDED STUDIES OF THE EFFECTS OF STIMULANT DRUGS ON CHILDREN: PEMOLINE, METHYLPHENIDATE, AND PLACEBO

Roscoe A. Dykman, Jeanette McGrew,
T. Stuart Harris, John E. Peters, and
Peggy T. Ackerman

## INTRODUCTION

THE BROAD PURPOSE OF the two studies to be reported here was to evaluate the efficacy of pemoline (Cylert®), a new drug under study by Abbott Laboratories. The larger study (N=99), done last, compared pemoline and methylphenidate with each other and a placebo; whereas, the smaller study (N=18), done first, had only two treatment groups, pemoline and placebo. In the text below, the larger study will be abbreviated S-99 and the smaller one S-18.

Pemoline, a mild central nervous stimulant, was first studied in Germany in 1956 (Schmidt, 1956). While pemoline is classified as a stimulant, it is structurally dissimilar to the amphetamines and methylphenidate. It has certain similar pharmacological effects to the classical stimulants without significant sympathomimetic activity. This report will not be concerned with the safety of pemoline and methylphenidate; both have been shown to be safe on administration for up to two years. Currently, methylphenidate (Ritalin®, Ciba-Geigy) is the drug most often prescribed for children with hyperkinesis, short attention span, and learning problems.

Knights (1972) reviewed stimulant drug studies attempting to locate psychological tests most sensitive to drug-induced behavior change. He grouped laboratory and psychometric data into the following categories: motility, complex motor, attention and vigilance, new learning, intelligence measures, visual-motor-spatial, auditory perception and memory, verbal fluency, simple motor reactions, language learning and achievement, and problem solving. He found that motility tests (stablimetric chair, actometer, tremorgraph), complex motor skills (maze, holes, pegboard, Lincoln-Oseretsky), and attention and vigilance tasks (continous performance, picture completion, paper and pencil mazes, embedded figures) more reliably demonstrated a drug effect than other measures. Surprisingly, he found that langauge, learning, and achievement tests (WRAT, reading speed, reading comprehension) and problem solving tests (picture arrangement, block design, object assembly) yielded fewer significant drug related changes.

Knights summarized his review by saying, "First, there is no clear trend for any one test, a test battery, or tests of a particular ability to emerge as differentially sensitive to drug-placebo differences." He concluded that some sort of a multivariate analysis or test profile assessment is needed (Conners, 1971; Knights, 1972). A second general conclusion is that since teacher and parent behavior ratings seem to be more sensitive to drug effects than psychometric tests or laboratory procedures, these should be given major consideration in drug studies. These ratings directly assess important aspects of social interaction and classroom behavior.

There are many studies showing that hyperactive children receiving methylphenidate make more correct responses and fewer incorrect responses on continuous performance tests (Conners and Rothschild, 1968; Knights and Hinton, 1969; Sprague, et al., 1970; Sykes, et al., 1971). Both Conners and associates (1969) and Douglas (1973) have concluded that the major effects of stimulants are increased capacity for reflective thinking and inhibited performance. We (Dykman, et al., 1970; 1971) have emphasized the ability of a child to focus or sustain his attention as the major effect of stimulants and have postulated that decreased motor activity that often occurs with stimulant medication is a concomitant of improved attention.

## METHOD FOR S-99

The larger study (S-99) was a double-blind study, in which dosages of pemoline and methylphenidate, assumed to be equally effective, were compared with each other and with a placebo. The study lasted eight weeks and consisted of a pre-drug evaluation, placement on medication or placebo, and evaluation after four and eight weeks of medication. Drug assignment was made on a double-blind basis with a predetermined randomization procedure. Pemoline, methylphenidate, and the placebo were administered as identically appearing tablets. For patients assigned to pemoline, the starting dose was two 18.75 mg tablets of the active drug in the morning, and one placebo tablet in the early afternoon. One presumed advantage of pemoline is that an afternoon dose is not required. Patients assigned to methylphenidate initially received two 5 mg tablets in the morning and one 5 mg tablet in the early afternoon. The placebo group, likewise, received two tablets in the morning and one in the early afternoon. Dosage was increased in accordance with a regular schedule, but not to exceed one additional A.M. tablet and one P.M. tablet each week. The maximum permissible dose was six A.M. tablets and six P.M. tablets; i.e. 112.5 mg of pemoline/day and 60 mg of methylphenidate/day. The mean dosage of pemoline in terms of mg/kg/ day ranged from 1.13 in week one to 3.24 in the eighth week of study. The corresponding dosage-range for methylphenidate was 0.46 to 1.67 mg/kg/day. The average dosage was two to three times what some workers (Sleator and von Neumann, 1974; Sprague and Boileau, 1973) believe is necessary for optimal relevant effects in children. Dosage was adjusted dependent upon side effects in addition to home and school improvement as judged by one or the other parent or guardian. Since side effects of medication were evaluated weekly, this encouraged communication with parents.

Parents were told at the outset that their child had one third of a chance of getting sugar pills rather than active drug. However, they were not to inform the child of this possibility, but rather were asked to be very positive in telling their child that the medicine he was to take would help him to pay attention at school. Most parents realized that a positive attitude could be helpful with either a placebo or drug.

### SUBJECTS FOR S-99

We selected 105 subjects who satisfied the following criteria: six to twelve years old, WISC full scale IQ of 80 or above, physician diagnosis of hyperkinesis due to minimal brain dysfunction, relative family stability, no obsessive, compulsive or phobic behavior, visual and auditory acuity sufficient for normal learning process, laboratory values within established pediatric norms, no current medical illness or past medical history contraindicating drug therapy, discontinuance of all prior medications at least eight days prior to beginning test medications, no demonstrable or suspected need for anti-seizure medications, no concurrent therapy for chronic illness, a total of at least fifteen out of thirty possible points on the initial parent or teacher questionnaire form on items defining a hyperkinesis index (see below).

Of the 105 patents, eighty-nine were male and sixteen were female, and eighty were Caucasian and twenty-five black. A further breakdown according to age follows: six children were six years old, eighteen were seven years, eighteen were eight years, twenty-three were nine years, nineteen were ten years, fifteen were eleven years, and six were twelve years. The social distribution of the families for whom sufficient information was available to calculate the Hollingshead Index of Social Position follows: social class I (highest)—4 percent, class II—22 percent, class III—31 percent, class IV—36 percent, and class V—77 percent. Most of the children were enrolled in the public schools of Little Rock, Arkansas, and surrounding communities.

Six subjects were excluded from data analysis because the initial parent or teacher questionnaire was completed while the patient was still on prior medication. This report will focus on the ninety-nine patients that were judged acceptable for analysis of safety and efficacy according to protocol.

Prior to entering the study, each patient had a history and physical including an evaluation of visual acuity (Snellen chart) and adequacy of hearing (audiogram). The physical examination was repeated at four and eight weeks. Laboratory measures were also obtained prior to medication and at four and eight weeks: white blood count and differential, hematocrit, SGOT, LDH, BUN, total bilirubin, and urinalysis.

### Behavioral Ratings

The rating scales used in this study were derived from a ninety-three item parent questionnaire and a thirty-nine item teacher questionnaire developed by Conners (1969, 1970) in earlier studies. The original scales of Conners were factor analyzed to produce a forty-eight item parent questionnaire and a twenty-nine item teacher questionnaire. Items retained for each questionnaire were those that had the highest loadings on each factor. The factors are listed in the results section below.

The items from teacher and parent questionnaires which were used to select children follow: excitable, impulsive, learning difficulty; restless in the "squirmy" sense; restless, always up and on the go; fails to finish things; childish and immature; distractibility or attention span a problem; mood changes quickly and drastically; easily frustrated in efforts; denies mistakes or blames others; disturbs other children; and demands must be met immediately. Not all of these items appeared on both questionnaires; the tendency to be moody and to deny mistakes appeared only on the parent questionnaire, whereas, the tendency to disturb other children and to have demands met immediately appeared only on the teacher questionnaire. Thus, only ten of the items listed above (not the same ten) appeared on both the teacher and parent questionnaires, and these are referred to in the study as the hyperkinesis index. Each item on the questionnaire was rated "Not at All," "Just a Little," "Pretty Much," or "Very Much" (a 0 to 3 scale). Parent and teacher questionnaires were filled out prior to medication and at four and eight weeks.

In addition to the rating scale judgments, the physician, teacher and one parent were asked to make global ratings of improvement. These ratings were obtained at the same times as the other ratings, i.e. before the study and subsequently at four and eight weeks. In addition, the psychological examiner responsible for a child's psychometric evaluation made global ratings at zero and eight weeks. Global ratings were on a five point scale: much worse (1) worse (2) about the same (3) better (4) and much improved (5) The initial evaluation was a rating of where the child stood relative to peers of the same age; subsequent ratings were relative to the child's premedicated status.

## Standardized Tests

The following psychoeducational tests were administered to the children prior to medication and again at eight weeks: Weschler Intelligence Scale for Children, Wide Range Achievement Test, Harris Draw-a-Person Test, Porteus Maze (Vineland Revision for pre-drug state and Extension at eight weeks) and the Wepman Auditory Discrimination Test. We utilized two different examiners, but each child had the same examiner for all tests, pre- and post-drug.

## Continuous Performance Test

This task of sustained attention was first described by Rosvold, et al (1956), and has been recently used by Douglas and associates (see review by Douglas, 1973; Sykes, et al 1972). Children were tested in a very dimly lighted, sound-shielded room. After a three to five minute dark adaptation period, an examiner pointed to the apparatus and said: "Do you see this viewer? When the machine starts to turn, you will see letters appearing one at a time. Your job is to say each letter as it appears and to press this key every time you see an X. Use the same finger each time. Hit it and let go as quickly as you can (We demonstrated and let the child practice). Remember, press this key every time you see an X, but not for any other letter." Some subjects required additional instructions and practice. In the second phase of the experiment, the subject was told: "Your job in this next part is to again say each letter and press the key when you see an X, but this time, only if the X follows right after an A. That is, when you see the letter A, then X, press the key on the X. Do not press the key for any other letter following an A except X, but always press it then. Remember now, when you see the letter A, get set. If an X comes right after it, press the key." The child was then given a trial run and, if he failed, he was given additional instruction and practice. Very few children required additional help.

For each phase of this experiment, we recorded the number of correct responses to X and grouped them into two categories, early and late detections. The child received credit for an early detection if he pressed the key before an elapsed time of 700 msec. Four kinds of errors were scored: the number of missed X's (failure to respond), the number of responses to letters other than X, the number of responses occuring between letters, and the number of times the child named a letter incorrectly, (e.g. looked at a B and called it E). In the first procedure, the child saw eight-one letters with twenty-one X's; in the second, he viewed eight-one letters with fifteen X's that were preceded by A's.

The viewer was a standard Lafayette memory drum (model 2301), and the letters were made with a Leroy lettering set (#1 pen, 61-0300-140CL). In our test, each letter was illuminated 0.1 seconds, and the interstimulus interval was 2 seconds. In the Sykes, *et al.* (1972) experiment, the stimulus (letter) duration was 0.2 seconds and the interstimulus interval 1.5 seconds.

### METHOD FOR S-18

The protocol for this study was identical to S-99 in all details except the following: (a) Criteria for subject selection were more stringent. The child had to receive a score of 18 on teacher hyperkinesis index items and a combined score of not less than 36 on the combined teacher and parent hyperkinesis index, and his WISC full scale, performance, or verbal IQ had to be 90 or above; (b) Clinical and laboratory evaluation were made at three, six and nine weeks; (c) There were only two treatment conditions, drug (pemoline) and placebo.

In general, subjects were relatively more homogenous in S-18. Of the twenty subjects selected, one on placebo (#13) was dropped on the 26th day, due to severe back pain, and another (#1) was dropped after it was found that both parents had psychiatric hospitalization in the patient's early formative years. There were no black children in this study; the ages of all subjects (all males) were between seven and twelve. The weekly mean dosage was 0.99 mg/kg/day in week one and steadily increased thereafter to a mean of 2.48 mg/kg/day in the seventh week, remaining constant thereafter.

In S-18 several psychological tests in addition to those used in S-99 were given: Bender Visual Motor Gestalt Test, scored by the Koppitz method (Koppitz, 1964), ITPA visual sequencing subtest and the Lincoln-Oseretsky Motor Development Scale (but only those items for Factor I, II, and III). These children did not, however, participate in the Continuous Performance Test procedure.

## RESULTS

Tables XII-I and XII-II present data on the global evaluations analyzed by univariate analysis of variance in S-99 and by standard $t$ tests for independent samples in S-18 (completely randomized designs). Raw mean global scores improved in all treatment groups in both studies, but did so to a greater degree in the active drug groups than in the placebo group. There was a much greater parent placebo effect in S-99 than in S-18, and several factors singly or conjointly could explain this. In S-99, parents were instructed that placebo could have an effect and were told to be very positive in telling their children that the medication would help them in school. S-18 parents were told only that their child might get a sugar pill. Also, while there were no black subjects in S-18, chance ruled in S-99 that the placebo group had a larger proportion of lower class black children than the drug groups.

As may be seen in Table XII-I, children on methylphenidate improved overall more than those on placebo or pemoline (see ratings at eighth week). Global ratings for both S-99 and S-18 indicate, however, that pemoline is beneficial.

Tables XII-III and XII-IV present the changes in mean factor scores on the teacher rating scales. While there were no significant

TABLE XII-II
GLOBAL RATINGS FOR S-18
PERCENTAGE OF CASES IMPROVED

|  | Week 3 | | Week 6 | | Week 9 | |
| --- | --- | --- | --- | --- | --- | --- |
|  | *Placebo* | *Pemoline* | *Placebo* | *Pemoline* | *Placebo* | *Pemoline* |
| Physician | 20.6 | 33.3 | 22.2 | 44.4 | 11.1 | 66.6* |
| Teacher | 33.3 | 77.7 | 33.3 | 55.5 | 33.3 | 66.6 |
| Parent | 50.0 | 77.7 | 37.5 | 66.6 | 37.5 | 77.7* |
| Psychologist | — | — | — | — | 33.3 | 66.6 |

*Pemoline $>$ placebo (p. 05)

## TABLE XII-I
### GLOBAL RATINGS FOR S-99
### PERCENTAGE OF CASES IMPROVED

|  | Week 4 ||| Week 8 |||
|---|---|---|---|---|---|---|
|  | Placebo | Pemoline | Methylphenidate | Placebo | Pemoline | Methylphenidate |
| Physician | 35.3 | 67.6 | 66.7 | 44.1 | 66.7 | 73.3* |
| Teacher | 37.5 | 43.8 | 54.8 | 38.7 | 53.1 | 78.6*** |
| Parent | 57.1 | 73.3 | 60.0 | 70.0 | 70.4 | 87.0 |
| Psychologist | — | — | — | 20.6 | 81.8** | 73.7** |

\*Methylphenidate > placebo (p. 05)
\*\*Methylphenidate and pemoline > placebo (p. 01)
\*\*\*Methylphenidate > placebo and pemoline (p. 01)

## TABLE XII-III
### CHANGES IN MEAN FACTOR SCORES IN S-99
### TEACHER RATINGS

|  | Pemoline vs. Placebo || Methylphenidate vs Placebo || Pemoline vs Methylphenidate ||
|---|---|---|---|---|---|---|
|  | 4 weeks | 8 weeks | 4 weeks | 8 weeks | 4 weeks | 4 weeks |
| I. Aggressive-Antisocial | NS | NS | NS | .01 | NS | NS |
| II. Restless-Hyperactive | NS | .01 | NS | .01 | NS | NS |
| III. Emotionalism | NS | .01 | NS | .01 | NS | NS |
| IV. Distractibility | NS | .01 | NS | .01 | NS | NS |
| V. Immaturity | NS | NS | NS | NS | NS | NS |
| Hyperkinesis Index* | NS | NS | NS | .01 | NS | NS |

*This *a priori* index had many items in common with Factor II

### TABLE XII-IV
### CHANGES IN MEAN FACTOR SCORES IN S-18

| | | Pemoline vs Placebo | | |
|---|---|---|---|---|
| | | 3 weeks | 6 weeks | 9 weeks |
| I. | Aggressive-Antisocial | .05 | NS | .05 |
| II. | Restless-Hyperactive | .05 | .05 | NS |
| III. | Emotionalism | NS | NS | .05 |
| IV. | Distractibility | NS | NS | .05 |
| V. | Immaturity | NS | NS | NS |
| | Hyperkinesis Index* | .05 | .05 | .05 |

*See footnote to Table XII-III

changes produced by either pemoline or methylphenidate at four weeks in S-99, by eight weeks, drug effects were obvious with little difference between the two active drugs. In S-18, we obtained significant drug effects at three weeks on two factors and on the hyperkinesis index. At nine weeks, in the smaller study, all teacher rating factors other than restless-hyperactive and immaturity were significantly improved. Interestingly, teacher ratings, grouped by factors, yielded more significant effects than their global evaluations. Thus, teachers may be better in rating specific items of behavior than in making global judgments.

Tables XII-V and XII-VI show the changes in mean factor scores for parent ratings. There are fewer significant differences than for teacher ratings. The major items of significance pertain to

### TABLE XII-VI
### CHANGES IN MEAN FACTOR SCORES IN S-18
### PARENT RATINGS

| | | Pemoline vs. Placebo | | |
|---|---|---|---|---|
| | | 3 weeks | 6 weeks | 9 weeks |
| I. | Aggressive-Antisocial | .05 | .05 | .05 |
| II. | Emotionalism | .05 | .05 | .01 |
| III. | Restless/Inactive | NS | NS | .05 |
| IV. | Somaticism/Aches & Pains | NS | NS | NS |
| V. | Nervous Habits | NS | NS | NS |
| VI. | Fearful | NS | NS | NS |
| VII. | Sociopathic | NS | NS | NS |
| VIII. | Somatic/GI Complaints | NS | NS | NS |
| | Hyperkinesis Index* | NS | NS | .05 |

*See footnote on Table V

## TABLE XII-V
### CHANGES IN MEAN FACTOR SCORES IN S-99 PARENT RATINGS

|  | Pemoline vs. Placebo 4 weeks | Pemoline vs. Placebo 8 weeks | Methylphenidate vs. Placebo 4 weeks | Methylphenidate vs. Placebo 8 weeks | Pemoline vs. Methylphenidate 4 weeks | Pemoline vs. Methylphenidate 8 weeks |
|---|---|---|---|---|---|---|
| I. Aggressive-Antisocial | .01 | .01 | NS | NS | NS | NS |
| II. Emotionalism | NS | NS | NS | NS | NS | NS |
| III. Restless/Inactive | .05 | .01 | NS | .05 | NS | NS |
| IV. Somaticism/Aches & Pains | NS | NS | NS | NS | NS | NS |
| V. Nervous Habits | NS | NS | NS | .05 | NS | NS |
| VI. Fearful | NS | NS | NS | .01 | NS | NS |
| VII. Sociopathic | NS | .01 | NS | NS | NS | NS |
| VIII. Somatic/GI Complaints | NS | NS | NS | .05 | NS | NS |
| Hyperkinesis Index* | .01 | NS | NS | NS | NS | NS |

This *a priori* scale has many items in common with Factor III.

TABLE XII-VII

MEAN GAIN IN PSYCHOLOGICAL TEST SCORES FOR S-99

|  | Pemoline | Methylphenidate | Placebo | Overall F Sig. Level |
|---|---|---|---|---|
| WISC Full Scale | 5.7 | 6.4 | 1.4 | .01 |
| WISC Performance | 9.6 | 9.7 | 4.0 | .05 |
| WISC Vocabulary | 0.0 | 1.1 | 0.0 | .05 |
| WISC Coding | 1.8 | 2.5 | 0.5 | .01 |
| WRAT Reading Grade | 0.4 | 0.4 | 0.0 | .01 |

aggressive-antisocial tendencies and activity. There the effects overall are more consistent for pemoline than for methylphenidate, which could reflect the longer lasting effects of pemoline persisting after school hours.

Table XII-VII presents significant psychological test results for S-99, showing the mean gains in scores from zero to week eight. The last column gives the overall F values testing the hypothesis of equal mean changes. Duncan's Multiple Range Test for the F values shown in Table XII-VII indicated that except for Vocabulary, there were no significant differences between pemoline and methylphenidate. Both active drugs produced significant effects on the other measures relative to the placebo. On Vocabulary, methylphenidate was superior to pemoline as well as placebo, while pemoline and placebo did not differ.

In S-18, Figure XII-VII all IQ change scores were significant, and the subtests contributing most were Information ($p < .05$), Block Design ($p < .05$), and Object Assembly ($p < .10$). Of the other standard test measures, only Factor II of the Lincoln-Oseretsky showed a statistically significant drug effect. This factor includes the following items: 19) making circles in the air with fingers; 17) making dots on paper without moving the arms; 27) paper and pencil mazes; 29) tapping feet alternately while taping with the index fingers in unison with movements of only the right foot; and 35) opening and closing hands while rotating palms one way and fists in the opposite direction. None of the WRAT change scores were significant in the smaller study, although all showed gains relative to placebo. In both S-99 and S-18, gains in performance IQ were greater than in verbal IQ. Unfortunately, as we have shown elsewhere, verbal IQ subtests relate more closely to school

TABLE XII-VIII
PSYCHOMETRIC DATA FOR S-18

|  | Change Scores From 0 to 9 Weeks |
|---|---|
| WISC Verbal IQ | .01 |
| WISC Performance IQ | .01 |
| WISC Full Scale IQ | .01 |
| WRAT Reading | NS |
| WRAT Spelling | NS |
| WRAT Arithmetic | NS |
| Porteus Mazes | NS |
| ITPA Visual Sequential Memory | NS |
| Wepman Auditory Perception | NS |
| Bender Visual Motor Gestalt Test | NS |
| Harris Draw-a-Person | NS |
| Lincoln-Oseretsky Motor Performance Factor I | NS |
| Lincoln-Oseretsky Motor Performance Factor II | .05 |
| Lincoln-Oseretsky Motor Performance Factor III | NS |

success than performance subtests (Ackerman, et al., 1971 a, b; Dykman, et al., 1973). Both verbal and performance IQ changes were greater in S-18 than in S-99; Figure XII-I shows the data for S-18.

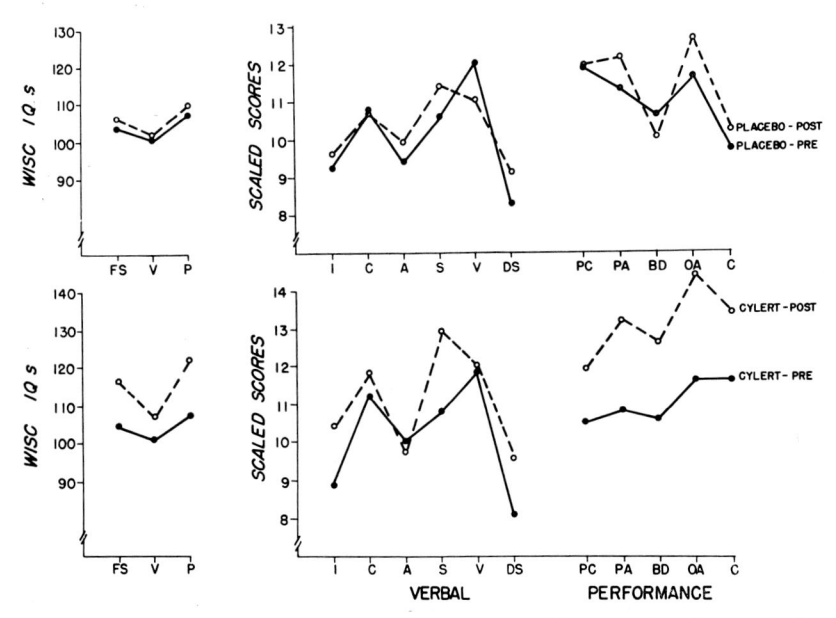

Figure XII–1. WISC measures for S–18 subjects. The interval between testing was nine weeks. Cylert® is the trade name for pemoline.

For the Continuous Performance test, we looked first at group means overall. In terms of correct detections, whether early or late, and for the X and AX conditions combined, 59 percent of the placebo patients showed some improvement or remained at 100 percent detection going from the pre- to the post-condition. The corresponding figures for the methylphenidate and pemoline conditions were 73 percent and 64 percent, respectively. Focusing on *early detection alone,* X and AX combined, the percentages of improvement were placebo 55 percent, methylphenidate 77 percent, and pemoline 48 percent. The mean gains in correct early detections from pre-drug to the end of the experiment were 1.2 for placebo, 5.6 for methylphenidate, and 1.4 for pemoline (Fig. XII-2). Of the three possible paired contrasts for the data, only the methylphenidate versus placebo effect was significant (Chi-square = 4.69, 2 df, $p < .05$, one-tailed test). That is, methylphenidate did not result in statistically superior performance than pemoline for X and AX combined.

Considering only the AX condition and early detection, however, methylphenidate was not only superior to placebo (Chi-square

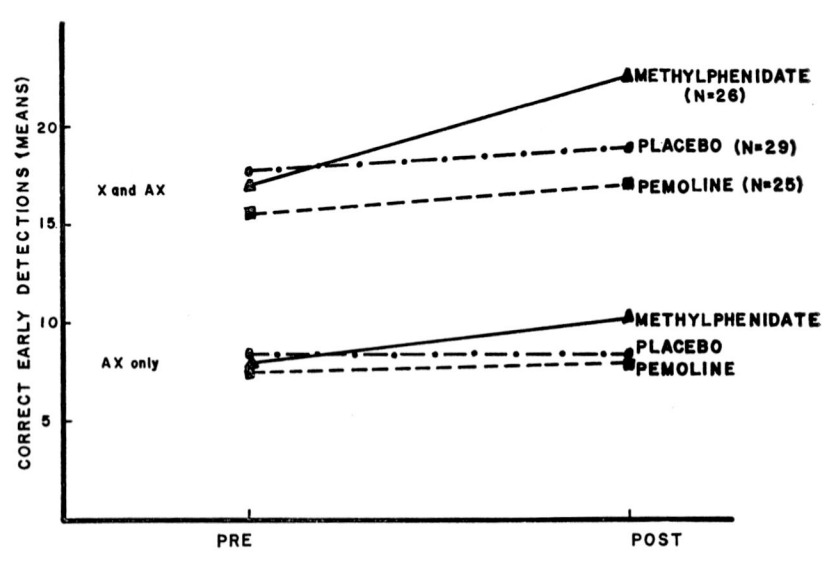

Figure XII-2. Continuous Performance test scores, pre- and post-drug. Mean number of correct early detections are plotted for the X and AX conditions combined and for the AX condition alone.

= 7.08, 3 df, p < .05, one tailed test), but to pemoline as well (Chi-square = 7.70, 3 df, p < .05, one-tailed test). Scores were divided into quartiles for these comparisons because of increased variability in the methylphenidate group.

Performance in the AX condition was age related. Considering pre-treatment scores, younger subjects in all groups made fewer correct early detections for the AX condition than did older subjects (Chi-square = 7.20, 1 df, p < .01, two-tailed test). This age advantage continued into the posttreatment condition (Chi-square = 8.45, 1 df, p < .01, two-tailed test). Moreover, there was a significant age and treatment interaction effect in the AX condition. It was older subjects on methylphenidate who improved most significantly, and more so than would be expected on the basis of age alone. This interaction was not true for pemoline subjects. Contrary to frequently voiced clinical opinion, then, methylphenidate may have a more desirable effect on performance of children above age nine than with younger children.

Because of pre-drug differences between groups for total error

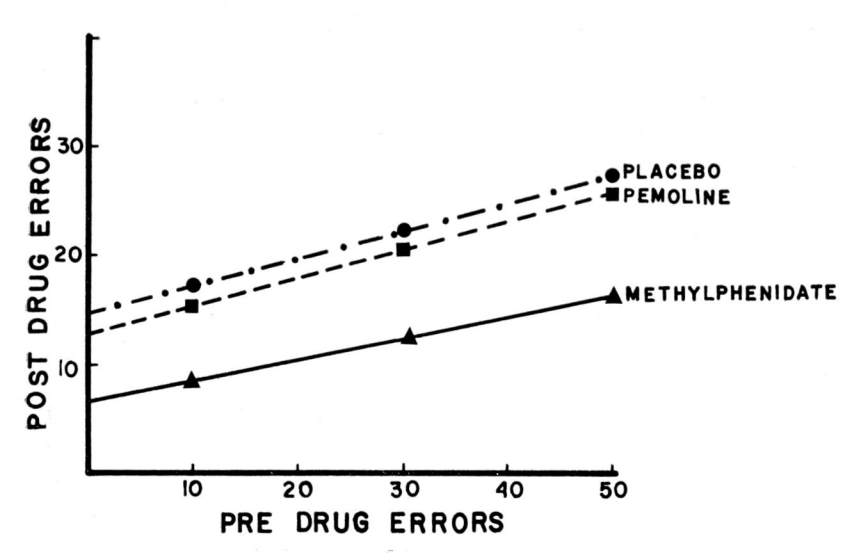

Figure XII–3. Regression equations for total error scores is the Continuous Performance test. In the equations below, X = pre-drug error score and Y' = expected post-drug score. For the placebo group. Y' — .213X + 15.3, while for the pemoline group, Y' — .250X + 13.3 and for the methylphenidate group Y' = .186X + 6.6.

scores in the Continuous Performance tests (X and AX), regression equations were computed to demonstrate change. Figure XII-3 shows, for example, that a subject who made twenty-five errors in the pre-drug condition would have reduced his errors to eleven in the post-drug condition had he been on methylphenidate, but only to nineteen had he been on pemoline and twenty-one had he been on placebo. Thus, on the error measure also, methylphenidate produced more improvement than pemoline or placebo.

## DISCUSSION

The two studies reported here have several advantages over many earlier studies of hyperactive children given stimulant drugs; in the one, a larger N, and for both a reasonably long period of observation (eight or nine weeks) and a rather well-defined subject population. The results are generally consistent with those reported by others for methylphenidate. Clearly, on the measures utilized in S-99, pemoline was not as effective as methylphenidate. While one main effect of stimulants is upon attentional processes (Douglas, 1973; Dykman, *et al.*, 1971), this is by no means the only effect. Indeed, considering the behavioral factors that were rated as improved, it would appear that both pemoline and methylphenidate had effects upon both attentional and *intentional* processes, behaviors that are presumably regulated by the frontal limbic cortex (Milner, 1963; Pribram, 1967).

While many of the psychological test results, including ratings, fall short of statistically significant improvement, nearly all variables studied changed more as a result of drugs than placebo. Thus, stimulants seem to have some general factor (G) effect on all aspects of behavior. One troubling problem in demonstrating particular drug effects on psychological test scores is that the subtests are too short to have satisfactory reliability (Dykman, *et al.*, 1974a). This is particularly true for the Digit Span and Arithmetic subtests of the WISC, the Visual Sequential Memory test of the Illinois Test of Psycholinguistic Abilities, and the three subtests of the Wide Range Achievement Test. Additionally, some tests do not have enough top to show drug effects. Such a problem was encountered in the analysis of our Continuous Performance data: several subjects performed at 100 percent in both pre- and post-drug evaluations. Certainly errors are a function of the amount of time in a situation as well as task difficulty. Had we kept the children at the Continuous Performance task a longer time, we possibly could have shown a pemoline as well as methylphenidate effect.

The above problems notwithstanding, the major fault of typical drug efficacy studies is that no attempt is made to identify the characteristics of individual children who do and do not improve on medication. For example, some children in our studies made very significant gains on pemoline, and, indeed, when they were transferred to methylphenidate after the study ended, they did not do as well at home or school. Their parents then requested transfer back to pemoline. The question we must carefully consider is not so much that of whether one stimulant is better than another, but, rather, what drug is best for which child. Our evidence overall indicates that pemoline would be a useful alternate to methylphenidate in the medication management of hyperactive-impulsive children (see also Dykman, et al., 1974b).

## REFERENCES

Ackerman, P. T., Peters, J. E., and Dykman, R. A.: Children with specific learning disabilities: Bender-Gestalt test findings and other signs. *Journal of Learning Disabilities, 4*:437-446 (a), 1971.

Ackerman, P. T., Peters, J. E., and Dykman, R. A.: Children with specific learning disabilities: WISC profiles. *Journal of Learning Disabilities, 4*:150-166 (b), 1971.

Conners, C. K.: A teacher rating scale for use in drug studies with children. *Am J Psychiatry, 126*:884-888, 1969.

Conners, C. K.: Symptom patterns in hyperkinetic, neurotic, and normal children. *Child Dev, 41*:667-682, 1970.

Conners, C. K.: Drugs in management of learning disabilities. In Tarnopol, L. (Ed.): *Learning Disorders in Children.* Boston, Little, 1971, p. 253-301.

Conners, C. K., and Rothschild, G.: Drugs and learning in children. In Hellmuth, J. (Ed.): *Learning Disorders.* Seattle, Special Children Publications, 1968, vol III.

Conners, C. K., Rothschild, G. H., Eisenberg, L., Schwartz, L., and Robinson, E.: Dextroamphetamine sulfate in children with learning disorders: Effects on perception, learning and achievement. *Arch Gen Psychiatry, 21*:182-190, 1969.

Douglas, V. I.: Sustained attention and impulse control: Implications for the handicapped child. In Sweats, J. A., and Elliott, L. L. (Ed.):

*Psychology and the Handicapped Child.* Washington, Office of Education, 1973.

Dykman, R. A., Ackerman, P. T., Clements, S. D. and Peters, J. E.: Specific learning disabilities: An attentional deficit syndrome. In Mykelbust, H. R. (Ed.): *Progress in Learning Disabilities.* New York, Grune & Stratton, 1971, vol. II, p. 56-93.

Dykman, R. A., Ackerman, P. T., Peters, J. E., and McGrew, J.: Psychological tests. In Conners, C. K. (Ed.): Clinical use of stimulant drugs. Excerpta Medica, 1974, p. 44-52. (a)

Dykman, R. A., McGrew, J., and Ackerman, P. T.: A double-blind clinical study of pemoline in MBD children: Comments on the psychological test results. In Conners, C. K. (Ed.): Clinical use of stimulant drugs. Excerpta Medica, 1974, p 125-129. (b)

Dykman, R. A., Peters, J. E., and Ackerman, P. T.: Experimental approaches to the study of minimal brain dysfunction: A follow-up study. *Ann NY Acad Sci, 205*:93-108, 1973.

Dykman, R. A., Walls, R. C., Suzuki, R., Ackerman, P. T., and Peters, J. E.: Children with learning disabilities: Conditioning, differentation and the effect of distraction. *Am J Orthopsychiatry, 40*: 766-782, 1970.

Knights, R. M.: *Psychometric assessment of stimulant-induced behavior change,* paper presented at the Abbott Laboratories "Symposium on the Clinical Use of Stimulant Drugs in Children." Key Biscayne, March, 1972.

Knights, R. M., and Hinton, G. G.: The effects of methylphenidate (Ritalin) on the motor skills and behavior of children with learning problems. *J Nerv Ment Dis, 148*:643-653, 1969.

Milner, B.: Effects of different brain lesions on card sorting. *Arch Neurol 9*:90-100, 1963.

Pribram, K. H.: Memory and the organization of attention. In Lindsley, D. B., and Lumsdaine, A. A. (Eds.): *Brain function and learning.* Berkeley, U Calif Pr, 1967, p. 79-122.

Rosvold, H. E., Mirsky, A. F., Sarason, I., Bransome, E. D., and Beck, L. H.: A continuous performance test of brain damage. *J Consult Psychol, 20*:343-350, 1956.

Schmidt, L.: 5-phenyl-2-imino-4oxo-oxazolidine, a control stimulant. *Arzneimittel Forsch, 6*:423, 1956.

Sleator, E. K., and von Neumann, A. W.: Methylphenidate in the treatment of hyperkinetic children. *Clin Pediatr, 13*:19-24, 1974.

Sprague, R. L., Barnes, K. R., and Werry, J. S.: Methylphenidate and thioridazine: Learning, reaction time, activity, and classroom behavior is disturbed children. *Am J Orthopsychiatry, 40*:615-627, 1970.

Sprague, R. L. and Boileau, R. A.: Are drugs safe? In Sprague, R. L.

(Chm): *Psychopharamacology of children with learning disabilities,* Symposium presented at the American Psychological Association, Montreal, 1973.

Sykes, D. H., Douglas, V. I., Weiss, G., and Minde, K.: Attention in hyperactive children and the effect of methylphenidate (Ritalin). *J Child Psychol Psychiatry, 12*:129-139, 1971.

Chapter XIII

# MEMORY ANALYSIS: SHORT-, AND LONG-TERM MEMORY IN LEARNING DISABLED CHILDREN

Philip H. Marshall, Robert P. Anderson
Philip A. Tate

ONE OF THE BASIC psychometric signs reported as a significant feature of the learning disability/minimal brain dysfunction syndrome relates to memory deficit, and a great deal of emphasis has been placed on the memory problems of learning disabled (LD) youngsters. The sequential memory subscales of the Illinois Test of Psycholinguistic Abilities (ITPA) for example, provide the clinician with data regarding the child's ability to process new information. The studies of Bean (1967) and Lewis, Bell, and Anderson (1970), among others, have affirmed that LD children do indeed appear to have problems in remembering material when immediate recall is expected from short term memory. An implicit assumption frequently made by clinicians and educators is that low scores on various measures designed to evaluate short-term memory (STM) mean that the youngster has a deficit and a poorly developed capacity in his/her ability to remember newly presented material. It is presented as evidence that the LD child is different from normal or non-LD children. However, if the child's memory storage system is different in some way then it is reasonable to assume that this deficit would appear under all conditions. Anderson, Beal, and Helabian (1974) factor analyzed the WISC and the ITPA scores for fifty LD boys. It was expected that all subtests apparently related to STM would factor out together, at least on one factor. Contrary to exception, the WISC digit span did not load on the same factor as the ITPA Visual Sequential Memory and Auditory Sequential Memory. An obvious conclusion is that these tests do not measure the same thing, contrary to accepted clinical assumption that they are measuring the same aspect of memory. A further implication, and one which provides the impetus for the research being reported, is that the memory processes in LD children are not very well understood and have not been scrutinized under rigorous experimental conditions.

The intent of the present investigation was to analyze the memory processes in LD children. The proposed research was viewed as a practical application of principles derived from basic research concerning memory. It was seen as the beginning of a series of investigations culminating in a more cogent and structured account of learning dysfunction.

The theoretical framework which provided the foundation for the study is centered on the currently discussed distinction in human memory between short-term memory (STM) and long-term memory (LTM) (See Adams, 1967; and Kintsch, 1970 for reviews). In applying this distinction to LD children, newly learned information is often forgotten in a relatively short period of time suggesting that the mechanisms for the transfer of information from STM to LTM storages are either nonexistent or seriously impaired. The task in this initial investigation was to ascertain if, and if so, to what degree, the transfer mechanisms from STM to LTM are impaired. To investigate these aspects of memory the procedure of free recall of word lists was utilized. Investigations of free recall typically find superior recall of items at the beginning primacy effect) and at the end (recency effect) of word lists, with poorer recall from the middle portions of the list. The superior recall from initial portions is usually attributed to the increased likelihood that such information will make it into the LTM through differential rehearsal. Superior recall of items from the end of the list is attributed to information in STM, which is at the time of recall still available to the subjects.

The research rationale employed in the study has also been used in other clinical situations. The experiment of Baddeley and Warrington (1970) closely parallels our own research efforts. These investigators were concerned with an analysis of STM and LTM in patients with clinically diagnosed amnesia with an organic basis. Six subjects were chosen, all of whom had a central neurologic impairment. Their performance on a free recall task was compared with six control subjects, comparable in age, and IQ, all of whom suffered from peripheral nerve damage. The investigators found the amnesic subjects displayed almost identical STM functioning with the normal subjects, however, their LTM, that is, the primacy portion of the free recall curve, was substantially reduced compared to that of the normal subjects. The results of that investigation illustrate very nicely that amnesics had "normal" STM but impaired LTM.

The rationale for our study was basically very simple and comparable to the Baddely and Warrington investigation. If two groups of children, one LD, the other normal, are similar in their recall of the end items of a word list, and different in terms of their ability to recall initial terms in the word list, with the normals being superior, it may be presumed that this difference is a function of a deficit in the transfer of information to LTM among the LD children. An information processing account would attribute this to differences in processing. If theoretical expectations are born out then "strategies" for helping the children to transfer newly experienced input to LTM can be investigated.

## METHOD

### Design

Two groups of children, one classified as LD and the other classified as normal, took part in a single trial free recall task. The task required individual presentation of a number of items which made up a list. After the last item in the list was shown, the child attempted to recall as many items from the list as possible, without regard to the original input order. Our interest was in a comparison of primacy and recency effects between the

LD and normal groups, with the expectation that the task would reveal deficient LTM transfer processes in the LD group.

## Subjects

The $Ss$ were thirty children diagnosed by school psychologists or counselors as LD, and at the time of testing the children were enrolled in special classes for LD children. The normal group was composed of thirty children having no demonstrable learning disabilities. Both groups consisted of boys and girls and ranged in age from seven to nine years. The LD group had a mean age of 8.55 years, and the normal group a mean age of 8.34 years. There were six girls and twenty-four boys in the LD sample, and eighteen girls and twelve boys in the normal group. In choosing $Ss$ all potential subjects with I.Q.'s below 85 were excluded from the sample. The mean I.Q. for the LD group was 97, and 105 for the normal group. The standard deviation of I.Q. for both groups was approximately eight points. The measures of intelligence for each group were obtained from school records and were derived from various instruments.

## Materials and Apparatus

The lists were composed of pictures of common objects such as "squirrel," "broom," "man," "school," etc. In this initial investigation a multi-modal presentation was utilized. In addition to the picture of the object, the name of the object appeared on the picture, and as a supplement, the $E$ spoke the name of the object as the picture was being presented.

Ten such lists were shown to each child, and each list was constructed by choosing randomly eleven different objects. There were no repetitions of objects across lists since each object was assigned to only one list.

## Procedure

The children participated individually in the thirty minute session. After being escorted into the laboratory, the instructions describing the task were read to the $S$. The child was first thoroughly briefed on the instructions, and then a practice trial was given consisting of the presentation and recall of a list of six objects. The pictures were exposed one at a time with an exposure duration of five seconds per picture. After the last item in the list was presented the child was asked to name as many of the items as he could remember without regard to any specific order.

The practice procedure was followed by the presentation of the ten criterion lists. The lists were presented according to a 10 x 10 Latin square with an equal number of children in each group receiving each order. The children were given forty-five seconds to recall the objects from the current list, after which a thirty second period elapsed before presentation of the next list.

### RESULTS AND DISCUSSION

The initial hypothesis stated that a flatter primacy (LTM) portion of the serial position curve would be found for LD children because of their hypothesized deficiency in transferring information to LTM. However, it was assumed that the recency (STM) portion of the serial position curve would be the same for both groups.

Figure XIII-1 shows the serial position curves for both groups with each point on that curve based upon 300 observations (thirty children in each group times the ten lists each). Both groups yielded clear serial position effects with quite obvious primary and recency effects, and with recency showing the usual superiority over primacy. The main information contained in Figure XIII-1 is that contrary to prediction, the LD group does not show a flatter primacy effect than the normal group.

It is also apparent from Figure XIII-1 that although the normal group recalled more items overall, the two groups were processing the input in the same manner. That is, whatever processes were at work to contribute to the development of primacy and recency, it is reasonable to assume they were the same for both groups. This fact obtains even more support from observation of the local variations seen in Figure XIII-1, which suggest that there were two parallel, but clearly separate, functions.

Figure XIII-2 depicts another aspect of performance on this free recall task. Whereas Figure XIII-1 described the probability that the $S$ would correctly recall the item given a particular serial position, Figure XIII-2 shows for each group the mean output

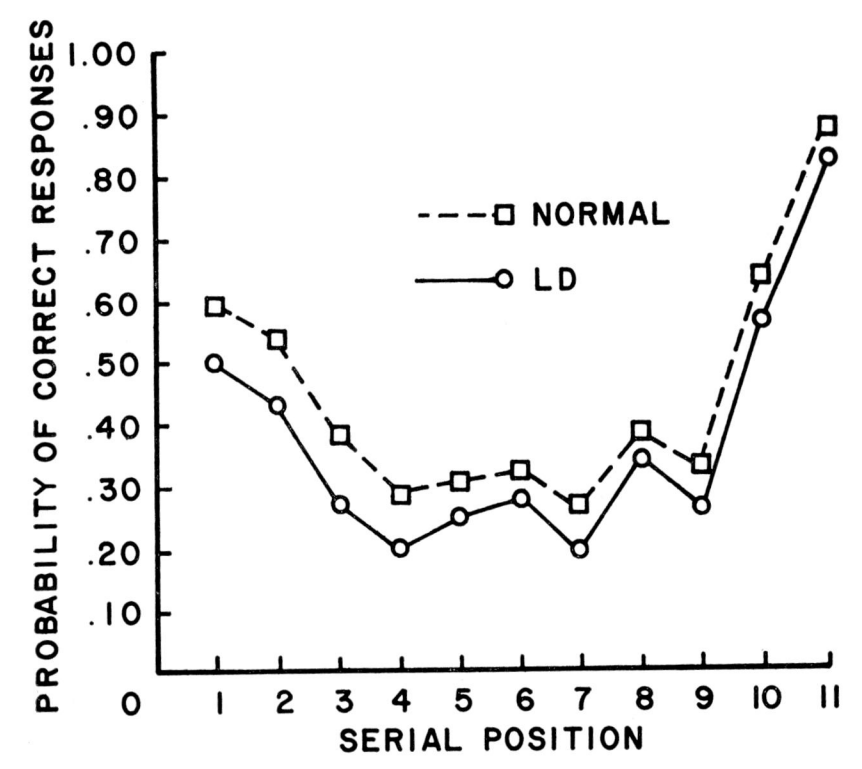

Figure XIII–1. Proportion of responses correct as a function of serial position for each group.

position for each input position. That is, given a response was correct, Figure XIII-2 gives its mean output position among correctly recalled items on the response protocol. For both the LD and normal groups the last couple of items are retrieved first and these are followed by items from the initial portion of the list, and finally by items from the middle of the list.

The number of intrusion errors from previous lists may be offered as a more subtle aspect of the recall data. The total number of intrusions was twenty-nine for LD and twenty-six for the normal. Thus, whatever factors were at work to differentiate lists, and the items in the lists, they appear to be the same for both groups.

Figure XIII-3 presents a plot of the serial position curves for

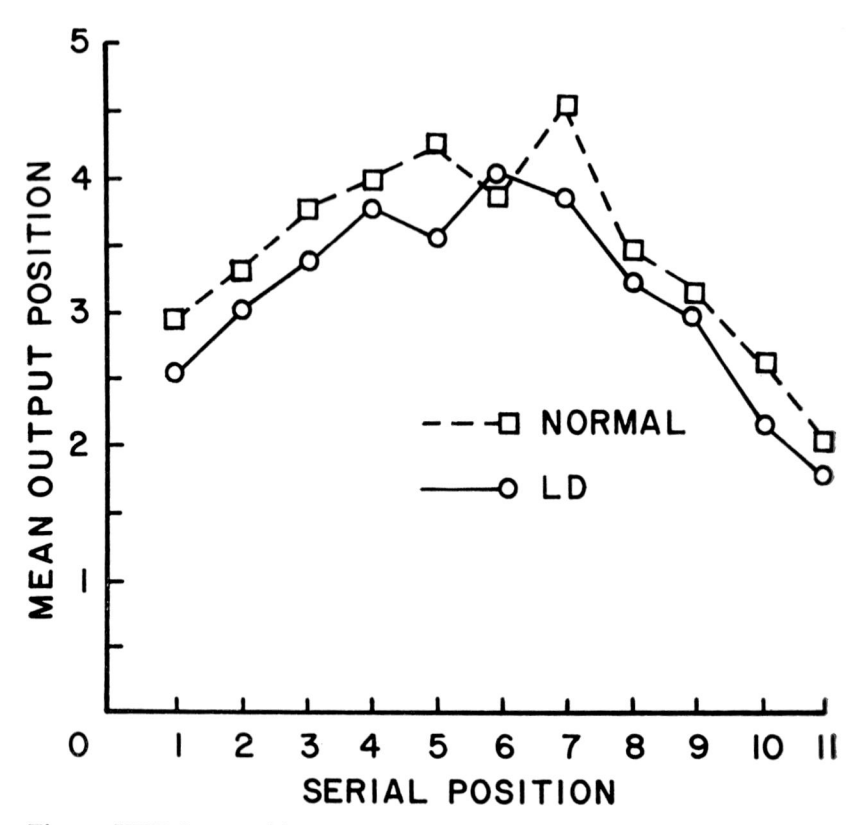

Figure XIII–2. Position on recall protocol as a function of input serial position for each group.

the LD and normal as a function of age. In preparing these curves the fifteen youngest and the fifteen oldest children within each group were chosen. Inspection of Figure XIII-3 suggests that there were differential age effects. The older normals showed a superiority in primacy, whereas both young and old normals seemed to perform at the same level in recency. Just the opposite appeared to be true for the LD group; the older LDs showed a superiority in recency, but primacy was not affected appreciably by age variations. To test the reliability of these effects, an analysis of variance was conducted with group membership and age being between-S$s$ factors, and primacy versus recency within-S$s$ factors. To obtain a primacy measure, the mean total number of correct

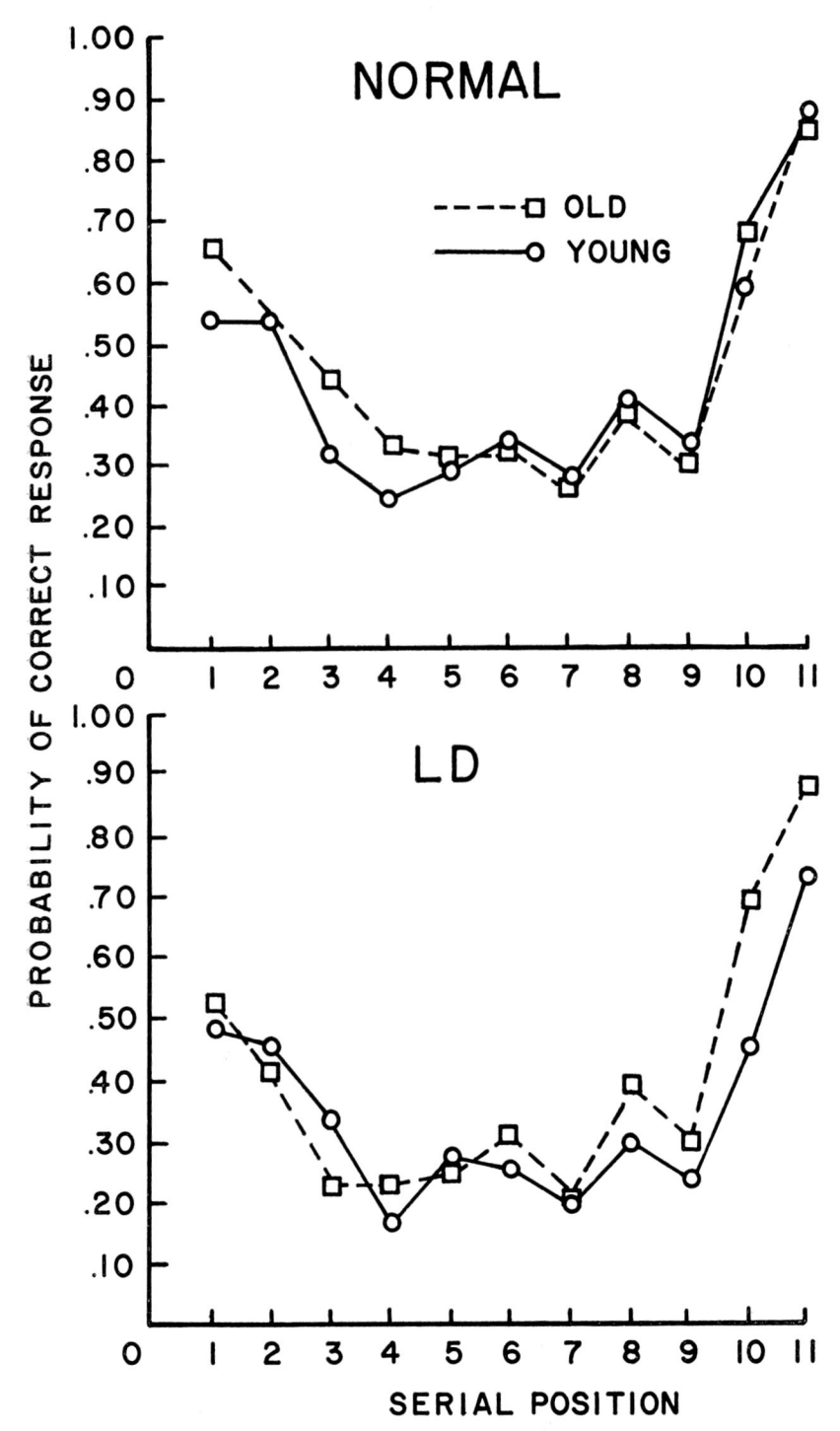

Figure XIII–3. Proportion of responses correct as a function of age for each group.

responses for each child over the first four serial positions was calculated. A recency measure was derived similarly from the last four positions. In effect, the procedure collapsed the primacy and recency effects into single points. The results of the analysis demonstrated that normals were superior to LDs in terms of the total number correct (20.1 versus 16.9), $F$ (1,56) = 18.65, p <.001; the older children were superior to the younger children (19.5 versus 17.6 correct) $F$ (1,56) = 7.25, p <.01; recency was superior to primacy (21.0 versus 16.1 correct) $F$ (1,56) = 28.24, p <.001; and that a significant second order interaction existed between group assignment, memory store and age, $F$ (1,56) = 6.04, p <.02.

Figure XIII-4 shows the significant interaction and clearly demonstrates the age effects suggested by the serial position curves in Figure XIII-3. If any improvement occurs with increasing age for the LDs, it is one of improving STM, as revealed by the increasing recency effects. The learning disabled LTM did not improve with age. Just the opposite was true with normals. Long-term memory improved with age, but STM remained stable, apparently reaching the ceiling for the age range under investi-

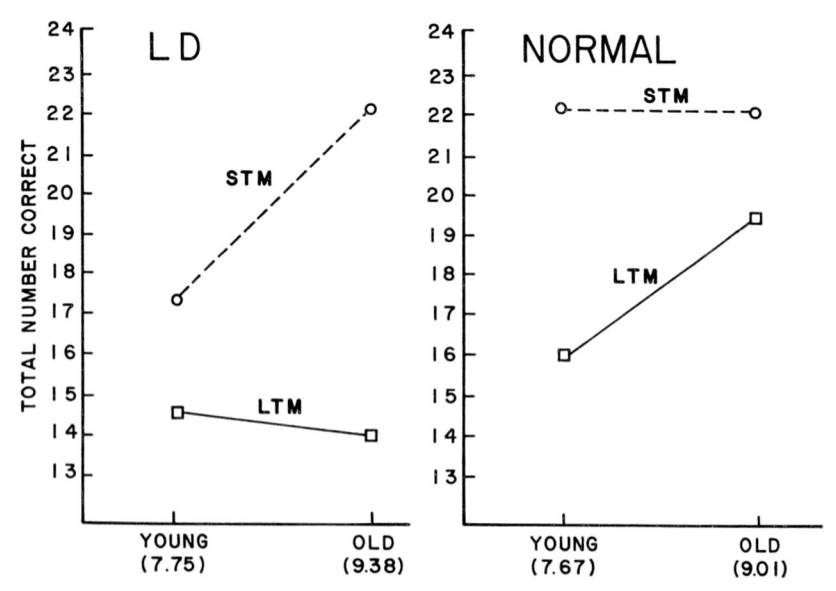

Figure XIII–4. Mean total number correct for each group as a function of primacy, recency and age (given in parentheses).

gation. It is also important to note that the improved STM for the older LD children reached a level of equality found in the normals. In terms of our original hypothesis the LD group as a whole did not evidence any difference in ongoing information processes. However, when age is taken into account, the performance of the older LD children tended to conform to expectation. These children demonstrated an equivalent STM but a deficient LTM as documented in Figure XIII-4. The younger LD children were inferior to normals in both LTM and STM. The reasons for this discrepancy are not immediately obvious.

## CONCLUSIONS

The goal of this initial investigation was to compare STM and LTM in learning disabled and normal children and to do so within a limited information processing framework. We chose for our empirical reference the free recall task that has been the subject of a great deal of study by laboratory investigators of human memory in recent years. Much of the theorizing concerning this task has explained the primacy effect in terms of recall from LTM and the recency effect in terms of recall from STM. The superior recall from the beginning of the list has been attributed to such processes as "selective rehearsal," "differential rehearsal," and "increased time for feature extraction." Explanations of recency seem to share the general theme of information "dumped" from STM, having been maintained in STM by a "rehearsal buffer," "less time for decay," or by "sensory persistence."

The results of this research give mixed support to the notion that LDs process information in a manner different from normals. Similarity between major groups is shown dramatically in Figure XIII-1 where the general serial position effects showed almost perfectly parallel functions. The overall superiority of normals may be attributed to a general I.Q. factor, which, however, would say nothing about differential modes of processing which was the concern of this particular study. It was fully expected that the normals would recall more than the LDs, and our primary concern was with the relative shape of the serial position curves; that is, as the recency and primary effects relate to STM and LTM functioning. Additionally, the serial position analysis, the output order analysis, and the intrusion analysis provided evidence contrary to the initial hypothesis.

The finding that different memory stages are affected by age differently in LDs and normals is, however, a very interesting and unexpected result. It appears that the LDs in the present study had retarded, but not permanently impaired, memory development. One is tempted to go beyond the immediate data for relevance to "real-life" problems. Perhaps the improvement in STM accounts for the phenomenon that the LD child appears to outgrow the problem in memory he manifested at an earlier age. This, by means of his ability to carry on conversations, to interact socially, etc., all of which may be aided by a more developed STM system. At the present time, however, one would be ill-advised to go beyond such speculation.

It must be pointed out, however, that other empirical frameworks could have been used to analyze memory processing in learning disabled children. The procedures developed by Peterson and Peterson (1959) on the short term retention of discrete verbal items, certain paired-associate learning paradigms, and other methods conducive to an analysis of LTM may have been employed. In defense of our own choice, the free-recall task was used because of the STM and LTM phases that are believed to be incorporated into this single task. Moreover, the free recall task is believed to reveal the operation of transfer processes at work when information goes from STM to LTM. Thus it is possible, as Anderson, *et al.* (1974) have shown, that LDs may perform differently in one memory task than another.

The greatest limitation of our own research, and certainly a problem for all LD research, (as pointed out by others during this symposium) is the sample of LD children being investigated. If possible one would restrict his investigations to one of the many problem areas subsumed under the heading LD; several such subgroups would be included in a single study for comparison purposes. With respect to our initial hypothesis, one would have predicted that LD's classified as *hyperactive* would have shown the most deficient LTM or primacy effects, because their attentional wanderings would have reduced the rehearsal needed to transfer

*Memory Analysis: Short- and Long-Term Memory* 247

the first few primary items to LTM. Unfortunately our sample included only five out of thirty LD children classified as hyperactive. Dr. Robert Doyle (V.A. Hospital, North Little Rock, Arkansas) was gracious enough to conduct an extension of our research at his facility. While that study is still incomplete, there are data which tend to support the hypothesis that hyperactive LDs would show a decreased primacy effect relative to normals. A comparison between the normal group from the original sample, and the five hyperactive LDs from that sample and the ten from Dr. Doyle's sample is presented in Figure XIII-5. Obviously more research is needed in this area before definite conclusions can be reached.

This study focused on only one aspect of memory processing,

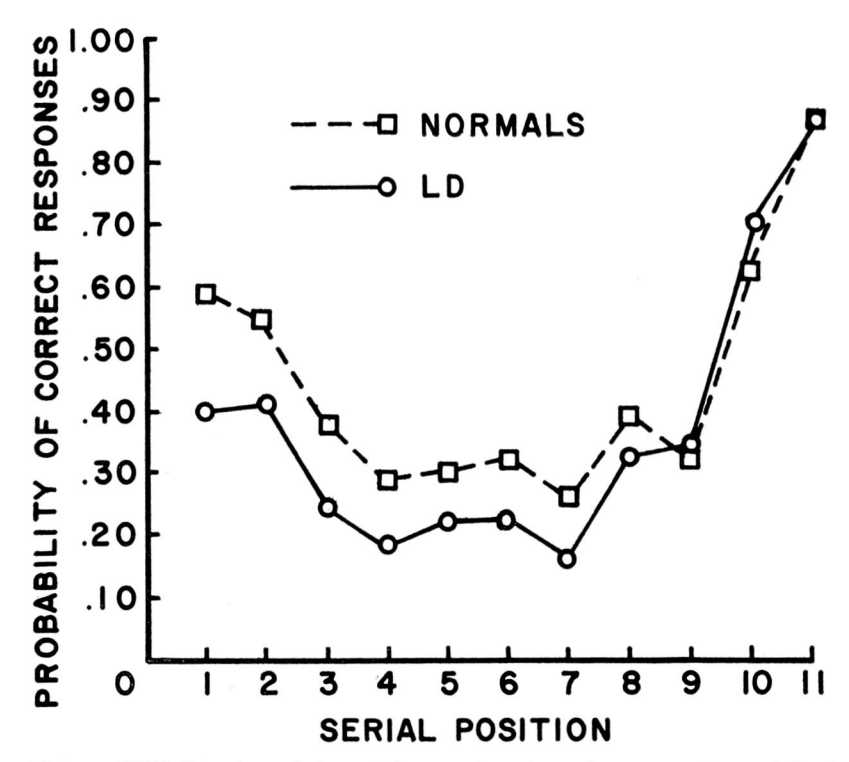

Figure XIII-5. A serial position comparison between the original Normal group (N=30) and the combined Hyperactive LD group (N=15).

the transfer from STM to LTM, and found some limited support for the notion that LDs and normals may process information differently when age is treated as a factor. In view of this success future research must be concerned with specific processing mechanisms and strategies (rehearsal, verbal mediation, etc.) before this approach to the enigma of the LD child can be evaluated.

## REFERENCES

Adams, J. A.: *Human Memory.* New York, McGraw-Hill, 1967.

Anderson, R., Beal, D., and Helabian, J.: *A factor analytic examination of the WISC and the ITPA with learning disabled children.* Paper presented at Rocky Mountain Psychological Association, Denver, 1974.

Baddeley, A. D., and Warrington, E. K.: Amnesia and the distinction between long- and short-term memory. *Journal of Verbal Learning and Verbal Behavior, 9*:176-189, 1970.

Bean, Wm. J.: *The Isolation of Some Psychometric Indices of Severe Reading Disability,* unpublished doctoral dissertation, Texas Tech University, 1967.

Kintsch, W.: *Learning Memory, and Conceptual Processes.* New York, Wiley, 1970.

Lewis, F., Bell, D. B., and Anderson, R. P.: *Predicting reading retardation: A cross-validational study,* Paper presented at Southwestern Psychological Association, St. Louis, 1970.

Peterson, L. R., and Peterson, M. J.: Short-term retention of individual verbal items. *J Exp Psychol, 58*:193-198, 1959.

## Chapter XIV

# FUTURE RESEARCH NEEDS IN LEARNING DISABILITIES

GERALD M. SENF

FOR CONVENIENCE, THE research problems I shall discuss have been divided into two broad categories: supporting conditions and procedural considerations. The former involves necessary prerequisites to the research effort while the latter deals with methodological concerns. While the procedural issues are intriguing and challenging, the supporting conditions place definite restrictions on the research effort and are just as important.

## SUPPORTING CONDITIONS

I have become particularly aware of the problems posed by supporting conditions such as financing, training research personnel, gaining cooperation from practitioners, and maintaining research's credibility during the past year or so. Being on leave of absence from a research and teaching position at the Psychology Department of the University of Illinois, Chicago, I have been working with an applied special education project called the Leadership Training Institute in Learning Disabilities based at the University of Arizona's College of Education. This position affords me some contact with the federal funding source for learning disabilities, the Bureau of Education for the Handicapped (BEH, USOE), and nation-wide consulting experience with learning disability service programs.

It has been an eye-opener for a psychologist contributing to the basic research literature in learning disabilities (LD) to attend conferences of the Association for Children with Learning Disabilities and the Council for Exceptional Children and to associate with prominent figures in the field of special education. In general, the future for research in LD is not optimistic.

## Financing

Nowhere is this opinion more fully borne out than in the area of financing. While service and training programs have also felt the pinch of meager allocations from the Learning Disability Act of 1969, research received no funding. Only one project involving learning disability research, itself a test development program has been supported by BEH. While LD monies were admittedly meager, it is significant nevertheless that a policy decision allocated all of the funds for service programs, reached into other funds for teacher training programs, but found none for basic research. The Research Branch of BEH historically has supported broad scale institutions such as regional centers rather than funding by competitive grants individual researchers who are typically housed in institutions of higher education where research training is a natural byproduct of the research endeavor.

## Research Training

Without research grants, the training of research personnel in learning disabilities becomes a nearly impossible task. Though the evidence in this regard derives from a limited range of experiences, it seems evident that learning disability programs at the University level do not attract students with research interests nor for the most part are they staffed by professors with active research programs. One must remember that teacher training is the primary function of Colleges of Education. The problems involved in promoting exemplary research are similar to those faced by clinical psychology; the students typically have applied interests and the staff's strength frequently lies in the theory and practice rather than research. Unlike clinical psychology, the subspeciality of Learning Disabilities lacks the host of research competent colleagues within their own department who can impart research skills to the practice-oriented students and try to instill in them the skeptical, inquiring approach of the scientist. Without the intellectual discipline and scientific method of inquiry provided by research minded colleagues, the practitioner-teacher can readily fall prey to unverified clinical wisdom or much worse to a cult of personality. The learning disabilities speciality and education generally have been particularly vulnerable to the hasty application of untested theories and to domination by a line of strong personalities. The result is that accepted practice relates more to personal influence than to the accumulation of knowledge. This problem is very serious since it is difficult to see how the field of learning disabilities will ever come to train researchers given the prevailing climate of a limited research emphasis.

My own belief is that research-trained persons from allied disciplines will accomplish the relevant basic research. In fact, they have been doing this right along. However, this presents problems. Researchers lacking intimate knowledge of learning disabilities may not ask very cogent or discriminating questions. Given our present level of understanding, better hypotheses will derive from experience with the phenomenon (LD children) than from the research literature.

A second problem attendent upon having noneducators accomplish the needed research involves funding. Funding agencies will have to become more open-minded vis-a-vis their grant recipients' professional affiliations. Competitive grants, judged by multidisciplinary committees, are a necessary step in buying the best research for the money.

A third problem is that of dissemination. How does research accomplished by psychologists, physicians, and scientists allied to other professions become part of the practice of special education? Our present professional institutions geared to dissemination such as journals, graduate degree programs and conversations typically lack an interdisciplinary focus. New institutions may have to be evolved to deal effectively with this problem. For instance, interdisciplinary post doctoral workshops may be necessary to acquaint practitioners with new applications drawn from research findings.

Grants and contracts may be necessary to support the complex task of bridging two disciplines. Few persons truly know the problems of practice and the intricasies of research. Such persons may need to act as "interpreters." Possibly grants to multiple agencies together representing research, training, and service capabilities could encourage new cooperative units where presently competition for monies further separates the various parties and, hence, reduces the dissemination of information. The complications introduced by professional jealousies tempers one's optimism; certainly research funding is needed to study the organizational psychology issues attendant on interdisciplinary cooperation and information exchange.

### Research-Practitioner Cooperation

A third supporting condition that creates problems for research in learning disabilities relates to the cooperation of practitioners. The simple mechanics of obtaining suitable subjects for research studies requires an investment in time and energy far in excess of the value of the knowledge typically gained. Schools seem more protective of *their* children's time than are parents! From the point of view of the school, it is easy to see how disturbing to everyday procedures a researcher's presence can be. Typically, schools receive nothing but headaches from researchers, unless of course the study finds significant results and then the thoughtful researcher affords the school principal a footnote. This parasitic relationship, which is exhausting to both researcher and practitioner, needs reexamination.

Researchers must consider alternatives which might enhance their reception. The "hit and run" tactic, while acceptable for producing publications, cuts one off from valuable longitudinal data and individual case studies that are so badly needed. A number of alternatives come to mind: researchers can provide schools psychometric services often required or useful for the research itself; they can conduct in-service training sessions for the school's special education staff or for all teaching personnel on any variety of topics, e.g. testing, research methods, the ongoing research programs, or review of research findings. Involvement of graduate students in such endeavors provides them valuable experience as well as an entree for their thesis research. The researcher with more applied interests and a flexible budget can enroll students for course credit and train them to provide tutoring to needy children, thereby creating a research sample which allows for continuous assessment. Alternatively, the researcher could associate with persons with applied interest and conduct his research under their aegis. The general point here is that we must become more atuned to the problems in one-shot research and learn how to develop more lasting, mutually profitable relationships with practitioners.

## Credibility of Research

The fourth supporting condition, the credibility of the research, underlies the other supporting conditions. Campbell and Stanley (1963) in their widely known book on research methods in teaching, place the credibility issue in a historical perspective. Their commentary, written more than ten years ago, is even truer and perhaps more timely today: They wrote:

> This chapter is committed to the experiment: as the only means for settling dispute regarding educational practice, as the only way of verifying educational improvements, and as the only way of establishing a cumulative tradition in which improvements can be introduced without the danger of a faddish discard of old wisdom in favor of inferior novelties. Yet, in our strong advocacy of experimentation, we must not imply that our emphasis is new. As the existence of McCall's book makes clear, a wave of enthusiasm for experimentation dominated the field of education in the Thorndike era, perhaps reaching its apex in the 1920s. And this enthusiasm gave way to apathy and rejecttion, and the adoption of new psychologies unamenable to experimental verification. Good and Scates (1954, pp. 716-721) have documented a wave of pessimism, dating back to perhaps 1935, and have cited even that staunch advocate of experimentation, Monroe (1938), as saying "the direct contributions from controlled have been disappointing." Further it can be noted that the defections from experimentation to essay writing, often accompanied by conversion from a Thorndikian behaviorism to Gestalt psychology or psycholanalysis, have frequency occurred in persons well trained in the experimental tradition.
> 
> To avoid a recurrence of this disillusionment, we must be aware of certain sources of the previous reaction and try to

avoid the false anticipations which led to it. Several aspects may be noted. First, the claims made for the rate and degree of progress which would result from experiment were grandiously over optimistic accompanied by an unjustified decreciation of nonexperimental wisdom. The initial advocates assumed that progress in the technology of teaching had been slow just because scientific practice was incompetent, just because it had not been produced by experimentation. When, in fact, experiments often proved to be tedious, equivocal, of undependable replicability, and to confirm prescientific wisdom, the over-optimistic grounds upon which experimentation had been justified were undercut, and a disillusioned rejection or neglect took place.

As noted previously, the field of learning disabilities acts as though it occurs with Monroe's disillusionment (1938) in failing to promote the research necessary to validate the basic principles upon which their remedial programs are based. At the same time, there is merit to the opinion that research has not taught us much. Researchers too often argue that the limited practical value of research is due to its "basic" nature. It is argued that benefits will eventually ensue from this basic effort. It is difficult to accept this argument. Can researchers dealing with psychoeducational phenomena credibly or validly claim that theirs is "basic research" which will some day contribute meaningfully to educational practice? The image of research is certainly not aided by the overwhelming number of one shot theses and dissertations that crowd the literature. Programmatic research, funded over extended periods of time under the direction of skilled and dedicated scientists is needed.

The credibility of researchers depends heavily upon producing usable information and ideas. I am in total support of scientists whose research has no immediate or even obvious potential relevance so long as there exists some rationale for the investment of tax dollars (granting that these distinctions are often hard to make in practice). The "basic research" arguement is often offered as a foil, an excuse for the researcher's failure to ask incisive questions or to discover and utilize a methodology that will advance knowledge. While it may appear that the integrity or at least the proficiency of many psychoeducational researchers is being impugned, my viewpoint reflects my understanding of the practitioners' problems. It is important to acknowledge the "unjustified denunciation of nonexperimental wisdom" (Campbell and Stanley, 1963) and to recognize that the "research emperor's clothes" may be improperly tailored if not nonexistent. The less researchers hide behind the "basic research" argument, the more likely will they be able to form more cooperative and productive relationships with practitioners, to see and respond to the challenge of tougher but more meaningful questions, and to regain once again the credibility and hopefully the tangible support needed for the orderly accumulation of knowledge.

## PROCEDURAL ISSUES

A second major set of research needs will be considered next, involving procedural issues. The first procedural need is that research in learning disabilities rely on established research paradigms in an effort to test competing falsifiable models. The second need involves finding ways to bridge the gulf between research based knowledge and the unknowns that the practitioners must face daily.

### Sample Difference Experiments

How many times have you read a research report characterized as follows: first it is alleged that LD children have an "X" deficit. A test or scale is constructed to measure X. A sample of LD children are compared with some contrast group and found to score more poorly on the X test. It is concluded that LD children have X deficit. A major variant on this approach is to adopt a previously existing test of X which likewise lacks the necessary construct validity to make conclusions truly "meaningful" in the logical positivist sense of the word.

### *Unvalidated Instruments*

Arguments against this type of research which so characterizes the literature, concern the meaningfulness of the test scores and the logical power of the research design. First, creating a measuring scale de novo represents the extreme case of adopting an unvalidated test. One simply does not know the empirical correlates of the measure. One may find that it distinguishes LD children from some contrast group (typically called normals) but that is all one knows. Further assertions made by the author rely on the face validity of the scale or upon the author's belief concerning what the scale measures; wanting to measure X, the researcher simply creates a scale which he thinks *ought to be* a measure of X. Finding that the scale differentiates LD from normal children, he asserts that LD children have disability X. He does so on faith in his own test construction abilities or in that of others. The study is basically meaningless, unless one wants to join in the author's guessing game. This type of study represents the "simple sample difference approach" utilizing an unvalidated, meaningless instrument.

It is mandatory that instruments used in research adopting this type of design have established meaning. Such meaning could be the result of test validation or could derive from a body of research utilizing the test paradigm in research studies. This latter procedure, the use of well-researched experimental paradigms, is potentially most fruitful by virtue of the power available through making small yet critical variations in the experimental paradigm. Dr. Marshall's paper (Chapter XIII) illustrates this point. His conclusions rest on the knowledge of the serial position curve and attendant theorizing. It is only from this knowledge base that he can assert that the LD children in his sample evidence greater long term memory problems on the average than his controls. Had he created his own test of long term memory, and not undertaken the lengthy task of validating it as a measure of long term memory, his paper would have been worthless in my opinion. On the contrary, his use of a well-researched experimental paradigm is exemplary for it has allowed him to interpret his results within the context of existing knowledge.

### *Logical Power of the Sample Difference Approach*

A second quarrel with research using the "simple sample difference approach," i.e. comparing LD children with normals, is independent of whether the test instrument(s) adopted has pre-established meaning. Predicting that LD children will perform more poorly than age and IQ controls is a pretty weak (though "safe") hypothesis. The fact is that LD children, like juvenile delinquents, psychopaths, and physically handicapped children, will perform more poorly than controls on almost any task given them. Their test taking abilities and attitudes together with their history of failure result in poor performance throughout. Consequently, the meaning of a difference between the score of an LD child and the normal control may not have the same meaning as the difference between the same two scores obtained by normally achieving youngsters. Said somewhat differently, the construct validity of the score may not hold for the disabled sample; method variance may obscure the content variance. This same problem occurs in practice where diagnostic testing may find the child to have ten or more psychoeducational disabilities where in fact he may have a single problem, an attentional deficit for example, which prejudices his performance on all tests administered. Aside from the fact that positing multiple deficits is not parsimonious, it is exceedingly precarious unless one can substantiate the construct validity of each deficit purportedly identified.

One solution to this problem is the utilization of falsifiable models which are tested using within child data or at least comparisons between groups of LD children, not between LD and normals. Again, Dr. Marshall's study is an excellent example; the more important point was not that LD children performed more poorly than the normal children, though they indeed did on the average, but that the within-subject data indicated that the long term memory rather than the short term memory (recency effect) showed weakness. Had, in fact, the LD children simply performed more poorly overall, no incisive conclusions could have been drawn.

The notion of a falsifiable model is that assertions exist for which invalidating data could potentially be found. The "simple sample comparison experiment" can only determine that the hypothesized difference exists or that the difference was not found but not that the difference does not exist.

It is more efficacious to design experiments which pit explanatory alternatives against one another. For example, one could assert that the hyperactive child selects inappropriate cues thereby making his behavior maladjusted. Or one could assert that the hyperactive child selects the same cues as the normal child but is inordinately rapid in acting, poor judgement being the essence of his maladjusted behavior. Parenthetically, it is interesting to note the diverse practical implications of these two hypotheses. The first, in positing a cue selection disability, would imply the need for special educational materials tailored to restrict task-irrelevant cues or suggest the need for distraction-reducing work cubicles utilized by Kephart (1960, 1963). The alternative hypothesis requires the production of no new materials; instead, training procedures would be espoused aimed at prompting reflection and delaying one's reaction until the alternatives had been considered. Whether or not this particular example has merit, the general point is the incisive knowledge sought required that we pose alternative hypotheses that can be shown to be false.

Certainly it is preferable to pit opposing viewpoints against one another which experimental data can distinguish between; such is the genius of great experimental science. At least we should construct experiments which tell us about the failing children's psychological attributes, a process which will be aided if we insist on validated, i.e. meaningful, instruments, and test alternative hypotheses within a disability group rather than between it and normal controls.

## Research Application Gulf

The final research problem concerns the gulf that exists between a lot of research and the knowledge needed by the practitioner. While it is all but necessary that research will always be seeking knowledge needed by the practitioner, the methods of research must change if we are ever to confirm a set of principles with attendant data useful to the practitioner. My major argument here concerns the level of classification that much research appears to have adopted. We have essentially accepted the categories "learning disability" and "minimal brain dysfunction" as appropriate blocking variables for research. As I pointed out previously, research has problems with these labels because they have changed markedly in practice over the years, differ from one locality to another, and generally lack succinct class principles to permit reliable classification. The most basic problem for research here is that incomparability of results can always be posited to lie in the discrepant makeup of the specific samples utilized, thereby undermining the possible accumulation of verified research findings.

In essence, the basic research problem confronting Learning Disabilities or Minimal Brain Dysfunction is that of sample definition. I have been concerned with this problem for a number of years during which I have tried to puzzle out its implications for research methodology. The problem essentially is more generic than the study of LD or MBD but concerns instead the creation of a methodology appropriate for the study of deviant psychological functioning. I would like to address some side issues important to practitioners, before discussing the problem of categorization.

There has been a growing emphasis over the years of individualizing instruction; the trend has been prompted as a more appropriate means for teaching all children than group instruction. There are at least two distinguishable issues related to individualization. First, should the administration of education resources be organized around categories of disability such as blind, deaf, mentally retarded, multiply handicapped, or learning disabled, or should the funding base be noncategorical? Second, should the child be taught as though he were one of a group of persons representing a certain category of disability, for example perceptually impaired, or should he be schooled as an individual, distinct from all other children. This issue has a second facet which is important to distinguish. Should the handicapped child *in all ways* be treated as an individual or are there some aspects of his behavior, notably his handicap, which if recognized as similar to other children's handicaps, could assist us in planning a sound educational program for him? Take a specific example. What comfort would there be in trusting a reading retarded child to a teacher who claimed that because she treated all children as individuals she really had no knowledge about the child's problem and would have to start from scratch and learn how best to deal with his reading problem. Would not a parent want a teacher who claimed, after an hour or two with a child, to have encountered problems such as his before and exhibit confidence that she were able to deal satisfactorily with problems of this kind? A medical analogy draws this distinction further: when visiting a physician, one certainly wants to be treated as an individual and be afforded all due respect from the physician and his staff; but when it comes to the treatment of the disorder, the patient prefers to have a disease routine in the doctor's experiences, one that he has seen many times before, and one that he knows how to treat effectively. Thus, complete individualization of instruction is a two edged sword if such individualization implies that we have learned nothing from past examples of the particular problem a child is experiencing.

Rather than holding such an extreme position, the practitioner is reaching against the category labels used for administrative purposes such as funding and is arguing that an appropriate education for the child in special need requires consideration of many distinctions not encompassed by such broad terms as learning disabled, minimally brain damaged, and culturally deprived. At the same time, some level of categorization takes place in the teacher's thoughts. The experienced teacher is one who has seen a wide variety of educational problems and is able to draw upon her past experience with children having similar problems.

All of this may seem quite obvious but when arguments are made to eliminate categorization and instead mainstream all handicapped children, the issue of administrative categorization appears to be confused with the natural human tendency to notice similarities between otherwise unique events.

### *Seeking Core Problems*

The issues of administrative categories, the question of the child's individuality, and the individualization of instruction are critical for research methodology. Viewing these problems as analogous to medical research is useful. From the set of crippling childhood diseases, medical researchers were able to isolate a syndrome which they called polio. Through extensive research, the Salk vaccine was eventually discovered that has proven an exceedingly effective deterrent. The fact that individuals contract diseases similar to those contracted by other individuals represents no threat to their individuality. The problems attendant on treating each case and, in fact, the specific ramifications of the disease within any given indivdual are varied. However, it is still possible to isolate a common core problem that can be named and once named can catalyze further research and knowledge about the disease. It is through the isolation of the common characteristics (syndrome) that we are able to begin amassing knowledge about a disease. In summary, isolating diseases does not deny the individuality of the people who contract the disease, nor does it claim that the manifestation of the disease is exactly the same in all individuals. Naming diseases (diagnostic categorization) does serve as a useful function in that it allows for the accumulation of knowledge obtained through study of similar cases, and thereby provides us with better methods to treat each individual contracting a sufficiently similar symptom pattern.

A similar approach is needed in the area of psychoeducational disabilities. Granting the philosophical stance that all children are individuals, behavior patterns still exist that allow us to see some children as more similar to each other than to other children. One encompassing symptom pattern involves the child's failure to accomplish satisfactory grades from the teacher. Such characteristics represent the grossest form of categorization within the educational disability area. The administrative categories used variously in different states such as "learning disabled," "perceptually handicapped," mentally retarded," "brain damaged," and so forth represent finer distinctions within this initial broad category. It has become clear from many sources and for many reasons that these categories are not especially useful; not only are there problems attendant on their use as administrative vehicles but they also lack utility for classroom management and remedial programming.

The researcher utilizing the sample difference approach has typically adopted this level of categorization or a level of categorization very similar to it. While adopting category groupings for the study of psychological deviance appears to be a very appropriate strategy, the level of specificity represented by the administrative categories has not been sufficient for the detailed answers being sought in the research as will be illustrated below. The practitioner needs to be assured that the goal of categorization is not to impune the integrity of the individual, but to enable an organized search for lawful relationships between aspects of the child's disibility and between the conditions which caused that disability and the steps that could be taken to alleviate it. Knowledge about the causative conditions can provide a preventative outlook. Moreover, understanding the best remedial procedures can provide substance for teacher training programs and direction for the individual teacher facing a child with a psychoeducational problem.

## Reliability of Classification

Why then has not the sample difference research approach produced very useful results despite its categorical nature? The basic problem is that researchers have focused their attention on the correlates of broad disability categories rather than upon an elucidation of the category system itself. A closer examination of the basic requirements of a category system will illustrate this point. Some years ago, Zigler and Phillips (1961) described some of the problems attendant on psychiatric diagnosis. Their conceptualization is useful in the present instance. In studying a specific problem area, such as learning disabilities, one needs a set of descriptors known as class principles which can be utilized to determine whether or not a given individual represents an instance of the class "learning disabilities." The more clearly the class principles can be stated, the more reliable should be the determination of whether or not the child belongs in or out of the category "learning disabilities."

If class assignment can be accomplished reliably, then one is in a position to examine the correlates of the class, i.e., the variables that relate lawfully to class membership. The sample difference approach is then typically utilized to determine whether individuals sharing class membership also share correlated characteristics of interest such as common causes leading to the problem, common response to various treatments, or common underlying process problems such as in attention or memory.

Within the framework of this research methodology, learning disability research could be expected to encounter problems. Reliability of categorization is a problem because of the changing face of the field of learning disabilities throughout the last decade. Multiple definitions exist, including the medically-oriented definition of Task Force I (Clements, 1966), the Northwestern Conference's educational definition (Kass and Myklebust, 1969), as well as a federal legislative definition.* None of these definitions have sufficiently clear, objectively stated class principles to permit reliable diagnosis. I do not know of any specific studies on diagnostic reliability but the problems are so analogous to those in the psychiatric literature that it is difficult to believe that diagnosis in the educational arena is much superior to that utilizing the carefully constructed psychiatric classification system (DSM-II) which in itself has not proven to be very reliable.

Some of the problems involved in learning disabilities research derive from the inequivalence of research samples caused by the absence of a set of shared class principles with which diagnostic reliability could be established. Without the assurance that samples are comparable, conflicting results remain uninterpretable. Also, unreliability restricts the magnitude of the empirical relationships one can find between class memberships and other variables of interest.

## *So-called Heterogeneous Categories*

While unreliability is certainly a serious problem it does not totally explain our inability to discover a greater number of important empirical relationships. Heterogeneity of the class membership is frequently cited as the cause of insignificant research findings; that is, one's hypothesis holding true for an insufficiently large subset of the total class to verify the hypothesis statistically. Heterogeneity of class members is assuredly a problem though one must be very clear about what is meant by "heterogeneity." Heterogeneity is either synonymous with unreliability of classification or invalidity of class correlates. In the first case, a class could contain members to whom the class principles do not apply, either due to

---

*Definition authored by the National Advisory Committee on Handicapped Children 1968:

> Children with special learning disabilities exhibit a disorder in one or more of the basic psychological processes involved in understanding or in using spoken or written language. These may be manifested in disorders of listening, thinking, talking, reading, writing, spelling, or in arithmetic. They include conditions which have been referred to as perceptual handicaps, brain injury, minimal brain dysfunction, dyslexia, developmental aphasia, etc. They do not include learning problems which are due primarily to visual, hearing, or motor handicaps, to mental retardation, emotional disturbance, or to environmental disadvantage.

inappropriate assignment or to inadequately specified class principles. The result is a class with members heterogeneous with respect to the class principles, i.e. unreliable.

Alternatively, a class could contain members all correctly classified who still differ on non-class principle variables. Because all persons are unique, all classes containing persons will be heterogeneous with respect to some variables. Framed in predictive language, class membership is an imperfect predictor of most variables and usually an adequate predictor of only a few variables. One hopes that the few variables that are predictable from class membership are theoretically important or useful. The point to recognize here is that all category systems are more or less heterogeneous with respect to class correlates. To bemoan this fact is only to admit that one cannot locate highly valid class correlates.

Heretogeneity vis-a-vis class correlates, i.e. lack of predictability, can be dealt with in two major ways. One is to intensify the search for correlates, concentrating on improving measurement, refining experimental procedures, evolving more potent treatment procedures or even at times looking to new ideas for clues about significant relationships. These steps have been taken. It is time now to examine an alternative approach, that of redefining or at least refining the category system itself. In predictive language, this second approach focuses on the predictor rather than on the criteria.

### Disparity of conceptual levels between category and criteria.

In learning disability research, we do not have predictor classes defined at a conceptual level appropriate to the variables we would like class membership to predict. Teachers will tell you that the term learning disabilities, just as the terms mental retarded, cultural disadvantagement, or minimal brain damage are not very useful. Typically, the teacher involved with such children must face the *differences between children within one of these broad categories.* To tell her that you as a researcher have found that learning disabled children have an attentional deficit compared to normals which is significant at the .05 level does her no good at all. She wants to know which of the children in her LD class have that attentional deficit, not whether the class as a whole is different from the regular classroom down the hall. This fact she already knows.

Whether or not the specific researcher is interested in providing data immediately relevant to the classroom teacher, he still wants to find empirically sound relationships between variables. When studying psychological deviance, the researcher must evolve a set of constructs at an explanatory level appropriate to his line of inquiry. Terms like "Learning Disability" are quite generic but may suffice if one is concerned about questions such as the relationships between school problems and (a) self image, (b) delinquent behavior, (c) attendant disruption of home environment, and so forth. However, if one is interested in the information processing capacities of the learning disabled child and in appropriate remedial techniques which interface with his strengths and circumvent or improve his weaknesses, the category "Learning Disability" would be a conceptually inappropriate choice of sample composition. For example, the class "Learning Disability" does not appear to be a strong predictor of memory disorders or of attentional disorders though both are certainly represented. Some more carefully defined predictor classes need to be evolved for determining which children will have memory problems and which will have attentional problems. Further refinement in each of these subclasses will likely be necessary to attain high level prediction of other criterion variables of interest.

Rather than view this category label as fixed, the domain of behaviors which define the broader category should be the focus of much of the researcher's theorizing and research. The creation of a class in the first place represents a belief that there are critical characteristics that persons so classified have in common and that these commonalities should allow us to predict other aspects of their behavior. If it turns out that the important behaviors that the particular researcher is interested in do not, in fact, lawfully relate to the class, then it certainly behooves him to reorganize the persons for study using different class principles.

It is important to keep in mind that the creation of classes such as Learning Disability or Minimal Brain Damage are intellectual constructions which may not be an appropriate, i.e. useful, way of looking at the world. Furthermore, it is important to recognize that such classes represent a complex variable which plays a key role in one's theory of educational disability. Unlike constructing a variable which has a number of levels, a taxonomic class asserts that all individuals so assigned are functionally identical. Persons assigned to the class "Learning Disabilities" do not appear to be functionally identical with respect to the dimensions that are of particular relevance to remedial intervention. In the broader scheme of things, the equalization of classes of individuals which are to be considered functionally equivalent represent an attempt to ignore nonessential commonalities. At one extreme, we must recognize that everyone is in fact totally individual i.e., there is some characteristic which distinguishes each individual from any other individual. At the other extreme, one can consider all human organisms as representative of the same class, homo sapiens, the assignment to such a broad class actually telling us many things about the individual, e.g. his dependence on food, water and so forth. The kinds of statements we wish to make about the educationally handicapped child fall somewhere in between. One can imagine a theory of individual behavior which is so detailed that it is able to predict unique outcomes for each individual. Considerably short of that, one can consider a theory of human functioning which makes predictions about a defined domain of behavior or a level which allows us to ignore some of the differences between individuals resulting in the creation of groups of individuals which are adequately similar for our level of study. Of course, the test of whether they are adequately similar for our purposes is determined by whether we can find variables of interest (class correlates) that lawfully relate to the group of individuals so isolated.

In the area of educational disabilities, research has shown that the categories being utilized, (Minimal Brain Dysfunction, Learning Disabilities, culturally disadvantaged, deaf, blind, and so forth) contain individuals who are dissimilar with respect to the important variables, i.e. the class correlates one would have hoped to exist. It is necessary now to search for alternative ways of grouping the failing children which may prove more fruitful.

## REFERENCES

Campbell, D. T., and Stanley, J. C.: *Experimental and Quasi-experimental Designs for Research.* Chicago, Rand McNally, 1963.
Good, C. V., and Scates, D. E.: *Methods of Research.* New York, Appleton-Century-Crofts, 1954.
Clements, S. D.: *Minimal brain dysfunction in children: Terminology and identification, phase one of a three-phase project,* bulletin no. 1415, Washington, U.S. Department of Health, Education, and Welfare, NINDS Monograph No. 3, 1966.
Kass, C. E., and Myklebust, H. R.: Learning disability: An educational definition. *Journal of Learning Disabilities,* 2:38-40, 1969.
Kephart, N.: *The Brain-Injured Child in the Classroom.* National Society for Crippled Children and Adults, 1963.
Kephart, N. C.: *The Slow Learner in the Classroom.* Columbus, Merrill, 1960.
Monroe, W. S.: General methods: Classroom experimentation. In Whippe, G. M. (Ed.): *Yearbook National Society Studies Education,* 37:319-327, Part III, 1938.
National Advisory Committee: Special Education for Handicapped Children. The first annual report of the National Advisory Committee on Handicapped Children. Washington, D.C. Office of Education, U.S. Department of Health, Education, and Welfare, 1968.
Zigler, E., and Phillips, L: Psychiatric diagnosis, A critique. *J Abnorm Soc Psychol,* 63:607-617, 1961.

# Chapter XV

# METHODOLOGICAL PROBLEMS IN WORKING WITH SPECIAL POPULATIONS

Charles G. Halcomb

Although I have long been an advocate of experimental psychologists' involvement in research of an applied nature, it came as a surprise when Dr. Anderson asked me to work with him to develop a methodology for investigating the alleged attention deficits of children with learning disabilities. While the vigilance task, which I had used in studying monitoring behavior for several years, provided an excellent vehicle for studying sustained attention (Anderson, Halcomb, and Doyle, 1973), my major concern was my lack of knowledge about the nature of the learning disabilities problem. An intimate involvement with research in the area during the past six months, has convinced me that my fears were unfounded. Many investigators who have worked with this special population for years are still expressing the same uncertainty about the nature of learning disabilities.

The ideas presented in the present paper represent some of the convictions which have grown out of the work that Dr. Anderson and I have been doing as well as some attitudes which have evolved over time concerning the proper approach to the systematic execution of research.

The first point to be emphasized is that it is extremely important to bring all requisite skills to bear on the solution of research problems. Too often people who have the important background knowledge to understand the problems which need to be investigated, do not have the methodological sophistication required to attack these problems. Conversely, research experts who have the methodological sophistication often lack an adequate knowledge of the problems and/or populations to be studied. Researchers and practitioners frequently failed to recognize the importance of the much discussed but seldom practiced team approach to research. Frequently in interdisciplinary research efforts, each participant works only within his area of interest; it is rare that problems are approached with a unified team. When faced with the task of attempting to develop a functional understanding of a complex set of problems, such as represented by the learning disabilities concept, it seems that a number of professionals, each with a unique set of skills, must cooperate if a solution to the riddle is to be found. Obviously physicians, educators, and psychologists must work together in this effort. However, there are other specialists who have much to contribute to research. Some of these overlooked professionals include mathematicians, engineers, computer technicians, physiologists and communication specialists.

A second conviction which has guided my research behavior is that research must proceed in a systematic and orderly fashion in order to be most productive. As the results of our research are presented to groups of parents, educators, and psychologists, the question is often asked why we have not attempted some application that might seem indicated by the results of the research. The answer to this type of question has always been that while many of the suggestions were potentially good ideas, we simply have not yet reached the point of being ready to move ahead without being sure that the recommendations have empirical support. One can always think of possible avenues of investigation and/or application faster than an orderly research program can move; however, a carefully conceived systematic approach will yield greater dividends in the long run. This does not mean that new avenues of investigation suggested by research results should not be pursued; rather, it simply means that one must walk before one can expect to run. Rarely do advances in our understanding of human behavior come in the form of dramatic breakthroughs. Most advances come from a careful, systematic and methodological investigation of the variables with progress coming in small increments which when organized with the aid of a model or theory provide the important answers to relevant questions.

The problem of selecting a specific methodology for investigating some aspects of the behavior of children with learning disability problems also requires attention As a rule of thumb, a person proposing to investigate some behavorial charactistics of a specialized population should determine whether there are tasks or procedures which have already been demonstrated to be reliable methods for looking at the behavorial characteristic to be investigated. This would suggest that a person must be familiar with the scientific literature, not just that directed to a specialized population or subject. The importance of a thorough understanding of the basic scientific work in our area of concern cannot be overstressed. The work of Marshall, et al. (Chapter XIII) illustrates this point nicely. His familiarity with the basic research in the area of memory aided his decision to use the free recall methodology as an almost obvious choice. In designing this experiment other investigators might have chosen to develop a creative, new methodology to look at the memory process of children labeled as learning disabled. Moreover, they might have done a good job of developing such a methodology. But, would anything be known about the reliability of such a procedure, and would the investigator have known how to interpret the results in light of the background literature?

It should be made clear that a program of research with a specialized population should not simply replicate all of the work done with normals using the special population. Rather, the researcher should work toward a careful selection of tasks which have proven useful and reliable. The information yielded should be both interesting and relevant to the area. Hopefully, the careful use of known procedures, in those instances where they are appropriate, will prevent re-invention of the wheel. (The basic problem with re-inventing the wheel is that the job may not be as good the second time around.)

Another advantage which occurs when an established methodology is used by a knowledgable investigator is that we will not only gain a real understanding of the data obtained, but we will also increase the probability that we will understand the limitations of the findings. Sometimes, the latter can be the most important understanding that can be possessed.

It is important to understand methodology and to be familiar with the relevant related research, but the investigator must also understand the populations with which he is going to work. The most salient thing I have learned about children with learning disabilities is that just a diagnosis that a child is an LD gives me very little information about the child. That is, my uncertainty regarding the characteristics of the child in question has not substantially reduced. A quote from the paper by Marshall, Anderson and Tate illustrates this point; I can only amplify the authors observations (Marshall, Anderson, and Tate, 1973). They said, "The greatest limitation of our own research and certainly a a problem for all LD research, is the description of the population being investigated." Certainly hetrogeneity is the rule and not the exception when one selects a random sample from a population of children labeled as having a learning disability. These observations point to a pressing need for parametric research aimed at developing an easily used taxonomical description of the population. Models such as the one presented by Dr. Dykman (Chapter III) represents at least a step in the right direction. The development of such a taxonomy would facilitate research toward developing an understanding of the problem, and also facilitate the development of meaningful diagnostic and remedial procedures.

Not only is it necessary for an investigator to be familiar with the population he is studying, but it is also essential that a person understands the data which he obtains. This does not mean that he should simply know the numerical values of the numbers he obtained. Rather, the investigator should understand what his numbers represent in behavorial terms. It is true that data usually reduces to some kind of number or symbol which is used to code the subject's behavior. However, it is not enough to be familiar with the relationships these symbols have with one another. One must also fully understand the relationship the numbers have with the behavior they represent. In other words, the investigator must be vigilant not to fall into the trap of letting his statistical tools make decisions for him. Instead, these tools should be used to assist in drawing meaningful conclusions that reflect the actual behavior which was observed.

I hold a strong bias that meaningful conclusions can only be reached if research time is spent during data collecting making simple visual observations of the spectrum of behavior that the subjects emit. This implies that subsequent data points should relate to the actual behaviors observed by the experimenter. If the investigator proceeds in this fashion he is less likely to arrive at conclusions which make little behavorial sense, or miss what careful observations may have told him about obvious behavorial differences or similarities among the subjects.

A corollary to this is that one must take the time to inspect the raw material data which is obtained. There is an alarming tendency on the part of graduate students and to some extent on the part of trained psychologists to accept the results of statistical tests and make decisions and/or interpretations without first making an adequate visual examination of the data points, the distribution and other important features of the data. I have become a strong advocate of the "eyeball test" as an important ingredient of any statistical analysis. Unless one is really familiar with the nature of the data some subtle, but important information may be missed. Even worse, statistically correct but behaviorally wrong or misleading conclusions may be derived. This point can be demonstrated by referring to the data presented in Figure XV-1 (Anderson, Halcomb, Ozolins, and Hopson, 1974). The authors were interested in contrasting the effects of auditory distraction on the behavior of normal and learning disabled children. Figure XV-1 represents the false alarm rate for the LD children during the vigil. Most of the children made few if any false alarms during the thirty minute vigil with the exceptions of seven children who made an unusually large number of false alarms. The effect of these extreme scores was, naturally, to pull the mean out in the direction of the seven extreme scores. When these data were originally analyzed, a statisti-

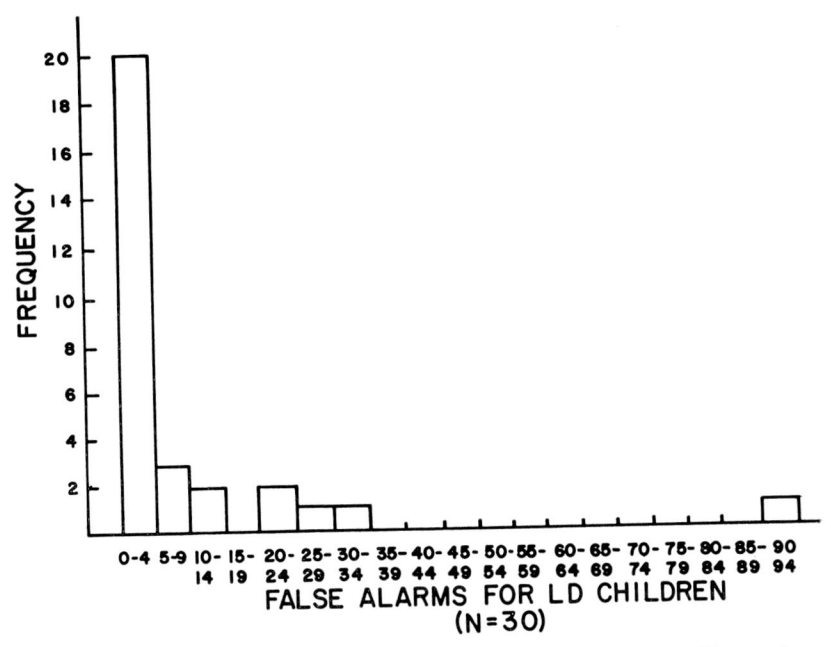

Figure XV–1. False alarms under conditions of auditory distraction.

cally significant difference was found between this mean and the mean number of false alarms for the normal group. However, examination of the data revealed that when these seven extreme scores were eliminated from the distribution the two sets of scores looked for all intent and purpose identical. In this case, the interesting results will probably occur when we examine the extreme scores of the seven children and identify the way in which they differ from the older learning disabled children in the sample. Since we have very sophisticated statistical techniques and procedures we often forget that very simple methods such as looking at, or thinking about the data may be quite useful. It seems safe to state that one cannot yet remove the requirement that there must be an intelligent investigator to make the final decisions about the meaning of statistical data.

As a final thought, the following premise is offered for consideration. We are trying to understand a very complicated phenomena. Simple solutions will not be found for complex problems. Methodology, theory and inferences will of necessity probably be as complex as the phenomena being studied. It is for this reason that I want to encourage, with tongue in check, the use of the technology available in the twentieth century. Probably, the most obvious example of this kind of technology is provided by the relatively inexpensive, small digital computers which can be used for process control and data acquisition purposes in the laboratory. Among the many advantages this technology offers is the ability to execute many types of experiments which would otherwise be impossible. I am currently involved in attempting to implement the techniques of adaptive training to the study of the attentional processes in the learning disabled child. The procedures, which adjust the difficulty of the task to the level of performance of the subject, would not be practical and in fact would be almost impossible, without the aid of a computer or a computer-like device. If succesesful, it is anticipated that this methodology will allow the circumvention of some of the problems associated with the relationships between such variables as age, IQ, and the difficulty of the changes which occur in the attention deficit as children mature, and it should allow meaningful contrasts among children with different intellectual capabilities.

Another advantage computers offer is that they make it possible to examine a more complex spectrum of the behavior being exhibited than is possible using more conventional laboratory procedures. It has already been suggested that the behavior we are studying is a very complex phenomena. Psychology is guilty of being the science of the bits and pieces of behavior rather than the science of behavior as we so glibly proclaim. This is not something that psychologists alone have been guilty of committing. Most scientists and other workers who have studied human behavior have also been guilty of this fragmentation. By taking advantage of the technology available today one can simultaneously examine the complex array of performance variables emitted by the subjects, the physiological variables which might be related to behavior at any given time, and the environmental variables any one of which might alone or in combination with other variables be important. The use of automated data collection procedures and proceses control systems also insures a greater degree of accuracy than can be afforded by other methodologies.

It may appear to some that there is a contradiction between my earlier comments that the investigator needs to become more intimately involved in the process of data collection and the present advocacy of the use of automated devices to facilitate the data collection process. However, they are not inconsistent at all. When the experimenter is freed from the responsibility of being directly involved in the simple mechanics of the data collection proceses, he is able to spend his time observing the behavior of his subjects as they perform their tasks in the laboratory.

It should be stated explicitly that we do not wish to imply that the computer is the only form of contemporary technology that needs to be taken advantage of. It only serves to illustrate one of the many new technologies that can be used. Of course, we need to realize that anytime we use a new technology we are in effect developing a new methodology and, as I suggested earlier, this must be done with a great deal of caution.

The learning disability phenomena is indeed complex and the solution to the problems confronting the learning disabled child and our understanding of the learning disabled child will be complex. Nevertheless, if we are careful, systematic, and diligent a solution to this critical problem will be found.

**REFERENCES**

Anderson, R., Halcomb, C., and Doyle, R.: The measurement of attentional deficits. *Except Child,* 39:534-541, 1973.

Anderson, R., Halcomb, C., Ozolins, D., and Hopson, J.: *The effects of auditory distraction on vigilance task performance in learning disabled children.* Paper presented to Southwestern Psychological Association, El Paso, 1974.

# Author Index

## A

Abstract reasoning, 142
Ackerman, P. T., 5, 86, 87, 188, 202, 229, 233, 234
Actometer, 218
Adams, J. A., 237, 248
Aftanas, M. S., 211, 214
Aggression, 145
Albert, J., 88
Alcuin, S., 176-178
Allen, R., 146, 148
Alley, G., 175, 178
Alluisi, E. A., 199, 202
Ambidexterity, 157
Amblyopic, 152
 refractive, 152
Amphetemines, 127, 128, 217
Amsel, A., 183, 186-187
Analysis of variance, 170
Anatomical reversals, 159
Anderson, R. P., 7, 8, 66, 85, 87, 186, 187, 192, 194, 195, 198, 200, 202, 203, 236, 246, 248, 268, 271, 272, 275
Anderson, R. W., 168, 178
Angell, R., 175, 178
Anthony, E. J., 129, 138
Arithmetic, 232
Arousal, 29, 36, 43, 48, 189
 physiological, 74
Association for Children with Learning Disabilities, 12, 13, 17, 22, 23
Astigmatism, 159
Atkinson, B. R., 66, 85
Attention, 29, 31, 33, 40, 141, 218, 232
 defects, 31
 deficits, 28-31, 82, 111, 112
 impulsivity syndrome, 142
 intention, 36, 43, 50
 out, 50
 selective, 69
 superior, 81
 sustained, 145, 222, 268
 switching mechanism, 51
Auditory discrimination, 142
Auditory-visual integration, 211

## B

Baddeley, A. D., 238, 248
Bakan, P., 189, 202
Baker, R. A., 200, 202, 203
Bakwin, H., 32, 33, 86
Bank Street Readers, 171
Bannochie, N. M., 90
Barnes, K. R., 115, 124, 234
Barr, E., 146, 148
Beal, D., 236, 248
Bean, W. J., 236, 248
Beck, L. H., 234
Becker, W. C., 117, 124
Behavior modification, 117, 147
Bell, D. B., 236, 248
Belmont, J. M., 109, 123
Belmont, L., 68, 86
Bender-Gestalt Test, 143, 211, 224
Bennett, R. M., 174, 178
Benton, A. L., 20, 26, 68, 93
Benton, C. O., Jr., 158, 160
Benzedrine, 127
Bereiter, C., 30, 86
Bevan, W., 200, 202
Bijou, S. W., 80, 86
Binocular coordination, 159
Birch, H. C., 68, 69, 86, 211, 215
Birnbrauer, J. S., 80, 86
Boileau, R. A., 148, 219, 234
Boll, T. J., 128, 138
Bourne, L. E., 182, 187
Boydstun, J. A., 36, 44, 74, 86, 92
Bradley, C., 30, 91, 127, 183, 187
Brain, W. R., 157, 160
Bransome, E. D., 234
Brown, J. L., 174, 178
Bruner, J. S., 38, 86
Bryant, D., 23

## Author Index

Buckland, P. A., 174, 178
Bureau of Education for the Handicapped, 12, 13, 17, 18
Burks, H. R., 183, 187
Butts, P., 204, 215
Butterfield, W. H., 204, 205, 215

### C

California Test of Mental Maturity, 81
Camp, B. W., 7, 80, 86, 204, 205, 207-210, 214, 215
Campbell, D. T., 163-165, 167, 178, 253, 255, 267
Campbell, S., 144, 147
Campion, G. S., 151, 152, 160
Cantwell, D. P., 91
Catecholamine, 77
Central processing units, 48, 55
Cerebral dominance, 156, 157, 159
Chair, stablimetric, 218
Chalfant, J. C., 12, 25
Chase, J. B., 93
Child Service Demonstration Programs, 18, 24, 25
Chinn, R. McC., 199, 202
Chlorpromazine, 121
Chomsky, N., 55, 86
Christensen, D. E., 80, 86, 114, 116, 123
CIBA-Geigy, 102, 127
Clemente, C., 44, 86
Clements, S. D., 12, 14, 15, 25, 86, 87, 183, 187, 234, 262, 267
Cohen, N. J., 59, 75-77, 86, 143, 144, 147, 155, 170
Cohen, S. A., 174, 179
Cohen, R. I., 161, 179
Concept formation, 142, 182, 183, 185, 186
  identification, 72
Conners C. K., 76, 77, 86, 116, 118, 123, 145-147, 218, 221, 233
  Abbreviated Teacher Rating Scale, 119
  Teacher Rating Scale, 118, 146
Continuous performance, 233
  task, 145
  tests, 218, 230, 232
Cornish, R. D., 168, 179
Cortical potentials, evoked, 189

Council for Exceptional Children, 16, 17, 23
Cox, C. A., 174, 179
Craik, K. J. W., 38, 86
Cratty, B. J., 162, 179
Critchley, M., 30, 32, 33, 86, 151, 161
Criterion Reading Levels Tests, 135
Cross-patterning experiences, 168
Cruickshank, W. M., 12, 25

### D

Dawson, D. K., 169, 179
Dawson, M. E., 31, 36, 91
Day, D., 88
Deblinger, J., 171, 179
Debus, R., 81, 87
Deem, M. A., 138
Defense mechanisms, 183
Delacato, C. H., 162, 166, 176, 177, 179
  mobility training, 177
  program, 177
  theories, 176, 177
De La Cruz, Felix, 9
Denhoff, E., 30, 31, 89
Detroit Learning Aptitude Test, 70
Deutsch, M., 30, 87
Developmental theory, 57
Dewaide, S., 180
Dexedrine, 77
Diagnostic-prescriptive approach, 21
Digital Equipment Corporation PDP-8/e computer, 193, 196
Doman-Delacato therapy, (see Delacato)
Dominance, 156
  crossed, 158
  eye, 156
  foot, 156
  hand, 156
  homolateral, 159
  incomplete, 158
  lateralized, 157
Donlon, G. M., 68, 89
Dopamine, 78
Douglas, V. I., 6, 8, 29, 31, 34-36, 59, 61, 65, 69, 72-76, 78, 79, 82, 86, 87, 93, 112, 124, 143, 144, 147, 148, 183, 184, 186, 187, 218, 222, 232, 233, 235

Doyle, R. B., 7, 46, 66, 85, 87, 187, 192, 195, 199, 202, 247, 268, 275
Draw-a-man test, 130
Duke of Wellington, 95
Dykman, R. A., 5, 8, 30-32, 34-36, 42, 43, 47, 59-62, 74, 76, 82, 87, 91, 92, 184, 186, 189, 192, 199, 202, 218, 229, 232-234, 271
Dyslexia, 33, 154, 159

**E**

Eames, J. H., 155, 161
Early, G. H., 164, 179
Edelson, R. I., 112, 124
Edwin, M., 176, 177, 179
EEG, 76
Ego strength, 34
Eisenberg, L., 233
Eisenson, J., 177, 181
Electronystagmograph, 154
Elementary and Secondary Education Act of 1970, Title VI-6, 17
Elkind, P., 171, 179
Emrich, C. D., 164, 179
Engelman, S., 30, 86
Estes, W. K., 214, 215
Evaluation Research Component at the Leadership Training Institute, 20, 24
Evans, M. B., 117, 124
Extroverts, 35, 36
Eysenck, H. J., 35, 36, 87

**F**

Falconer, D. S., 33, 87
Falik, L. H., 167, 179
Farnham-Diggory, S., 87
Far sightedness, 159
Faustman, M. N., 169, 179
Federal Advisory Committee, 16
Feldman, R., 203
Ferinden, W. E., Jr., 165, 179
Finel, M. W., 72
Firestone, P., 143, 148
Fishbacks, S., 92
Fivel, M. W., 90
Footlik, S., 170, 172, 181
Forester, J. M., 177, 179
Fox, B. H., 9
Frankenhaeuser, M., 88

Freibergs, V., 72, 78, 87, 183-187
Freundl, P., 92
Friedman, F., 93
Frostig, M., 162, 166, 175, 180
  Developmental Test of Visual Perception, 143
  exercises, 163
  Figure Ground Tests, 130
  program, 166, 174, 175
  test, 163, 174-176
  training, 165, 167, 174, 176
Frustration, 144

**G**

Galbrecht, C. R., 87
Gates, M. F., 46, 74, 88
Gates Basic Reading Test, 166
Gates Word Survey Test, 169
Getman, G. N., 162
Gilmore Reading Test, 174
Glaeser, G., 176, 180
Glaser, R., 213, 215
Gold, M., 99, 102, 109, 110, 123, 124
Goldberg, H. K., 154-158, 161
Good, C. V., 253, 267
Goodenough Draw-a-man test, 143
Goodman, J., 81, 147, 148
Goodwin, W., 204, 215
Gordon, W. J., 194, 202, 203
Gorelich, M. C., 170, 180
Gray, J. A., 45, 88
Greenberg, L. M., 92, 138
Gruber, J. J., 173, 180
Guilford, J. P., 70, 71

**H**

Haber, R. N., 54, 88
Habituation, 189
Hagin, R., 172, 181
Haider, M., 92, 202
Halcomb, C. G., 8, 85, 87, 187, 192, 194, 195, 198, 200, 202, 203, 268, 272, 275
Halgreen, M. R., 172, 180
Hallahan, D. P., 12, 25
Halliwell, J. W., 171, 180
Hardesty, D., 199, 202
Haring, N. G., 12, 26
Harris Draw-a-person test, 222
Hartlage, L. C., 200, 202

# Author Index

Hawthorne effect,
Hebb, D. O., 44, 88
Helabian, J., 236, 248
Heredity, 30, 32, 33
Herjanic, B. M., 32, 88
Hersch, M., 172, 181
Hinshelwood, J., 150, 151, 161
Hinton, G. G., 218, 234
de Hirsch, K., 7, 35, 87, 88
Holes, 218
Hopson, J., 198, 202, 272, 275
Hopwood, J., 92
House, B. J., 79, 93
Hubel, D. H., 153, 161
Hull, 214
Hunter, E. J., 75, 81, 88
Hyperactivity, 30, 32, 33, 46, 59, 110, 114, 116
  medication effects, 116, 139, 194
Hyperopia, 159
Hypoactivity, 30, 46, 59

## I

Illinois Test of Psycholinguistic Abilities, 12, 142, 232, 237
  sequential memory subscales, 236, 237
  visual sequencing subtest, 224, 237
Impulsivity control, 82, 141, 144
Index of Social Position, 220
Induction phenomenon, 62
Information Processing Model, 29, 48, 49
Intelligence, 169
Intention, 28, 29, 33, 39, 40, 232
Introverts, 35, 36
Ismail, A. H., 173, 180

## J

Jacobs, J. N., 174, 180
Jacobs, N. T., 62, 88
James, W., 29, 34, 40, 42, 51, 52, 58, 88
Jansky, J., 87, 88
Jensen, A. R., 70, 84, 88, 213, 215
Jensen, N. J., 170, 180
Jerison, H. J., 189-191, 202, 203
Johansson, G., 77, 88
Johnson, D. J., 182, 187
Johnson, E. G., 88
Johnson, L. C., 75, 88
Johnson, N., 90

Journal of Learning Disabilities, 14

## K

Kabot, R. R., 176, 177, 180
Kagan, J. I., 81, 88, 89, 93, 148
Kahana, B., 147, 148
Kahn, C., 211, 215
Kaider, M., 189
Kaplan, M., 6
Kass, C. E., 13, 14, 16, 23, 26, 262, 267
Katz, L., 65, 89
Keim, R. P., 167, 180
Keefe, F. B., 75, 88
Keeney, A. H., 159, 161
Keogh, B., 69, 89, 163, 164, 180
Kephart, N. C., 11, 26, 110, 125, 162, 164, 167, 179, 258, 267
Kesner, R., 48, 54, 72, 89
Kidder, J. D., 86
Killen, J. R., 90
Kindergarten Screening Test, 135
King, E. M., 170, 180
Kintoch, W., 237
Kintsch, W., 248
Kirk, S. A., 12, 13, 26
Kleuver, R., 70, 89
Knights, R. M., 218, 234
Knobel, M., 74, 89, 129
Kogan, K., 93
Kohlberg, L., 34, 89
Koppitz, E., 224
Korsakoff Syndrome, 70
Kovalinsky, R., 165, 179
Kuhlman-Anderson Tests, 211

## L

Lacey, B. C., 89
Lacey, J. I., 44, 52, 57, 89
LaFontaine, L., 82, 92
Landeen, J., 215
Langford, W., 87
Larsen, N., 160
Laterality, 156-158
Lateralization, delayed, 30
Laufer, M. W., 30, 31, 36, 89
Laybourne, P., 6
Leadership Training Institute in Learning Disabilities, 13, 18, 23
Learning Disabilities, history of, 11, 165
  recent history, 17

Learning Disabilities Act of 1969, 13, 17
Learning quotient, 212
Lehtinen, L., 11, 26, 110, 125
Leshin, G., 23
Lesser, L. I., 91
Levi, R., 180
Levine, A., 96, 124
Levine, M., 96, 124
Levine, E. A., 82, 89
Levitt, M., 89
Lewis, H. M., 75, 88
Lewis, J. N., 165, 180
Lincoln-Oseretsky Schedule of Motor Development, 143, 218, 224
Lindsley, D. B., 92, 189, 202
Lindsley, O., 20
Linn, S. H., 175, 180
Lovitt, T. C., 80, 89
Lucas, A. R., 30, 89
Luria, A. R., 45, 47, 57, 82, 89, 187-189, 192, 203
Lyle, J. C., 88
Lytton, G. J., 74, 89, 129

### Mc

McCall, 253
McCann, J. W., Jr., 158, 160
McCarthy, J. M., 16, 17, 26
McCollum, P. S., 184, 186, 187
McCormack, P. D., 200, 203
McCormick, C. C., 170, 172, 181
McGrath, F., 166, 167, 181
McGrew, J., 234
McLees, M. P., 168, 181
McMahon, S., 138
McQueen, M., 91

### M

Mackay, D. M., 38, 89
Mackworth, J. F., 189, 203
Mackworth, N. H., 189, 190, 203
   Clock Test, 189
Magnusson, D., 88
Malmo, R., 44, 90
Manley, M., 168, 169, 180
Mann, L., 110, 124
Marshall, P., 72, 90, 256, 257, 270, 271
Maslow, P., 166, 180
Masterman, J., 176, 177, 180

Matching Familiar Figures Test, 69, 83, 144, 145
Maturation, 164, 165
Maudsley Personality Inventory, 35
Maze, 218
Mechanisms, 51
Meehl, P. E., 33, 90
Meichenbaum, D. H., 81, 90, 147, 148
Memory
   drum, Lafayette, 223
   leaky bucket theory, 213
   long term, 48
   short term, 48, 142
   tasks, 67
Mendolson, W., 32, 90
Mentally retarded, 152, 164, 199
Methylphenidate, 64, 75, 80, 114, 116, 118, 127, 129, 130, 145, 217, 218, 219, 224, 226, 230-233
Metropolitan Reading Readiness Test, 175
Miller, C. A., 12, 26
Miller, C. B., 174
Miller, G. A., 53, 90, 213, 215
Millichap, J. G., 129, 138
Milner, B., 40, 74, 90, 232, 234
Minde, K., 31, 90, 93, 111, 124, 143, 144, 147, 148, 235
Minden, H. A., 155, 156, 161
Minimal Brain Dysfunction, definition, 14, etiology, 30
Minke, K. A., 204, 215
Minnesota Multiphasic Personality Inventory, 34
Minnesota Counseling Inventory, 35
Minsakoff, J. G., 129, 138
Miracle, F. B., 176, 181
Mirsky, A. F., 234
Mitchell, C. C., 155, 161
Model Centers Program, 13
Monroe, W. S., 253, 254, 267
Morgan, W. P., 11, 26
Morgenstern, G., 86, 93, 143, 144, 147, 148
Mortality, 164, 165
Moss, H. A., 89
Muscle imbalances, 159
Myklebust, H. R., 4, 9, 14, 16, 26, 71-73, 90, 182, 187, 215, 262, 267

## N

Namy, E., 81, 90
National Advisory Committee, 26, 126, 138, 267
National Institute of Child Health and Human Development, 102
National Institute of Neurological Disease and Blindness, 102
Neural maturation, delayed, 30
Neurodevelopmental lag, 31
Neurological training, 168
Neurological training program, 168
New York Academy of Sciences, 102
Nonparametric statistic, 173
Noonan, J. D., 167, 181
Norepinephrine metabolism, 78
Normoactive, 59
Northwestern Conference, 14
Nystagmus, 152, 159

## O

Occam's Razor, 29
Ocular
  fatigue, 159
  motility, 155
  motor apraxia, 159
O'Donnell, P., 177, 181
Olds, S. W., 127, 138
O'Leary, K. D., 117, 124
Olson, H. C., 155, 161
Oltman, P. K., 93
Operation Moon Shot, 169
Optometric visual training, 163
Orthoptics, 154
Orton, S. T., 11, 26
Osler, S. F., 72, 90
Ozolins, D., 194, 198, 200, 202, 203, 272, 275

## P

Painter, G., 164, 171, 172, 181
Paley, 147
Palkes, 81, 147, 148
Parenting, inadequate, 30
Parry, P., 59, 73, 78, 79, 90, 143, 144, 148
Parucka, M. R., 7, 72, 73, 79, 90, 182-187
Patterson, G. R., 80, 90
Pavlov, I. P., 45, 91
Pearson, L., 88
Pegboard, Purdue, 218
Pemoline, 217, 219, 224
Penfield, W., 45, 91
Penick, E. C., 32, 88
Perceptual-motor, 143, 144
Perryman, R., 199, 203
Peters, J. E., 48, 65, 87, 91, 92, 183, 188, 202, 233, 234
Peterson, L. R., 246, 248
Peterson, M. J., 246, 248
Phillips, L., 262, 267
Phillips, W., 88
Piaget, J., 34, 47, 57, 91
Pihl, R. O., 80, 91
Piper, G. L., 166, 181
Placebos, 217
Poetker, B., 170, 181
Pontius, A., 39, 45, 91
Porteus Mazes, 31, 144, 145, 222
Pribram, K. H., 37-40, 42, 43, 55, 91, 232, 234
Psychoeducational, 11
Psychomotor abilities, 168
Public Law, #88-164, 12
Pursuit Rotor Test, 143

## Q

Quay, H., 79, 80, 91, 118, 125

## R

Rao, C. R., 209, 215
Raven Progressive Matrices Test, 211
Rawson, M. G., 32, 91
Reaction time, 59
  simple, 58
  task, 144, 145
Reading
  achievement, 176
  comprehension, 170
Reality scale, 35
Reciprocal inhibition, 47
Reese, W. G., 87
Reinforcement, 207
  contingencies, 147
  continuous, 183-185
  delayed, 183
  no, 180
  partial, 183-186
  positive, 199
Reiss, S., 25

Reitan, R. M., 128, 138
Release latencies, 60
Research design
　control group, 167
　crossover, 172
　one group pretest-posttest design, 164, 165
　one shot case study, 164
　posttest, 167
　pre-experimental design, 164, 167
　pretest, 167
　pretest-posttest control group design, 164
　true experimental designs, 164
Retarded, training, 102
Reticular activation system, 31
Riddle, I., 95, 124
Ritalin, 77, 130-132, 194, 217
Rivalry, 158
Roberts, Richard H., 9
Robbins, M. P., 177, 181
Robinson, E., 233
Robinson, Jeffers, 85
Rodin, E. A., 89
Roessler, R., 34, 91
Romine, J. S., 91
Rosebaum, A. L., 89
Rosen, C. L., 174, 181
Rosenfield, G. B., 30, 91
Rosman, B., 83
Rosvold, H. E., 222, 234
Rothschild, G. H., 147, 218, 233
Royce, J. R., 211, 214
Rubino, C. A., 155, 156, 161
Rudnick, M., 211, 215
Rutter, M., 152, 161
Ryback, D., 204, 215

S

Safer, D., 146, 148
Santasphano, S., 81, 91, 147, 148
Sarason, I., 234
Satterfield, J. H., 31, 36, 77, 91
Satz, P., 30, 91
Saudergras, R. A., 117, 124
Saul, R. E., 91
Scates, D. E., 253, 267
Schain, R. J., 150, 155, 161
Scheffelin, M. A., 12, 25
Schiffman, G. B., 154, 157, 161

Schmidt, L., 217, 234
Schnobrich, J., 170, 172, 181
Schwartz, L., 233
Scott, J., 92
Scott, K. G., 110, 124
Selection, 164, 165
Senf, G. M., 5, 8, 12, 16, 20, 21, 26, 67-69, 92
Serotonin, 78
Seunath, O. H. M., 66, 85
Shannon, C. E., 29, 92
Sharpe, T. M., 164, 179
Shetty, T., 30, 78, 92
Shields, D. T., 77, 92
Silver, A., 172, 181
Silver, L. B., 78, 92
Simon, H. H., 48, 51, 92
Simson, C. B., 89
Sinton, D. W., 92
Sipowicz, R. R., 200, 203
Sleator, E. K., 219, 234
Sloane, A., 152, 161
Snellen chart, 220
Snider, W., 175, 178
Socioeconomic variables, 169
Sokolov, E., 38, 42, 92
Solan, H. A., 171, 180
Solomons, G., 30, 92
Sonies, B. C., 92
Sparrow, S. S., 30, 91
Spencer, J., 175, 178
Spitz, H. H., 82, 92
Spong, P., 77, 92
Spong, R., 189, 202
Sprague, R. L., 5, 6, 8, 31, 80, 86, 91-93, 102, 111, 112, 114-116, 123-125, 145, 146, 148, 218, 219, 234
Spring, C., 63, 64, 92
Sroufe, L. A., 75, 76, 92, 146, 148
Staats, A. W., 204, 205, 207, 215
　Motivation Activation Reading Therapy, 204, 207
Stake, R., 209, 215
Stanford-Binet Test, 135, 211
Stanley, J. C., 163-165, 167, 178, 253, 255, 267
Statistical regression, 164, 165
Stayton, S., 81, 91, 148
Sterritt, G. M., 211, 215

# Author Index

Stevens, D. A., 31, 86, 92
Stewart, M. A., 31, 32, 78, 90, 93, 127, 128, 138
Stewart, W., 147, 148
Strabismus, 152
Strauss, A. A., 11, 26, 110, 125
Sundermann, R., 87
Suzuki, R., 87, 188, 202, 234
Sykes, D. H., 59, 90, 93, 111, 124, 143, 148, 218, 222, 223, 235
Symbolic material reaction time, 63

## T

Task Force I, 14, 15
Tate, P., 8, 271
Taxonomic diagnosis, 15
Taxonomic structures, 25
Teacher's rating scale, 146
Theory of frustration, 183
Thioridazine, 116
Thorazine, 131
Thorndike, 253
Tizard, J., 161
Toppe, L. K., 122, 124
Transactional analysis, 35
Trauel, N. N., 36, 93
Tremorgraph, 218
Trumbo, D., 199, 202
T test, 173

## U

US Office of Education, 13
Underaroused, 74

## V

Validity
  external, 164
  internal, 165
Vandervoort, L., 20, 26, 68, 93
van Doorninck, W. J., 204, 208, 215
Van Handel, D., 165, 179
Vigilance, 189, 218
  task, 46, 66, 143, 186, 189, 268
Vineland Revision for Pre-drug State and Extension, 222
Visual perception, 153
Visual-spatial test of perception, 211
Vivian, Sister M., 176, 181
Vocabulary, 170
von Neumann, A. W., 219, 234

Vygotsky, L., 47, 58, 93
Vygotsky Block Test of Concept Formation, 74, 83

## W

Walls, R. C., 87, 188, 202, 234
Walzer, S., 4, 9
Ware, J. R., 200, 203
Warrington, E. K., 93, 238, 248
Weaver, W., 29, 92
Webb, G., 90, 111, 124
Wechsler, D., 70, 93
Weidenfeller, E. W., 200, 203
Weiner, B., 200, 203
Weiss, G., 93, 143, 144, 147, 148, 235
Welch, L., 88
Wender, P., 30, 36, 78, 93, 127, 128, 138
Wepman Auditory Discrimination Test, 222
Werener, H., 11
Werry, J. S., 31, 91, 110, 111, 115, 116, 118, 125, 134, 145, 148, 234
West, W. D., 92
Westberg, W. C., 155, 161
Whitmore, K., 161
Wiener, E. L., 203
Wiesel, R. N., 153, 161
Wicklund, D. A., 65, 89
Willerman, L., 84, 89, 93
Winterhaven program, 168
Wirthlin, L. D., 174
WISC, 41, 50, 57, 69, 70, 71, 76, 77, 81, 135, 142, 166, 211, 220, 222, 232, 236
Wisconsin Card Sorting Test, 31, 37, 73, 83
Witkin, H. A., 82, 93
Wolf, M. M., 86
Wolff, Peter H., 4, 9
Word Discrimination, 170
Wide Range Achievement Test, 211, 212, 218, 222, 228, 232
Wright, F. S., 92

## Y

Yando, R. M., 81, 93

## Z

Zeaman, D., 79, 93
Zigler, E., 262, 267
Zigmond, N. K., 211, 215

DISCHARGED
MAR 3 1973          DISCHARGED

DISCHARGED

DISCHARGED 1977      DISCHARGED
                     JUN 30 1988

MAY 1978

DISCHARGED 1978

AUG DISCHARGED 1978

AUG DISCHARGED 1978

DISCHARGED 1991

MAR 15 1984

DISCHARGED
DISCHARGED 1984

OCT 1995
DISCHARGED
JUN 24 1986

DISCHARGED
DISCHARGED
NOV 12 1991